DANCE OF THE ANCIENT ONE

DANCE OF THE ANCIENT ONE

How the Universe Solves Personal and World Problems

Arnold Mindell

DANCE OF THE ANCIENT ONE

How the Universe Solves Personal and World Problems

ARNOLD MINDELL, PH.D.

Cover design by Elzbieta Kacprzak

Book Design by iWigWam

Deep Democracy Exchange
Portland, Oregon USA
415-729-4333
deepdemocracyexchange.com
ddx@deepdemocracyexchange.com

Library of Congress Control Number: 2012956463

ISBN: 978-1-61971-015-3

Deep Democracy Exchange

CONTENTS

LIST OF FIGURES

ACKNOWLEDGEMENTS

Thanks to NASA, the US National Aeronautics and Space Administration, for images of the Universe used in this book and for Appendix 2.

Thanks to Apollo 14 Astronaut, Captain Edgar Mitchell, one of the 12 astronauts to walk on the moon for his vision:

> ...if our political systems and our leadership at the political levels could ever see earth from that point of view we'd have quite a different leadership on earth. What that was, was utter magnificence of seeing earth as a little planet in a larger picture of the heavens.[1]

Thanks to Albert Einstein for saying:

> Now it appears that space will have to be regarded as a primary thing and that matter is derived from it, so to speak, as a secondary result. Space is now having its revenge... is eating up matter.[2]

And for his 1920 statement:

> According to the general theory of relativity, space without ether is unthinkable...[3]

Thanks to physicist John Wheeler for the black hole concept and for connecting space–time to Taoism. He quoted from 10th century Su Tung-p'o in a poem about sailing:

We let our boat drift as it would... felt that we were sailing in empty space and riding on the wind... were light as if we had forsaken the world, and free of all support, like one who has become an immortal and soars through space... [4]

Thanks to Prof. Edwin Taylor of MIT for work with Wheeler and for their Exploring Black Holes: Introduction to General Relativity.

Thanks to Prof. Max Tegmark of MIT for the idea of *mathematical democracy*. [5]

Thanks to the Processwork Institute of Portland and Processwork institutes and students worldwide for your ongoing support. Thanks especially to those individual people who have enriched this book through allowing me to use their own words.

Thanks to Susan Kocen for your labors writing up the notes for this work. Thanks to Margaret Ryan, once again, for your invaluable editing help. And many thanks to Susan Newton for your editing expertise and attention!

I am indebted to many people for allowing me to keep their personal stories in this book! Thanks for your insights into Islamophobia, kidnapping in Colombia, problems in the Philippines, discussions about Buddhism, understanding military leadership and dozens of other personal, social and organizational situations.

I am indebted to Drs. Max and Ellen Schupbach and Dr. Stanford Siver at the Deep Democracy Exchange for their dedication to and support of the publication of this work in English and around the world.

Thanks to you, dear reader, for applying *Dance of the Ancient One* to worldly matters.

Dear Amy (Amy Mindell), thanks for living, exploring, discussing, and helping me research, experience, and teach every aspect of this work! I could not have done it without you.

PART ONE

The Universe Dance

CHAPTER 1

The Process Paradigm Shift

> *...the whole of this existence of ours will some day have its single, central principle spring to life, that will be so natural we'll say to ourselves: How could it have been otherwise and how could we have been so stupid all these years not to have seen it?*
>
> —John Wheeler (physicist, creator of the black hole concept)[6]

Just about everyone experiences complex health issues, personal and organizational relationship problems, diversity problems, war, and climate change. We all know that many problems can be solved independently of other problems. Have a headache? Take an aspirin! But some of our biggest headaches, such as global climate change, require more than just turning down the global temperature by using less carbon, by producing less CO2. Reducing global warming is not so simple because it is not *mono-causal*, that is, caused by one thing. Resolving global issues such as climate change is connected with worldwide economic and social issues as well as with scientific facts. I realize from my experience working with military groups, with government and United Nations groups, and with big city open forums and conflicts that many personal and global problems require more than one solution and more than one discipline. We need more than physics or psychology, politics or diversity consciousness, and cosmology or inner work to resolve today's problems. We need a more universal, interdisciplinary approach to resolve individual and global issues.

We need a global *system mind* to deal with individual and world problems. Better leaders would help. But we don't just need new leaders. Each of us needs to learn to facilitate conflict within ourselves, at home, at work, and for the crucial issues facing our world. Such facilitation is, in principle, not that hard to do! Most of this facilitation work could be taught in kindergarten. To begin with, notice, then express, the two (or more) main conflicting viewpoints in a given situation. Just about anyone can play the *good guys* and the *bad guys*! Then find some distance or detachment from both viewpoints so you can listen fairly and help each express yourselves more completely and more deeply.

What did I say? "Find some distance or detachment from both viewpoints?" Ha! Sounds easy, but just about everyone favors one side over another. Of course, favoring the good side (in our subjective opinion) over the other side is important to begin with. That is basic to just about everyone's ethics. However, there is a problem with such *good* ethics. Rarely do the good people remember that the so-called bad guys have ideas that need to be heard too, which they feel are good. Therefore, without even realizing it, most of us contribute to little fights, big battles, and world wars by being one-sided! How then will we ever manage to facilitate conflict by understanding and moving authentically between opposing parties?

This book calls the solution to ongoing, complex personal and global issues the *Dance of the Ancient One*. The solution is not a fixed state; it is a process or a *dance*. Who is that ancient one? This most ancient one is the universe of course, but it is also you and me! Yes, it is you in your deepest dreams and you near the end of your life! It is you, if you lived 1,000 years. It is you, in a relaxed and open state of mind. The solution to complex global issues is your most detached wisdom: it is you moved, or danced, by the universe.

WHAT? MOVED BY THE UNIVERSE?

Yes! Just as the earth is moved by the universe, you, me, every human, every life form, and every thing is moved by the universe as well. This movement feeling, the sense of the universe's gravity field or what Einstein called *space–time*, is not just felt by astronauts. All of us feel moved by gravity all the time. When you let gravity move you, when you are moved by space–time, you are moved by the universe. When you are moved in this way, you are showing the "dance of the ancient one," and are in contact with the space between us, with the subtle experience of being moved by what I shall explain is a *system mind*—possibly the most powerful system mind available to us.

Everyone has this dance of the ancient one in her or in him. But to get there, we need to go deeply into our feelings, our movements, and imagination. It's easy; everyone has experienced her or his own dreammaker in action while dreaming at night. This book shows how this dreammaker also appears in the experience of being moved by gravity, that is, by Einstein's space–time. Our experience of being moved by outer space and our experience of dreaming are similar, or even the same. The dance of the ancient one is your space–time dreaming, your sense of being moved by space, and your meditation of being moved by the universe.

Facilitators need the dreammaker's mind, this universe mind or system mind. If you deal with global problems, you need a system mind that works for all that you can observe, for the whole earth, and not just one part or one side. In my previous book, *ProcessMind*,[7] I spoke of this system mind in terms of the feeling of being moved by the earth. Now I will generalize the powers of the earth in terms of the powers of the universe's space–time.

Because space–time dreaming is within and around you—indeed it surrounds all people and our whole planet and the entire universe— it is a psychological experience of a global or even universal system mind. Let's talk a little about processminds or system minds.

Every living system has a kind of organizing intelligence. James Lovelock's *Gaia* concept is an example of a planetary system mind. Physicists such as Einstein and others hoped that science would discover the mind of god.[8] Everywhere, people seek unified fields that organize events. Some call it god and use prayer or meditation to reach this *mind*. I call the intelligence of this field, the *processmind* and its power and manifestation, *space–time dreaming*. It's no big mystery. If you note your dreams, you might wonder, "What is that mysterious mind giving me these outrageous dreams to make sure that my everyday mind considers new things and to make me move this and that way in life?"

I said that gaining access to your most detached dance of the ancient one and resolving conflicts is not hard to do! Ha, ha, ha! Some spiritual or psychological traditions tell us that we need to meditate for 10 years, or even a whole life, to find this detached viewpoint. This new method of space–time dreaming, which depends upon our experience, our imagination of the spaces around us, of gravity and space–time itself, will fit just about anyone. It gives all viewpoints a chance and makes everyone and everything feel that they are all parts of our universe — which they are!

I began searching for this natural, unifying, system mind principle after graduating from MIT. At first I went to Zurich, in the 1960s, to study physics at the Swiss ETH (Eidgenössische Technische Hochschule, the European MIT) . But to my surprise, I ended up becoming a Jungian analyst! Why? Science by itself ignored feelings and dreaming! I loved Jung's fascination with dreams and with the principle of synchronicity: that is, the connection between psychology and physics. I appreciated that he and Nobel Laureate, physicist Wolfgang Pauli tried to put psychology and physics together. They, too, were seeking some sort of interdisciplinary system mind to understand and untangle the mystery of synchronicity.[9] They were looking for a system mind that included both psychology and physics!

Another Nobel Prize winner, physicist Werner Heisenberg, intuited this system mind years ago. He knew that psychology and physics were one discipline:

> The same organizing forces that have shaped nature in
> all her forms are also responsible for the structure of our
> minds.[10]

I call these organizing forces the dance of the ancient one or space–time dreaming. The goal of this book is to find and use these "organizing forces that have shaped nature in all her forms" and to use them as a home for world problems. We need to bring the problems of our world home to the universe, to our sense of the dance of the ancient one.

Psychology helped me understand these forces: quantum physics, with its inexplicable self-reflection in its basic equations, helped me understand how awareness might infuse the universe and cosmology, with its curved spaces, reminded me of psychology's altered states of consciousness. Physics and psychology, however, are not alone in pointing to these altered states. Five thousand years ago, Taoists spoke of "the Tao that can't be said." In their minds, this Tao was the essence, the mother of the universe. They said that the Tao came before heaven and earth:

> There was something formless and perfect
> before the universe was born.
> It is serene. Empty.

Solitary. Unchanging.
Infinite. Eternally present.
It is the mother of the universe.
For lack of a better name,
I call it the Tao.[11]

Space–time dreaming is a formless power like the Tao that manifests in the dance of the ancient one. This dance is best approached by overlapping or interweaving scientific, psychological, and spiritual disciplines. But our world today is described mainly by separated disciplines. More than ever, we tend to live in separate universes, so to speak. When psychologists ask about dreams, they rarely try to see them expressed in the body or connect them to the sense of gravity. Medical people rarely ask about the dreams behind symptoms. Physicists are often taught to follow empirical observations but not feelings. All conflicting parties see themselves living, in a way, in separate worlds. In other words, our separation of disciplines, wonderful as their products and achievements have been, is also part of our present world dilemma.

We need a paradigm shift. Older paradigms devoted mainly to separations between inner and outer, psyche and matter, mind and body, individual and group, social and universal, and so forth, are *state-oriented*. We need a process that includes and moves within, between, and beyond inner and outer, mind and body, psyche and matter, you and me, bad guys and good people. Process? Yes. Our awareness of change, of process, moves between inner experiences and *outer* observations about the body, the mind, the psyche, science, and psychology. Best of all, *process* can be simply defined as the observation of signals. Just follow process in terms of what you see, feel, hear, and dream. Process! Follow events, follow what people do, follow nature, follow the river.

Processwork is awareness work: the work of becoming aware of how individuals, groups, and nature herself change, starting with ourselves. For example, if you don't notice your own aggressive signals, you are going to think that the other person is aggressive! But processing your signals will show you that whomever you gossip about is not just living in a separate universe. They are part of your process, here and now. The good guys and the bad guys overlap! I am excited by the process paradigm that connects psychology, medicine, physics, small and large groups, organizations, inside and out.[12] I love art, music, psychology, medicine, organizational work, chemistry, politics, and geology, but when the separate paradigms of these disciplines don't work because we are often dealing with overlapping local and global system problems, Processwork becomes a necessity. I love all the divisions of life into this and that, physics and psychology, chemistry and dreams, but sometimes these divisions are more of a problem than a help.[13]

Space–time dreaming lies at the essence of Processwork and may be one of those single principles mentioned by Wheeler. Remember his quote at the beginning of this chapter:

> ...the whole of this existence of ours will some day have its single, central principle spring to life, that will be so natural we'll say to ourselves: How could it have been otherwise and how could we have been so stupid all these years not to have seen it?

I hope that the theory and experiences in this book will convince you that space–time dreaming is one of those principles.

In the following chapters, I will show you how to use space–time dreaming through a series of about 40 inner work, relationship, organizational, financial, and ecological meditation exercises. I shall present new movement and feeling experiences tested from practical teaching experiences with classes in Portland and large group work in enumerable cities world-wide. Much of the work in this book is taken verbatim, directly from teaching classes, seminars, and doing large public group work in Portland and around the world. These various experiences will provide a common human ground that will allow you to communicate cross-culturally, and possibly nonlocally, to resolve inner and outer conflicts. I suggest making notes on paper to keep track of each exercise. In this way, you can apply this work to personal problems, body symptoms, relationships, community diversity issues, global financial and ecological difficulties, as well as to space travel problems encountered by astronauts.

Summary of the Six Parts

I divided this book into six parts.

Part 1: The Universe Dance

Here I introduce the *dance of the ancient one*. I speak about Processwork theory and practice and ask about the origins of the universe. I show how process theory and practice include parallel world theories, Einstein's universal space–time, entropy, and quantum theory.

Part 2: Who Are You? Jung, Einstein, Pachamama, Dalai Lama
Cosmologist Stephen Hawking asks, "Why is there something, rather than nothing?" I'll explain some basics of relativity theory and its connections with Tibetan Bardos (intermediate states of existence) and Jung's understanding of the alchemical *unus mundus* (one world). Here we explore timeless body experiences in the dance of the ancient one as it appears in physics, psychology, and various spiritual traditions.

Part 3: Symptoms, Madness, or World Dance?
In this section, we consider our fear of body problems with the help of space–time dreaming, which, like a spirit let out of a bottle, is shown to help body symptoms. I also provide an overview of how this new space-time dreaming can be used to help what medicine refers to as psychotic states.

Part 4: Relationship: Beyond War and Peace
The worst inner and world problems may also be hidden gifts pointing to a most powerful inner teacher! This insight and the experiences of this section may allow you to detach enough to work with difficult inner or world social issues and conflicts.

Part 5: Process Oriented Ecology (POE)
POE integrates psychology, earth-system thinking, experience of the quantum world, and the universe. POE is both an art and a science. I'll talk here about the gods that work in trash and in the stars. Here, new ideas appear about how to apply space–time dreaming to street work, global finances, and the planetary environment.

Part 6: Earth, Money, and the Big Picture
Bringing separate parts and parallel worlds in psychology, ecology, sociology, and economy *home* with new space–time dreaming methods is the work of a psychologist, economist, ecologist, and politician who has a big picture. Here I will show how a big picture emerges from the foregoing chapters and can be used in practice with earth's problems, financial crises, and world events.

Since I began this chapter with a quote from the visionary physicist John Wheeler, perhaps I can end with another. This great physicist was a mentor of Richard Feynman and Hugh Everett and a friend of Einstein and wrote a book about journeying into space–time. In that book, Wheeler quoted the 10th century Su Tung-p'o poem about sailing:

> We let our boat drift as it would… felt that we were sailing
> in empty space and riding on the wind… were light as if we
> had forsaken the world, and free of all support, like one who
> has become an immortal and soars through space… [14]

The challenge and promise of this book is to make this far-out space a palpable and necessary experience that everyone can feel moving them on earth in order to help with relationships and world tensions.

....

Σ   *FOR REFLECTION ON CHAPTER 1*

- World problems are interlinked. We need a new kind of interdisciplinary facilitator.

- We get tied up with parts, and we need more distance to see the big picture.

- To solve problems we need a paradigm shift from parts to process so that we can appreciate and also move beyond the parts.

- Einstein's space–time universe can be experienced or imagined by everyone as a psychological and physical feeling: a force field, which, like gravity, moves us.

- I call that field *space–time dreaming*: it moves us to the *dance of the ancient one*.

- Space–time dreaming is an interdisciplinary concept that connects psychology, physics, politics, and spiritual experience.

CHAPTER 2

The Universe's Wonder, Diversity, and Dance

Most sets of values would give rise to universes that, although they might be very beautiful, would contain no one able to wonder at that beauty.

— Cosmologist Stephen Hawking[15]

I have been involved with policy makers in various governments, with top scientists, and with large organizations from many different nations. From these diverse contexts, one point stands out for me: Our planet is split into parts. Scientists live in one world, ordinary citizens in another, the politicians in another, and businesspeople in still another. We live in separate worlds and that is one reason why our planet has developed so many problems. We not only have several wars going on in one place or another but also an entire global environment in a mess, and we have science over here and we have government over here, and we have business over here. There is little understanding between one and the other.

Today there are about 7 billion people on this planet. By the end of the 21st century, if things keep going the way they are, there will be 9 or 10 billion. That is a large number for such a little place. How come we are slow to awaken? Why don't we sometimes get along very well? A few people do get along very well but many don't and never have.

What is that due to? Everyone, of course, will have her or his answer and those answers are important. We need to ask these questions and find answers.

Perhaps our problems are connected to the nature of our universe. How did we get here? How did the earth get here? Where are we to look for answers to such big questions? Do we even ask these questions? Most people don't ask. They have enough troubles of their own without pondering such matters. But these are important matters because if we had a general theory or belief or system that really worked, we would have a system mind—and it would be remarkable!

Inside yourself you have your own mind, your own dreaming, and there is something that is organizing you most of the time. You can get in touch with whatever that is and you feel better, at least temporarily. It is my hypothesis that there is a system mind in the background, but we don't know how to use it well to bring things together more on our planet.

People are born, and people die. What happens at death? Why do so many people worldwide believe in some form of life outside of the *consensus reality* of life here on earth as physical creatures? How did we develop a consensus reality in the first place? And how have we managed to evolve in such a manner to split our world into billions of parts and peoples? Each of you will have your own answer. I will tell you a story later in this chapter (taken from one of my classes) to explain my own answer. My story corresponds to five or six general themes that you can find in many Aboriginal creation myths from different parts of the world. My story also will correspond to aspects of quantum physics and relativity theory. If we can find a story that fits many people, then we have a beginning—only a beginning. That story always needs revising and updating because there may be no one permanent story for anything.

In the quantum world, people talk about elementary particles. What is a particle? We usually think of a particle as something that hits something else and goes ping. Actually, in quantum physics a particle does not really know exactly where it is or how fast it is going. Since we cannot precisely measure it, in some sense, it does not exist until it is observed. Did you get that? A particle is not a particle until it is looked at. That is something to think about. It's like the story of the tree in the forest, if there is nobody there to hear a tree fall to the ground, does it make a sound? Does something exist before someone hears or sees it?

In quantum physics, a particle is not only a particle but it also has wavelike characteristics. What is a wave? Mathematically and graphically, it goes up and down. If you were a particle, that is, a fixed thing, where are you until you are observed by others? Now we are talking psychology. Where are you until you observe yourself and suddenly say, "Aha, I am here."

Someone in my class answers: "Pregnant!"

Arny: I had not thought about that! A fantastic example! You are a feeling, then a little thing incubating, and then pop! You are here!

Audience: There is a time in early infancy, a developmental phase, where they speak about the time when the ego comes.

Arny: Right! The child, like new ideas in us, is in a kind of dream-like oneness and then suddenly it pops out and can be seen by all!

MY OWN CREATION MYTHOLOGY

In my own universe creation story, in the beginning, in the earliest phases of consciousness, there was something wiggling and curious. It was wondering. I imagine it to be a kind of wiggly sine wave.

2.1 Wonder, a curious something, wiggles around.

This curious something was wondering or divining. The word *divine* means something marvelous and spiritual, but I use the word *divining* to mean looking for something. In my story, in the beginning there is the process of wonder, a divining something that is pondering things. We are all diviners. We are always wondering and trying to figure things out. Look at little kids: they walk around asking question after question: "What is this? What is that?" My dog was always sniffing in my advanced calculus book and chewing on it (which was not good) when I was at MIT.

One reason you cannot sometimes understand your own behavior, feelings, or dreams is that you don't know the diviner in yourself who went to sleep. The biggest problem with understanding dreams is not the issue of each dream's content. The biggest problem is not knowing who is asking the question that the dream answers. If you want to understand your dreams more easily, then, before you go to bed at night, become more conscious of what it is you are asking. "What am I wondering about? What is on my mind? Is it about life, is it about work, is it about relationship, about death?" Write those things down. Become a conscious diviner.

A story that fits many stories is that in the beginning something was going, "Mmmm?" This something was wondering, divining, but not quite conscious and it wanted something. Then it pondered, "Who am I?" and a big bang occurred! A big, big bang! And it said, "Aha! I am this, and I am not that!" And that is a short-cut version of how the world of bits, pieces, and parts got created. Wonder's original oneness broke itself up into parts. Pictures may help us understand this idea better. Wonder's wavelike oneness was divining and humming...

Again and again, the wave began to wonder,

"Who am I?"

Then the wave developed parts

and suddenly there was a very big bang and the wave separated into parts!

Now there was a + and a –
The original unity temporarily forgot itself as the plus (or the minus) said to the other,
"I AM NOT YOU!"
So the world began with a big bang,
and since then we have been trying to remember the original oneness.

I remember my daughter Lara, for example, when she was 2½ or 3. One day she got up and she walked around like she normally did, talking to herself and playing. And then she said to me, "Pappi!" she said, "I am Lara, I am not Robin (my son)!" "Well, of course," I said, "Yes." "No! No!" she protested, "I am me, I am not him!"

In my work with people over the years, I have seen little tiny children and also older people say again and again, "I am not that, I am this!" and usually some form of a big bang occurs. Bang! And the world begins. And our problems begin as well because, "I am me and not you!"

But now, as we psychologists who look at dreams have always advised you not to forget, you are a little bit like the other who is in your dreams. This process of awakening and feeling, "I am me and I am not you!" is thus a huge psychological and world issue. Why does this splitting happen?

Breaking the original symmetry and creating parts is a huge big bang moment. We develop an *edge* to parts of ourselves and create the beginning of a multiverse.

Multiverse is a physics term but it has been picked up by science fiction to mean parallel universes. The reason parallel universes are so named is because parallel means lines that never intersect; they don't meet or touch or connect in any way, ever. So our *oneness* breaks itself up into various parts that don't connect, into parallel universes and psychologies.

Radical cosmologists speak about parallel universes. They talk about other universes, possibly in our neighborhood or very far away, that run parallel—that is, never intersect—to our universe. This is so exciting to me! I never realized—I'm almost out of breath when I say this—all these years I have been working with people in all states of consciousness and situations; with families, organizations, and cities; and I never realized until now that the problem of parts can be understood in terms of parallel universes.

Our tendency in adult life to make a stance and take a fixed position that defines what we are and what we are NOT is common to all of us. How did our world get to this point? My answer is that in the beginning there was a sort of field. Fields are powers that move you, like a magnetic field or the gravity field, a kind of field the Taoists called the Tao: forces or energies that move us around. Fields occupy space, and they contain energy so there can be no true vacuum. Fields fill space so that any material thing in that field can feel a force upon it.[16]

Fields are without physical form. So, in my creation myth, when the field asked itself, "Who am I?" the power of formlessness becomes this and not that. In that moment, parallel universes get formed and splits happen!

Do you see this story in Judeo-Christian or Islamic thinking? Take the creation story of Adam and Eve. God created something: we don't know the details of how he or she did that but suddenly there were people, two women, or two men, or a man and a woman called Adam and Eve. They were smooching together and a snake appeared and said, "Do it! Eat that apple and forget what God suggested!" In other words, forget that oneness.

Where did the snake come from (at least in the Judeo-Christian traditions)? If God created everything, then oneness or God also created the snake, who was out to subvert God's wishes! God created parallel universes, so to speak. So in some versions of the holy books, God or wonder got upset and forgot Itself and said, "You guys leave heaven and go to the earth!" The planet earth is over there, and heaven is over here. And parallel universes came into being. Very, very early on we see the concept of parallel universes in many mythologies.

When my psychology teachers asked, "What did you dream last night?" they were interested in what they viewed as the parallel universe, that is, my dream last night instead of seeing me as combination of universes that are awake and also dreaming with my body right here and now. For them the dream was not here. It was *there* in the unconscious—a fantastic idea. I still love that idea of the unconscious, but I just want to point out that when you take this view, you are maybe seeing psyche and matter as parallel universes. With awareness however, you can see psyche and matter together as a process or unity in and around anyone flowing from one to the other!

So, modern cosmology, many religions, and psychologies speak about split, parallel universes without calling them that. Belief in parallel universes causes physicists to say, "physics is not psychology" and psychologists to say, "psychology is not physics." We need parallel worlds or universes and we also need bridges: we are missing the bridges between us. We need oneness and differentiation, that is, the experience of being this and not that. But we've had huge amounts of differentiation and specialization and approaches that break things down into parts. What we need now is a way to appreciate diversity and to simultaneously re-experience the original unity again.

How can the intelligence of the universe, the universal or individual processmind, the god or the deepest part of us which is supposed to be all-conscious, forget itself? We walk around in parallel universes perhaps in part because the divining processmind seems to want to forget itself so that parallel universes exist. Why? It needs them. Why do you think the divining process wants parallel universes?

It loves diversity!

The big bang helps the universe awaken! Oneness needs and loves diversity and multiplicity. It loves—excuse me for saying this—it loves conflict. Eeek! Who wants conflict? But there is so much of it, somebody must be liking it! I am just an empiricist here! I have to say, if there is so much conflict, something must be saying, "Hurrah for conflict!" When I realized this, the easier it is for me to work with conflict. Parallel universes want to remain parallel, like the differences between us; nature wants her diversity to be seen. That diversity is part of the beauty of the universe. It shows itself in terms of apparently fixed opposites.

If you are a facilitator working with a lot of conflict, it can be helpful to think that *something* needs these polarities to see itself: it uses them to *self-reflect*. Self-reflection seems to be built into everything in the universe. Physicists and psychologists don't know yet where consciousness comes from but it's there in the equations. Now, I am saying that consciousness comes about as parallel worlds emerge and self-reflect upon one another. Can you follow me here?

Audience:	Are you saying that oneness cannot be seen as oneness without having diversity in the field? Otherwise it is not oneness?
Arny:	Perfectly said! Yes, perhaps oneness gets bored with itself. With a heaven and hell there is more to do, more action, and the need to find the unity again! Something about our universe wants to forget its state of oneness and create diversity processes, conflict, and remember the need for unity again.
Audience:	Since there is diversity, and it is always present and we create it, why does it have to be conflictual?
Arny:	Well, conflict makes a bang! It wakes itself and everything up. "Yikes! There is another side to things!" Sometimes you wake up in the morning with a very heavy dream. That heavy dream is saying, "Hey, don't you neglect me for one minute!" So if you wake up with a very big dream, you should be proud of yourself. Even a nightmare can be a wonderful thing in the sense of remembering the other

energies you have forgotten to appreciate inside yourself. Without conflict, we tend to be unaware or else unwittingly one-sided.

All this goes along with John Wheeler's whale. This great physicist who just died a few years ago pictured the universe as a whale (I have spoken about this elsewhere[17]). He said that the universe is like a whale in a way. Its eye looks at its tail and it says, "Aha, the tail. I am not the tail. I am the head. I see the tail." In that moment it has forgotten its oneness. In Wheeler's picture, we are all part of one body but forget it and get focused instead upon the opposites in our universe.

This choosing one side and not another appears in our choosing our everyday body, instead of our dreaming experience. That is why when people get very sick, or especially near death, they fear the loss of their body, which is one part of themselves, and forget the whole of themselves including the experience of dreaming. Much of our thinking operates like that. When we are alive we are here, so our typical thinking goes, and when we are dead we are not here. Instead we might think, "Maybe we are here when we are *alive*, and when we are *dead* we get closer to our dreaming and to the oneness field." We forget and then sometimes need to remember this background field, this oneness.

Where do you see parallel worlds in Processwork theory? There are a lot of them.

- **Primary and secondary processes**: Things are closer to awareness and further from awareness. So we try to say, awareness is there, is unified, instead of conscious and unconscious, which could be a little more split.

- **Channels and channel theory**: I am seeing things, and usually when I am seeing I am not feeling. Now, if I use sensory grounded awareness, I can see, then move, feel, relate, et cetera as a moving process. In most people around the world, body feeling is marginalized. Frequently that is why having people focus on body feelings is such a huge thing—another channel is like another world.

- **Consensus reality and dreamland**: The world everyone says is *real* and another world, the world of dreams.

- **Double signals**: One signal you realize you are sending and the *double* signal you barely notice. Again, two worlds happening at the same time.

As you may know from previous work, I call our *primary process* the feelings, ideas, and signals you or *u* identify with. X is a kind of abbreviation for *secondary process*, that which is *not-me*! In everyday consensus reality there is a *u* as well as this other part of yourself, X, that is further from awareness and appears in double signals and dreams as if it were a parallel world or a separate entity.

PARALLEL WORLDS IN QUANTUM THEORY

In quantum physics, two opposing realities can be present simultaneously. As you know, you can be both dead and alive at the same time according to Erwin Schrödinger. He told us that, using a cat in his example. He said, in essence, "This possibility that the cat can be dead or alive is certainly proof that my wave equation theory of quantum physics is wrong." But Schrödinger's self-doubts were wrong. In quantum physics, as in dreams, you can have parallel worlds and a cat can be both dead and alive depending upon the observer. Two very different and apparently irreconcilable states such as death and life can both be present at the same time.

Let me tell a personal example that happened a few weeks ago to bring the theory to life. Amy and I were about to leave Yachats (a town on the Oregon coast). We had been on the coast, working and doing our Worldwork seminars, growing vegetables and watching sea lions and whales, but then we were leaving to come to Portland. Yachats for me is often a very split off parallel world, very different and separate from the parallel world of Portland. In Yachats, there is the sea with whales that come up and say hello now and then. You don't see many of those in Portland. But Portland has Starbucks, 23rd Avenue, lots of people, and all sorts of things that you don't see in Yachats.

I had just been studying this idea of overlapping states as Amy and I were setting out to drive to Portland. Imagine this. We enter the garage and push the button so the garage door will go up. But there was no power! A tree had apparently fallen in Yachats and the result was that there was no power. We had an appointment in Portland but the garage door was down and would not move without electric power. It couldn't move. The tree had broken the electric lines and our garage door had no power and could not open. I began to sweat, worrying about getting to Portland on time.

Then I remembered parallel, separated worlds. Yachats = inside, and Portland = outside in the world doing this and that. Split worlds. And then I remembered that maybe they both exist and overlap at the same time: How can I be like Schrödinger's cat, both dead and alive, both inside and outside at the same time? How is that possible, and how is that deep quantum world, or "quantum wave world" going to help?

I tried to lift the garage door but the mechanical part was jammed. I could not lift the garage door. I would have needed a crane to lift that door. We were in a terrible rush and I said to myself, "I have got to remember my deepest self, my connection to the whole universe." Each of you will do this in your own way. I went down deep inside myself until I felt, "Oh, two parallel worlds are overlapping, and one part is inside and one part is outside." Then I remembered, "I am not either inside or out, these are overlapping worlds," so I am inside-outside: both at the same time. Yachats and Portland are both here at the same time. Inside and outside in the world, I am with you and I am not with you. All of you do it in your own way.

I went deep inside-out and then for some reason Amy handed me a pair of pliers (neither of us had spoken) and something in me took the pliers and went clunk clunk to the garage door. In a kind of dreamy state, my pliers seemed to work on something almost by themselves, on something I couldn't see and the door opened to the "outer world" as if by magic! This sounds like a good story, but it is true story! The garage door opened! It really happened, I cannot explain it, and I am not sure how it happened. It is not quite reasonable that inside in Yachats and outside in Portland are simultaneously present, but there is an essence or unity that is beyond parallel worlds. It is as if you can be inside and dreamy while you are outside clear and precise at the same time without a barrier or garage door between these inside and outside parts.

Audience: Did the door go back down?

Arny: Yes! I cannot explain it. There was a lock and gears in there, and something happened between the lock and gears. I don't know what I did but *it* did!

Audience: Would you consider that to be a bridge between worlds?

Arny: Yes! That is my point. This deepest part of us, like quantum waves, can be in two states at the same time. These subtle, wave-like experiences in us seem to be the bridge missing in the parallelism of our everyday life. There are inner and outer worlds I associate with the feeling of Yachats and the city of Portland. Yet, there is a kind of *bridge* between them. I am going to call it a common ground between diverse parts of myself and of everyday consen-

DANCE OF THE ANCIENT ONE

sus reality. We need to get to that bridge, that common ground.

Audience: Are you saying that your everyday self did not know how to make that work?

Arny: Yes. I know a lot about mechanics, but I could not get that garage door to go up or down. It is interesting and powerful to realize that there is something trying to tell me, "Arny, inside means Yachats, and Portland is the outside world and at the deepest level they overlap right now!" We need to rediscover that dreaming-oneness bridge, while also being very clear and awake in everyday reality.

But what about the times when we just can't find the bridge? Do you know about those times? Everyone I have ever met has had periods in their life when they say to themselves, "I am split, I cannot get my parts together. My God! Why am I working on this problem again? Why is this happening again?" My teachers told me this story about Jung. They went with him to a church in Basel, Switzerland, where he was giving a lecture and trying to explain the psychology of religion. He was a nervous wreck! He was in his early 70s at the time, and he was a nervous wreck, fidgeting, and so forth. Finally Barbara Hannah said to him, "C.G.! Why are you so upset?!" She was very, very clear about things. She said, "C.G., it is just your negative father coming again!" Quite irritated, Jung said, "What do you expect! I have been working on this all my life and it is coming again to make clear that it is here!"

So Jung, the icon, struggled in the same annoying way with lifetime polarities as did the cobbler down the street from the church. Why do problems that we could have solved, should have solved, have solved already, come back? [The class was suddenly silent.]

I love that silence. Working on your problems to solve them is a great idea, but at a given point the problems are no longer the point but their implicit energies and viewpoints are: that is their diversity! It seems that the universe loves diversity, she loves conflict. When old diversity tensions reappear in your life, it is because nature is trying to tell you that those powerful, different energies in you are still there and are part of your beauty and your overall process. From one viewpoint the different figures and energies represent problems but from another they are part of the wave going up and down. Those energies are part of your beauty. They are what make you look like an ongoing, amazing process.

Audience: Could you also just say that they want to be seen?

Arny: Wonderful! They want to be seen and recognized, they want to really be seen. Hey! Hello! So that you can sometime flow from being this into that with less conflict!

For example, the most difficult thing for the kind of person who says, "I want to be a kind, happy, loving person" is having another, apparently opposite kind of energy like this [Arny mimes explosion]. This explosive energy can be seen as part of inner beauty but because of trauma from the past, or whatever, it is seen as *not me*. Yet, from the most detached viewpoint, there is simply a oneness in the background appearing as diversity.

When I wrote *Earth-Based Psychology* the American Psychological Association decided to review it. The reviewers liked it as a whole but one of them made a comment that is still on my mind. One of the reviewers said, "This is really new, those exercises really work, Mindell seems to know what he is talking about." But then the reviewer said, "But what is physics doing in a psychology book?"

Parallel Universes!

What is physics doing in psychology?! My rebuttal was, "I am *this* and *that*." We live with and are parallel universes; they are incredible and they are part of our beauty and part of our difficulties. Our job is to dance and to find the unifying flow that is this and that, psyche and matter.

The dance puts it all together. There is a dance underneath that unifies these parallel worlds and makes them phases of the overall flow, like the *wave* I spoke of earlier in this chapter. This wave is a symbol of process.

Process

When I first studied psychology, there was psyche and there was matter and no one knew how to put them together. How do psyche and matter link? And I said, maybe psyche and matter are dual fixed things is the wrong paradigm. Maybe we just need to focus on process. Forget these splitting paradigms. Process says, for example, "Now I am feeling something in my body. Now I am having an imagination." The fact that your dreams appear as body symptoms is the unifying dreambody idea in the background. Process is the bridge between parallel worlds, between opposites, between dream and body, and a bridge that puts the worlds together.

ALCHEMY

Many spiritual traditions have put these ideas together and one was alchemy. As some of you know, in Europe and Asia and different parts of the world the alchemists tried to put things together. They had various goals. They put the opposites in their kettles and cooked them: they put hot stuff with cold stuff; they were trying to resolve diversity issues and worked out and sensed some kind of one-world quality behind the world of parts they called the *unus mundus*.

TAOISM

Putting the opposites together is a central issue also in *Taoism*. The Taoists spoke of "The Tao that cannot be said." The Tao was imagined to be a field-like undulating wave, a power. This wave-like processmind power moves back and forth between polar opposites. The Tao that can be said is yin and yang, really simple and easy. The Tao that can be said is what happens if I ask the Tao to tell me whether I should go to the right or left. So I flip my pen into the air. Should I go to the right or should I go to the left in life? Let me spin my pen in the air now. (spins pen). To the left, it says. Left! That is the Tao that can be said.

That is one opposite, one decision for now. But what is the Tao that cannot be said? Something was imagined, some Tao or field-like power that moves the pen in the right way. Watch, when I throw something up in the air. Watch it fall. People have always believed that there is some power in the air that moved things in the right manner. It is this field thing I am talking about. It is this Tao, this field, this space-time presence or dreaming field which we can experience and which appears as one or the other opposite, but in principle is neither. The unifying power or field in the background can be called, "the Tao that can't be said," or process moving between parallel worlds!

2.2 Yin Yang.

WORLD TREE

Being in touch with the living thing that connects worlds is a spiritual thing. People in Northern Europe, way north near the arctic, for centuries and centuries talked about parallel worlds and different universes. Their mythology says that there is a wavy magical tree called *Yggdrasil* that connects all the different universes together.

In some versions of this myth, ladders appear connecting the worlds. In Estonia, for example, the mythic shamans used to say, "We don't know what to do, let's climb a ladder." And a ladder came down and connected them. We find the same theme in the mythology of Africa's bush people, the oldest known civilization. They have a ladder that goes up connecting the different worlds. The ladder is an image of the processmind, the feeling that moves us back and forth between the universes. Being a ladder implies that this back and forth flowing movement process between the worlds is something that all of us human beings can develop in ourselves.

2.3 Yggdrasil, Mythic Tree Between Worlds (Wikipedia).

Audience: So flowing energy itself can be the bridge between worlds?

Arny: Yes, energy is process. The classical shamanistic tree grows and flows between worlds, bridging various polarized universes.

The ancient Chinese oracle, the *I Ching* is based upon the implicit belief that the power of space-time, the Tao, influences a flipping coin. Einstein called the gravity field, or the space around us, space–time. It is our common ground. This common ground is the only space in which we can talk about the diversity that is present and not go to war. Getting to this space and flow is important for facilitators.

The feeling of this space-time dreaming, of this field that moves everything is both smoothly predictable and, at the same time, somewhat unpredictable. We will practice this. We will work with different energies and problems that you have. If I let myself just be moved by space, for example, here is how it looks (Arny moves about in a slow motion, then jitters a bit). Each of you will have your own experience of the space and the movement through it. Some people will stand still. But right now, being moved by space means, for me, that I am moving more or less back or forth. More or less and oops, there is also a bit of a jitter every now and then and there may be a little extra something. Perhaps I can draw this movement on the board.

2.4 Our movements are smooth and a bit unpredictable.

To let yourself be moved by space, or spacetime, relax and let yourself be moved! If you suddenly bump into something a little bit, or jitter a little, that movement can be important. Can you explain why, psychologically, a little jitter may be important? Watch very young children. They can be suddenly very unpredictable. When you are down deep in yourself and close to sleeping, dreams can move you and may even awaken you with a so-called myoclonic spasm. When you are really relaxed, you may feel a little bit altered, sometimes even a bit "drunk." One of the great desires for people, behind most addictions, is to get to this state. But you don't have to drink to get here, you have this open space-time dreaming deep inside yourself.

How come a moment like that can be important?

- It is new and unpredictable.
- It is unintentional—a bug.
- It is part of the bang.
- It is surprising.
- It is a shock that comes out of the clear blue sky.

Yes, jitters are important because they are stochastic. Stochastic means partly determined and partly random. Your movements in space-time cannot be completely predicted.

2.5 Space-time Dreaming.

The spiral in the air is a picture of the powers moving us, of "space-time dreaming," a mixture of gravity, dreaming, and the Tao behind events.

For example, I can just about predict from your childhood dream what is going to happen to you in the large things in life. I can guess at the relationship scenes, at the body problems, and so forth. The deeper part of us is partly deterministic and partly random. I cannot predict however when, how, or exactly where you will have met your partner or done these things in your life. I don't know and have not met anyone, even shamans, who can predict such things because the exact moments are random. There are deterministic aspects in us and there are parts of us that are totally random and it's up to the grace of god or moment in the universe. This is, or we are, a stochastic process.

Einstein might have called the smoothly flowing part the deterministic part, close to his understanding of relativity theory. This random aspect of space is closer to quantum theory which physicists have not yet integrated into relativity. Or the random aspect may appear eventually in what we today call, the mysterious and unknown dark matter and energy of the universe.

In any case, the idea of a connecting space between everything in the universe is what modern physics presently calls *space–time*. Space–time is also a universal connecter, a kind of universal common ground between all observers. It is a needed concept not only in conflict work but also in physics. If two people, one on the moon and the other on earth, both measure a meteor speeding by in the universe, without space–time their measurements will not agree. Space–time is a common language for the universe, so to speak. I'll speak more about the physics later, but let me just suggest at this point that our experience of space–time is like the altered state feelings of dreaming.

Like space-time, dream talk and dreaming are a common ground, a language everyone speaks, everywhere. That is why you find healers, dreams, and shamans all around the world! In any case, your experience of how space moves you is similar to the way you are moved at night to sleep. Space–time (like the Tao) pushes and pulls things in the air; it moves the coins you flip, it is one of the forces determining how the coin will land.

Space–time dreaming is a mixture of the Taoist's idea of the Tao moving things unpredictably and Einstein's idea of space as space–time from his general theory of relativity.[18] Space–time dreaming is a transdisciplinary physical and spiritual characteristic of the universe. As I just said, it is like the Tao, a force field we all sense, especially at night in dreaming, in the day as a subtle sense of being moved, and as a power breathing us into life. Space–time dreaming is an experience everyone already knows about. This experience occurs during the day-time in moments when you allow yourself to be moved effortlessly, feeling both detached and at home at once. It is the core of many spiritual traditions.

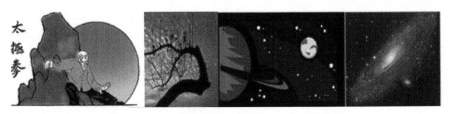

2.6 The Spaced Out Feeling Between Us.

(Thanks to http://www.intermartialarts.com/styles/tai-chi-chuan and Nasa)

Space–time dreaming gives the sense of feeling at home in the universe. You will find aspects of space–time dreaming experiences described in spiritual traditions, in psychology, in physics theories, and in peak or ecstatic as well as near-death experiences. Space-like psychological experience is perhaps one of our greatest, yet little known, gifts. It is not just for those who are interested in the psychological, spiritual, or physical nature of the universe. It is a basic experience, a gift, a specific altered state of consciousness, which is available to anyone needing detachment and creativity,whether for their inner life or for leading meetings! It is implied by the feeling of being spaced out!

My point is that many people, including Einstein, have always felt that the space between us is magical. It can give us distance we need to access the kind of detachment that is based upon the common ground between us.[19]

INNER WORK

Now let's put all this to practice and work on your worst problem! Actually, it is the energy of that problem with which we will work. Some of you may be shy to tell your worst problem to somebody else. If you are shy to tell your personal problem, you don't have to tell the details. I have been lucky in recent times. I don't have a lot of problems. But one of the worst that I do have, relative to not having any, is getting tired after exercising. I do a lot of running. So my worst problem is I get tired afterwards. It is a lucky thing to have, as problems go, and it sounds normal to get tired after running. But for me it is a problem because if I express that tiredness I go down like this (Arny bends forward, arms hanging downward). And the part that most dislikes that energy jumps up in the air a bit and says, in essence, "Let's get going!" The two parts are in conflict.

You are going to be working on the two energies involved in your worst problem. Get some paper to make notes. OK. After you identify those two energies, I am going to ask if you can see those energies in a favorite earth spot. For me, both my conflicted energies are in the coastal area. And I want you to be there in your favorite spot (for me it is the coast), and let the earth there breathe you and move you around. Now comes the big moment. I want you to move away from the earth a little bit, like an astronaut, getting distance from things. Getting distance is extremely important. This movement out into the distance will bring out a tiny bit of an altered state. Don't be nervous about it. Get away from the tensions and the opposites and all and just let your-selves be moved by space as if you were a coin being moved freely. Once away from your problems, and in that distant area, while you are being moved by space-time I want you to stay conscious and use your awareness to notice how your movement dance gives you spontane-ous, dreamlike, and very quick insights. Catch those insights, and they will help you with the problem on which you are focusing.

Here is a summary of the steps of this exercise, which, as all ex-ercises in this book, can be done alone or with a helper. As I said, I'd advise you to keep a record on paper of each of these exercises for use at a later time.

....

EXERCISE

1. Identify your worst problem.

2. Identify the most disturbing energy—let's call it X—contained in that problem.

3. Express X with your hand motions and quickly sketch X's energy on paper.

4. Note which part of you most dislikes this X energy—let's call it u.

5. Feel u in your body, express u in hand motions, and then sketch it.

6. Have X + u energies appeared in a childhood dream or memory or in a recent body problem?

7. Go to a favorite earth spot and find the X + u energies somewhere there.

8. Let the earth breathe you between the X + u spots on the earth as you express them in movement.

9. Now rise up above earth into space and let space begin to dance and move you unpredictably until this dance gives you insight into how X + u are somehow parts or phases of that oneness dance.

After the exercise, an audience member asked:

Audience: How come I am not more like this altered state all the time?

Arny: The problem is that we forget the flow part of ourselves. We forget the dance, the flow. It is absolutely natural to forget. We need to forget the dance to be a normal, everyday person in consensus reality. There we have separate parts. That is ok, there is nothing wrong with being a part. It just isn't comfortable all of the time. It's important that you get to know this movement-dreaming part of yourself that will eventually put your parts together into a flow.

When the universe dances you, the u and the X energies appear as if they were phases of the dance. *Phases* means that the energies are in the dance. There is no fight from the dancer's viewpoint. In a way, you are a dance looking like a person. You are not a person who dances only. You are a dance looking like a person. It is another viewpoint. It is a more universal viewpoint. You are a process acting like a particular person, a normal person in conflict with other parts. Everyday or consensus reality is a dimension of fixed, separate particularities. But you are a dance, and in your dance, you will find everything that you are.

Audience: Could we also say that we are a wave looking like a particle?

Arny: Oh, how beautiful! We are waves acting like particles. I love it! The most dangerous moment, Don Juan says to Castaneda, comes when we reveal our personal history to somebody because that person will identify us with it. And as soon as we are identified with it, as Ms. So-and-So or Mr. So-and-So, or Arny and Amy, you are that, and you forget the dance.

....

Σ   *For Reflection on Chapter 2*

- When the oneness of the universe wakes up, it is as if something curious and wonderful breaks into parts and forgets itself. Space awakens and tends to identify as this or that, makes a big bang, and creates the universe of parts!

- Then we have space–time dreaming, as well as an X and a u and everyday reality.

- Perhaps our job is to find and use that oneness again, that world tree, the Tao, or space–time dreaming to put the world parts together again.

DANCE OF THE ANCIENT ONE

CHAPTER 3

Illness, Time Reversal, and Parallel Worlds

I love to hug. Here is a big hug to all of you in various parts of the world online and here in Portland. Wait, I am saying this… I don't feel it yet. Let me say it when I feel it… lol! I almost forgot relationship work. Relationship is not just about two or more people, it is also about something else inside of you that you share with others. So to just work on a relationship as if you are two people is not enough. That is obviously important, but it can be missing the relationship field. This is a nonlocal field between you.

Normally, I identify with this person running around, giving a talk, and neglect that part of me, that parallel world, the dreaming field that is still present when I am waking up. It's normal to forget that parallel dream world, but today I want to stress that neglecting parallel worlds is a source of unwellness. Remember, when you wake up in the morning, a crucial moment occurs when you make decisions about who you are. Be careful how you make those decisions and remember, if you can, more or less your whole self.

Last time (i.e., the last class from which the prior chapter was derived) I was saying that one way of understanding a lot of quantum physics, a great deal of mythology, and a lot of psychology is to comprehend the wave hum: the deep background that is wondering. It is a *wonder*. Wonder may be the essence of the images called by the names of the various goddesses and gods. Wonder has an amazing quality. When wonder wakes up, it says, "Who am I?" Usually I am this and I am not that. As I said in the last chapter, the moment you make that choice, you are divorcing a part of yourself. That's quite natural. But the X that you divorced upon awakening will look like a problem or a problematical person or group later in the day.

LOVE

Someone online just asked, "Where does love fit into the basic idea that the universe tends to marginalize its own parts? Where does love fit in here?" Each of you will have your own answer to that question. My answer is that *love*, for me, is living in this world of ours, full of diversity, and now and then finding that oneness that "ties the knot" and holds us together. Love is an appreciation of diversity and an experience of the oneness that is our essence. The spiritual traditions say that god is love. So, in Processwork terms, love is associated with the processmind's space-time dreaming experience. For me, love is present when we remember the processmind, the dance between our diversity in this world.

In my mind the word love is also connected to compassion: compassion toward the various sides of yourself and others. *It* wants. It loves this direction and that direction. It is open to all of the directions. It gives birth to them and it is the mother of your parts. Compassion and love can mean so many things to me. You might wake up in the morning with an agitated feeling of being chased by somebody and say, "Whoa! That was a difficult dream." You wake up in yourself taking one role and then you remember that love produced the dream. The energy chasing you—maybe abuse issues, childhood wounds, adult grievances—is really love saying, "Wake up to this other energy! Wake up to all of yourself! Wake up to fighting this other thing! Wake up to eventually integrating this energy!" It's love or wonder that produces all these parts and is very generous to you in a way.

That perspective is something to keep in mind especially if you plan to facilitate large groups. Because as the facilitator, if you are a normal person, you will turn against one part of a group, one or another, sometime or other, and then you become part of the difficulty. Instead of one part, the earth has room for all parts including your resistances and everything else's—all the parts are present from the grandest viewpoint.

That is why I say that wherever you have trouble, make that trouble part of your family. Bring that trouble home to the universe, to your universal mind, to the processmind, and to love so that you can work with it. This kind of love is a *metaskill*, as Amy says. It is a feeling thing.

Now let's think about the parallel worlds theory of theoretical physics. I am going to talk about theoretical physics but will focus on the psychology behind the physics. First, I want to tell you about Max Tegmark, a cosmologist studying the universe at MIT. He is now saying things that are almost generally accepted as mainstream science today. (He was just published in the Scientific American.[20]) Tegmark says that even though we don't know exactly what events some of the math behind quantum physics and string theories predict, we must consider the possibility of there being parallel realities to the one we usually identify as this world or universe. Why does he think this? Because of the equations of quantum physics and because of what he calls a *mathematical democracy*.

As I said in *Quantum Mind*, the equations of physics point to realities we don't understand and yet are in many ways like dreams and fantasies. In a certain sense, Tegmark is saying that all our dreams and sudden fantasies are *real* even though we don't know exactly what each of them refers to in the moment. This is a radical idea. Physicists are beginning to say something to the effect that dreaming is real, that we have to be open to the possibilities in the background, and that we must be open to the dreaming—the unfathomable realities to which the equations point—even if we cannot see them. This is the beginning of a huge culture–paradigm change. In some ways we are going back to where we were thousands of years ago.

Audience: Why do the physicists call these multiple realities a *democracy*?

Arny: Max Tegmark is trying to say, in part, that although we see only reality, or what I have been calling *consensus reality*, other realities are also *mathematically real* in some way. So, be democratic. Open up to the other possibilities as well. Open up to the one you see and remember that the others are around even if you don't see them. Of course, Aboriginal people have known about these parallel worlds since the beginning of time, but physicists are just catching on to them. I think this may be happening in part because I criticized science in my book *Quantum Mind*, where I suggested that Einstein and other physicists marginalized various possibilities and were against the different worlds in us. One physicist was especially hurt by my suggestion. He told me that physicists were always open but just shy about saying that the other worlds are there. We just don't see them all the time.

Amy: In *Quantum Mind* you talked about deep democracy and they may have picked up that concept of democracy from there.

Arny: Yes, physicists now speak of the "democracy of particle paths," et cetera.

Parallel worlds exist: Let's say there is a little kid in the background of my behavior and I am saying, "Be democratic. Be deeply democratic!" Where do you see that little kid? I am an adult! But in my double signals you can see the kid. You see him in the fluctuating minimal cues that you cannot put your finger on! That kid appearing in my double signals of dancing around is a parallel world, though usually not identified as such.

To be deeply democratic with yourself, you need awareness and openness to all that you are. Otherwise, you can marginalize parts of yourself that you don't think belong in consensus reality! Because not recognizing or not accepting parts of yourself that you think should not be here can be a kind of internalized childism, sexism, racism, et cetera. Or you can be ageist: people over 20 often think they should not be kids. Be careful of how you look at your parts. Be deeply democratic.

The idea of parallel worlds was first implied by quantum physicists such as Niels Bohr. In his *Copenhagen interpretation* of the quantum world, he stated that once we observe one of the many background possibilities, they all *collapse* but the real one. That principle is a central part of physics. Other possibilities collapse. Where does this happen psychologically to you and me? By stressing consensus reality, we collapse or marginalize our double signals! Or organizations may say one way is right and real. The rest? Forget 'em!

In 1957 physicist Hugh Everett spoke of parallel worlds that fluctuate. Where do you see your parallel worlds fluctuating? In dreams and flirts! You are walking along the street and something catches your attention quickly; it fluctuates in your attention. Look at that! I call those things flirts; they catch our attention quickly. Those are quantum like, fluctuating parallel worlds. If you want to have a good day, I suggest that you catch those flirts. For example, Amy and I were looking into a hat store on 23rd Avenue the other day, and there was a woman working in the store looking very serious about selling those hats. We had never gone into that store before. Something about her flirted with me and so Amy and I went in, and I acted out a signal that I saw in her that had caught my attention. I said to the saleswoman, jokingly, "Would you like to buy my hat, the one on my head?" The saleswoman was shocked and looked at me wide-eyed! "You don't have to answer this," I said, "I am just making fun. $2.50 please!" and she broke out laughing uncontrollably.

Parallel worlds are nonlocal; they are in the air. The saleswoman acted serious, but she seemed to me to give signals of wanting to be more playful and to buy a hat for herself. Amy and I wanted to play. So Amy and I walked into the store, made a little 2-minute scene, and played with her. All the things that catch your attention, all those parallel worlds are your family: the person selling the hat, the imagination of someone wanting to buy the hat, the dog on the street, the tree, and the kid inside you.

Don't be shy about living within your own feelings. I like doing it. Try it, in a way that is safe and good for you, acting out things that may have caught your attention. Bring the world back to life. That is my suggestion. It is a fantastic universe, and we should really bring the life that is in the background of these parallel worlds out to the forefront!

Richard Feynman, a Nobel Prize winning physicist, said that the elementary particle that we pictured going one way or another is not really doing what we saw. Instead, elementary particles are in a continuous process of trying all paths. The particle goes forward, backward, and everywhere before deciding to move in the way we see it. This is another interpretation of quantum life and of what today we might call parallel worlds. Try all worlds, all paths, all signals.

How do you try all paths before choosing what to do? Remember standing in front of the mirror in the morning and deciding what to wear? You probably said, "I don't want to show this part; better put on a jacket that covers that part." You are trying the different parts of yourself and choosing one of them. Also, before you make decisions about something, you are thinking all sorts of things: "If I do this, it might come out bad there; if I try that, it might come out good here," and so on. We try all paths so quickly we barely notice them. It is very important to notice, though, because knowing ourselves means catching and appreciating these teeny-weeny things, these parallel worlds we take part in all day long. Self-love is meditating and noticing the little things that we do as well as the big ones.

Entropy

Missing signals means you are missing information. If you think that what happened in a dream only happened in a dream, you may start to feel confused, uneasy, or fatigued during the day. You may get tired or fear that some illness is coming your way. Depending on your age, you may fear death, or, independently of your age, you may feel criticized by somebody and worried about her or him. The basic idea is that uncertainty creeps in. If you marginalize any one of these signals or their worlds because they don't seem to belong to you, then the energy of that world will spook you from the background. "Hahhaha!" You think that information is in the dream or in another person or the other person does not like you—all of which may or may not be true—but there is information that is missing, and missing information is a very serious thing.

Let's talk about information theory. In 1948, physicist Claude Shannon said something very simple. He said that when information gets bungled up, entropy increases. Entropy is a measure of disorder. That is how to say it simply. For example, when I put some soymilk into my coffee, you might see little images swirl in there with the soymilk! When you look at my coffee with that milk looking so nice, you might say, "Isn't that beautiful?"

What happens over time? Disorder. The soymilk mixes with the coffee, and you might say, "Well, it is not as pretty, all I can do is drink it now." Entropy increased. The original order of putting the cream into the coffee went to pieces. It was beautiful and that beauty was lost. Entropy increased, disorder increased.

So what? Who cares about entropy increasing? The reason you should be upset about entropy increasing is because you no longer know the image the soymilk made. The same thing happens in the morning when you get up; you may be clear sometimes about what you dreamed and what bugged you. Perhaps some person you dreamed was doing some stupid thing that upset you. That order and information are in a state of low entropy or high order first thing in the morning. If however you forget it, you may walk around all day wondering, "Why am I doing these stupid things?" And you may be bothered by allergies as if you were allergic to yourself. That is because disorder has happened, the cream dissolved into the coffee. You have lost the clarity of the parts and forgot that a part of you does stupid things that upset you. If you were clear, you would change your behavior.

Entropy generally increases in closed systems. It is normal to go into a mood during the day, feeling like this or that, and that is because there is a lot of entropy happening; you have got to go back and find out what it is that is bugging you. That is really important. Dreamwork reduces entropy and increases awareness of order.

Entropy happens in communication. If two people understand what one other said, that is low entropy. But if communication channels, like a bad telephone connection, distort someone's voice, that creates too much entropy! Lots of entropy means too much *noise* in the system.

If you have too much disorder inside yourself, you are not just moody; your body may also begin to trouble you. A lot of body symptoms (perhaps all) are preceded by months of ignoring or losing information about yourself. Then entropy increases, you no longer know what it is that was bothering you and that lost information may appear as a body signal that bothers you like something bothering your stomach, a cramp in your neck, and so forth. Entropy increased!

Can we reverse entropy? Physics says that it is improbable that nature herself will reverse a disorderly process in a closed system. This disorderliness is a natural law; as entropy increases, the universe will—in principle—end up in a *heat death*. Have you ever heard that? This is one of the most outstanding and dreadful laws in physics. It's called "the second law of thermodynamics," but no one can prove or disprove it yet. This law implies that the whole universe will end up in a shambles. That means that there will just be noise and chaos, nothing and nobody left. What do you think about that?

I have never heard of anybody clapping for that future! You pour milk into your coffee and at first it is very, very beautiful. Then, in time, it becomes mushy. The reversal of this process has never been observed. It is very unlikely that the milk will pull itself together and go back into the bottle all by itself. Or will it? Can we reverse time? That is the question. Can we go backwards in time? My answer is "Yo"—yes and no!

If you get a big symptom, is it true that without normal medicine you are going to go downhill and the universe is going to end up in a big mush? Is there any chance for you to have a spontaneous healing? Yes! Of course there is. This phenomenon might be called spontaneous healing. This is rare but happens. Spontaneous healing is a kind of metaphorical entropy reversal.

Can you reverse the entropy flow inside yourself and create order where there was disorder? We are not exactly closed systems, as humans, so I shall answer, "Yes," there are several ways of reversing disorder just with your mind. Bringing more awareness of your body to your mind sometimes seems to reverse symptoms. Some symptoms reverse temporarily, whereas other symptoms seem to disappear altogether, but both require consciousness to achieve the reversal and to hold onto it afterwards. Healers and shamans have been speaking of this kind of healing for centuries and, although it is hard to prove statistically using the scientific method, I have seen it happen. Process-mind awareness that flows between the parts may have good effects on your body, not just your everyday psychology. I want to leave that idea as a hopeful possibility for you to prove or disprove in the future.

Trying to understand ourselves and communicate with ourselves and others clearly without double signals reverses entropy. The whole point of psychology is to reduce entropy in the mind and emotions, but can we also reduce entropy in the body so that it does not die? Maybe we can slow time down. That is exactly what our exercise today is about: slowing time down. Isn't that the most exciting thing! Slowing time down!

By assuming that, "I am this and I am not that," we forget our parallel worlds, we ignore some information about ourselves, and we, as physical systems, become entropic. Remember:

1. For closed material thermodynamic systems, entropy is a measure of available energy.

2. It is also a measure of the disorder or randomness in a closed system.

3. It is also a measure of the loss of information in a transmitted message.

4. The entropy law, the second law of thermodynamics, says that in our consensus reality universe there is a tendency for all matter and energy in the universe to evolve toward a state of inert uniformity.

Entropy describes physical and informational disorder. A little disorder can be psychologically stimulating and make you work with yourself and others better. But too much entropy is disturbing to everything and everyone.

Instead of pushing away or neglecting signals, following your body signals will give you more energy for work. Sometimes, if you are really aware of all your signals, you can do *not-doing*. That means, things sort of happen and you don't feel that you are doing them. In a doing mode, you are pushing against an unknown, which creates entropy and reduces the energy available for working. But if you are in your processmind, that means you are close to your dancing mind; you feel the deepest part of yourself, experiencing it partially as a dance, and what you do seems to get done, as if by itself.

The solution to unwellness and entropy—a solution to a lot of body problems and relationship problems—is to get deep inside yourself and let the universe move you in whatever ways it wants. Sometimes it does things spontaneously with a lot of energy in it: unpredictable things like what I was calling stochastic in the last chapter. The universe will move you in predictable ways and sometimes unpredictably and in an apparently chaotic manner. The point is that when you are consciously close to your processmind your entropy is very low. You are with all the different parts of yourself. They are not split off from one another, and you feel well.

You can find your processmind dance at any time. For example, when I work with an organization or a business, I don't show my processmind dance all the time, but I will suggest to participants, "Loosen your neck muscles, let your neck go," and they will do it. Just that one simple shift in awareness that creates the loosening is the beginning that allows new things to flow in.

The Not-Doing Exercise to Reduce Entropy—slowing down disorder and not doing—that's what we want to practice. The point is getting to know yourself. I am trying to bring the worlds together. Physics and psychology belong together. As they come together, they get closer to shamanism. Being close to processmind allows you to do amazing things. The following exercise is about wellness and it is about becoming conscious of when you become unconscious. We will be working with the energy of pushing—I call that X—and with the one who is upset by that pushing—I call that u. We shall then move into the universe to gain distance from these polar opposites and look at things from a great distance so that we are not so involved in the polarizations. Also, distance gives us a little detachment, which is really the same thing. It is the feeling of being at home and that everything else is a part of you, not the whole of you.

....

EXERCISE: EXPLORE TIME AND WELLNESS

1. When you push yourself to do things, what disturbing body sensation (X) do you feel or fear?

2. How do you look and act when pushing?

3. Feel and draw that X energy. What does time feel like then?

4. What part of you (that is, who in you) is most disturbed by this X? This is u. Feel and sketch this u energy.

5. Why does X forget u and why does u forget X?

6. In your imagination, go to a favorite place on earth and try to find the X + u energies there somewhere in the wind, trees, water, or in the city, et cetera.

7. Now leave the earth and its parts. Let go and move from that earth spot into the universe. Let the universe dance or move you unpredictably.

8. Then, when you feel totally in your dance, look back at earth and give yourself some advice.

9. Feel your unpredictable dance movements and body sensations. What does time feel like now? Make a sketch of your movement on paper. That movement, that's not-doing, a kind of "healing" and perhaps even a kind of time reversal.

(Commenting on a participant's drawings)

What different motions do you see in her drawings? Curving versus linear and inwards and outwards. The most classic aspects of us.

Why do you think she needed to work on that? Why do you think all of us need to work on this conflict process between linear and curved motion?

- We get caught in one role like the curving feeling and forget the others.

- We forget where we are coming from.

- We forget our mother, where home is, the universe.

Each of you may have discovered your own wisdom that comes out of this experience. Some people sing or hum something. Other people will blow a fart! Whatever people do, just catch it.

Many people seem to have near-death experiences in order to gain this connection to the universe. That dance is, in a way, indeed something to die for. There is a slang expression in English: "I could just die for that." Does anyone have a question about the exercise, or does anyone want to describe that subtle state?

Audience 1: I experienced the universe dance as a state of totally undefined vastness and endlessness. The motion that came out was this (demonstrates vast, sweeping motions, with a smile). It was as if something was moving me. As if every-thing significant, the night sky, the morning sunrise was loving me.

Audience 2: This dance is a health issue for me. When I am close to the universe, I can breathe freely and that deep breath-ing brings more oxygen and more consciousness into my body.

....

Σ   *For Reflection on Chapter 3*

- Splitting off information into a parallel world makes things con-fusing, and we may feel unwell as a result.

- The universe creates disorder through breaking things into parts, and mixing them all up. But the universe also inspires us to create more order and to reverse the inevitable entropic increase and disorder around us.

- Use the universe dance to know yourself and give yourself some advice about how to deal with polarizations.

CHAPTER 4

Relationship, Atmosphere, and Kairos

How are you all today? I can feel that the answer is mixed. I like that. That is diversity for you! Everyday seems to be busy to me but then I remember, "Aha! Something else can help me with all this."

This class is about what I call the *process revolution*. It is about the *relationship spirit*, the spirit of relationships. There is no one spirit of relationship, of course, but the idea is to think about and sense the background to relationship. For me, that background is also a spirit.

Or you could say this class is about, "Who spilled the coffee? Who spilled the water?" In other words; who, you or me, did the thing that wasn't good? And the answer, in reality, is you or me but from a deeper perspective it is us.

As you know, I have been speaking about a possible metaview of the origin of the universe that fits some characteristics of quantum physics and that also fits some creation myths. The reason I take physics and mythology both equally seriously is because I feel that people have always felt and known, without actual evidence, what is actually happening in the universe. Many peoples have always felt that there was something in the beginning that may have had some form of consciousness that wanted to self-reflect. It awakened itself, like we awaken in the morning, often saying, "I am this, and I am not that."

Perhaps we all need an overview or metaview when we are dealing with the many problems and tensions around the world. These problems can bother us at night and day, inside of us, inside our nervous systems. We need something like *wonder* to center us in order to continue that work. A philosophical viewpoint of almost any kind is extremely important to manage to move through things. Everybody has one. You can find yours in your dreams.

Here is one possible metaview: The universe creates conflict and the opposing sides exist not just because there is good and evil—each to his or her own—but because *it* or wonder wants to self-reflect. Believing that opens me up, and hopefully you too, to not make war with wars, with sides you don't like. If you can open up just a little bit to the other side; wow, it is easier in your body and easier in the world as a whole.

The universe, the processmind, creates polarities I have been calling $u + X$. They conflict and the conflict then escalates and creates a lot of bloodshed. We know this from history. Most of us are sick of it. But re-beginnings happen. Remember, after the Second World War? Remember Egypt recently fighting for democracy? (Over 5,000 people from Cairo and Alexandria recently joined my Facebook page wanting to know, "What now after democracy?")

In the creation myths there is always a godhead or Adam and Eve figures that choose to forget where they came from temporarily and thereby contribute to creating the world. But then, there is almost always a deluge on earth. And the deluge means a lot of entropy but then it also reawakens the world and miraculously there is a re-beginning. *Deluge* means a big flood, a big catastrophe, a lot of trouble. In some traditions the deluge is created by the essence or godhead figure that says, "Oh! I'm fed up with those guys down there!" and then a whole lot of trouble comes and a re-beginning occurs again and again.

Of course, I hope that $u + X$ can awaken, find the processmind, and avoid some of these terrible entropic phases. Can we help short-cut the troubles before they get really bad? And in relationships and group process, when I see conflicts beginning to happen, can I short-cut them a little bit by getting clearer about what is happening by coming back to the essence level and re-beginning? Sometimes it is possible.

Audience: On National Public Radio this morning, somebody was talking about Syria and said, if we only talk to our friends and never to our enemies, then the issue does not resolve.

Arny: If you only talk to your friends (u) and not to your enemies (X), that is it! One of our topics in the second training is,

"How does your worst enemy evaluate you?" And remember I said, "Go where the conflict is. That is where your home is. That is where your family is."

Audience: If home and family are where the conflict is, why do we sometimes marry someone we love rather than someone we are bickering with?

Arny: Well, most of us usually first relate to or marry somebody we are bickering with! Most people create first relationships or marry with unfinished conflicts from their family system. So we are unconsciously trying to work out some of that old stuff. You don't have to marry the conflict, though! If you feel there is a lot of conflict or difficulty someplace, to begin with, work on it in yourself as if it is you. That is the first step.

We have been talking about using the space–time dreaming approach to global problems, and I want to continue studying how to find more order. By *order* I mean finding the polarities in a mood or finding the polarities in a bad atmosphere and feeling that atmosphere. Finding the polarities already reduces the disorder. Just getting clear if there is a bad mood in a group can help you focus your work on changing the climate between group members.

Work on the atmosphere to begin with, otherwise things get disorderly. And if you are in a mood for a while, which is absolutely natural, see if you can find some order: "What is bugging me and who's against it?" See what is in that mood. It might be good for your health. That is the entropy connection that I was talking about. When entropy increases, so does disorder. More entropy = more disorder. Get back to the source of things. Polarization is not yet disorder. However, polarization that goes unconscious creates the conditions for disorder.

Every place you move there is diversity! Be clear about it. Process it, at least with yourself. That creates more order. That is the basic idea. Becoming aware of the source of your (u) responses is good for you, and it is surely good for the atmosphere. Some people are too quiet or too shy to talk openly about the inner work they do on themselves in this regard. That is ok. That is their style. Just know that inner work may have nonlocal effects because space-time is a common ground. Working on myself is, for me, an inner spiritual and also a realistic worldly endeavor.

I want to mention James Clerk Maxwell (1831–1879), one of the greatest scientists responsible for our understanding of thermodynamics, which is the field of physics that deals with heat flow. Maxwell, along with others, defined *entropy* as a measure of disorder. The greater the entropy (inertia), the less energy there is available for work. It was also his idea that the universe, left to itself, runs downhill. As I said in the last chapter, the second law of thermodynamics implies that the universe is going to pieces. It means that there will be less and less available energy. It is difficult to prove such a thing because the universe is a very big place: how are you going to do an experiment with it? But we do know that closed systems degenerate.

Clerk Maxwell created a thought experiment in which he sought to invalidate this second law of thermodynamics through the imagined actions of what came to be called by others *Maxwell's demon*. Maxwell conceived this unknown force as able to actually decrease entropy by somehow getting into the closed system. In my terms, Maxwell realized that there must be some form of awareness demon, some *mind* that could go inside these closed systems and reverse their physical things so that time slows down and so that order can be reestablished. No one has ever found that demon, but it was still in his mind.

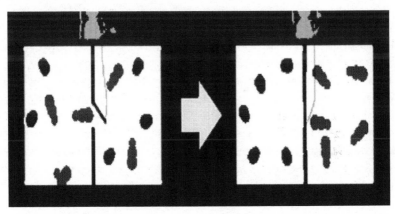

4.1 The Maxwell Demon.

The Maxwell demon's Awareness opens and closes the door reducing the X + u conflict and reversing time and the law of disorder. (Thanks to Wikipedia)

Maxwell sensed that he, or anyone, could get inside a mess and clear it up. Though they have not found such a thing in physical reality, it is possibly inside of us. Just think about it: Inside your own body, with your own self, you can, within reason, slow time down a little bit. You can feel better. That is what therapy is all about. There is a potential for order. When you become aware of the parts working against each other and you are beginning to feel unhappy or disagreeable or irritated, that's when you know you need to take some kind of conscious action.

In Processwork we know you have two choices at least. One is to go inside and ask what kind of energy is bugging you and who is against it? Then have the conflict out more consciously. And the other choice is to go with the misery for, say, depression or oppression and exhaustion. If possible, go with the degenerate feeling: "I am exhausted. I cannot go on. The deluge is coming and it can be helpful!" Say, "OK, I am a mess. I am dying." in the sense of letting go of everything. Going into the fatigue state can be very illuminating and exhilarating. Letting go of your $u + X$, drop out of the world of polarities. Just letting them all go can be very regenerative. Say, "OK, let's just go with the impending deluge." Go inside and then at some point, let go!

These are two different types of people and two types of processes, and both are fine. Work directly on the polarity, fight, get medicine to overcome the X or just *sink* into the dance of the ancient one and dance between the polarities.

Maxwell projected that inside every physical system is the possibility of consciousness. Even in a dead-looking lump of matter is the potential for consciousness and the process of separating things out and working with them.

Maxwell's demon is the processmind! Maxwell did not believe the prediction that the universe is simply going downhill. He hated that prediction. He knew that physics says, if you can reverse entropy, it is equivalent to reversing time. If you create order where there was disorder, you slow time down and if you do that enough, you can reverse time and even go backwards in time. In principle we know that that is a possibility but it is not too likely. I will go for the slowing down part. I am uncertain that we can or want to reverse time all together.

If you could, you might go backwards 100 years and tell your grandfather not to fall in love with your grandmother. That would be a problem! You can't reverse time completely, because you would make yourself disappear! If you went back and stopped your grandfather from having a relationship with your grandmother, you might not be here. Total time reversal may be unlikely but making more order and creativity in the world—Yes! That is definitely possible!

Buddhism and Taoism

When you are deep enough inside yourself, the concept of polarities makes you giggle and then you land in the world of Buddhism and other traditions that say that things are not fixed. Suddenly, you get close to Buddhism and to Taoism in that moment. There really are no permanently polarized polarities at the essence level. When you begin to dance from the deepest dreaming mind inside of you and you begin to get in touch with space–time, like we have been practicing, in that moment what used to be u + X polarities are not polarities at all, just aspects of your dance.

I remember a number of years ago while doing worldwork in India, there was a spiritual master who got up and said to us, "Oh! You are always working with all this conflict. Why are you doing that? So silly! Ho ho!"

"Ggggrrrr!" I was a little irritated. He had created a conflict with his statement! But now I am sharing his view, which is also one of my views. It took me many years to understand him, and now I do. From the deepest viewpoint, the polarities are not permanent realities but parts or phases of a dance. In consensus reality, we need to be very serious about polarities. If somebody is approaching you with a fist and is about to hit you, you better stop him any way you can and not meditate just yet. It is important to pay attention to the polarities that abound in our consensus reality. At the same time, it is equally important to hold the background sense of the larger dance that is free of all polarities. Then you might even predict that someone is about to punch you, and you might step over to where that person is standing and starting yelling at yourself as well… part of a dance… where you also roll over to your own side.

The little u is a natural dictator. Why don't we do this more often? The little u is a dictator! It is horrible and wonderful. By that I mean, the little u part of you says, "I am me, and I am not that, and I really don't like that!" Nature loves that differentiation! She produces us and makes us do that to self-reflect. We know that she is against X. There are good things about having a good strong ego. Everybody knows that: "Be strong. Be intelligent. Do the things you want to do!" OK! Woof! But it is exhausting after a while.

But everyone's little u can learn. Sailing might help. Let's imagine going sailing. See the diagram below. Look at the left hand side first, the Parts View. Let's say Z, my goal, is to the right, let's say west. The wind, X, however, is going from north to south. For u to get to Z when the wind, X, is blowing from north to south means that I must steer my ship a little towards the north, that is upwards, into the wind! Into X! I can't just go straight to my goal Z because this wind X is troublesome. X, the wind, comes at me, whoosh-whoosh, so I must push against X to get to Z! That's normal sailing. That is tiring! You have to push against X to try to reach your goal.

CR Parts (vector) View

u can't go straight because of X. So *u* fights X to get to Z.

Processmind (curved) Space View

No forces on *u* in curved space, so *u* goes forward with processmind dance.

4.2 Two Ways to Sail.

OK, that is one way to do things. Now let's look at the processmind curved view. This second way to do things as the little *u* is to head towards Z as before. But as I go in this direction toward Z, I feel the X wind in my face and now with my processmind I go deeper in myself and say, "I know where my goal is but *it* has to get me there. My old way of doing things is tiring." So I will start out against X, so to speak. I move and relax but let my processmind spin me around to get me there. *It* will get me there in its own way. This path is nonlinear. The little *u* is a linear personality structure and that is just fine but little *u* doesn't know the best way to get to Z in the face of X so it begins to fight, then relaxes and flows.

The problem is the little *u*. It normally thinks that it has to get you there. But if you are connected with yourself deeply enough and you just remember your goal and *it*, the dance of your most "ancient one," the dance of the universe will get you there on its own. There are always at least two ways of doing something. When you are straining, you have too much stress and your body is complaining. Those are clear signs that your little *u* needs to remember space-time dreaming.

Know your goal! Know as best you can where you want to go in life and then get in touch with *it* bringing you there. Sometimes you must first use your fist and force your way and sometimes you can do things more easily by following space-time dreaming! That is one of the most important points I have ever learned. Did I get it across?

Audience: How do you reconcile that idea with the everyday consensus reality expectations that by a certain age you should be doing this or by a certain time you should have done that?

Arny: Try the *should* as best you can, and if the should wears you out; if you start to do it and something steps in the way all the time; well, good. You can try harder still but then at another point, *it* has got to do it or things won't work well. Shoulds only work for us when they resonate with our deepest parts, with our processmind.

Audience: So you are saying that the deepest teacher is our own process, not anything outside?

Arny: Yes, thanks for saying that for me. There is nothing like your processmind.

Audience: That idea just undid all the socialization and conditioning I've ever had.

Arny: Normal consciousness is like a square around my head. My head is inside of a box. I think only in my head.[21] It's all about my head, my head, my head. Another state of consciousness involves taking the box off my head and letting the entire environment; the earth, the universe's spaces; be my head. Some people can achieve this new perspective by visualizing it. Others feel it. Some of us must use movement to get out of the head box.

We are surrounded by, held by, a magnetic field. A *field*, in this sense, is something that we cannot see that moves us, like gravity. Who of us has ever seen gravity? So, in one state of consciousness, I do things. And in another state of consciousness, I am moved as if there is a field moving me, like space–time. Fields are mysterious, and the final word on fields is yet to come.

Being moved by space–time and other fields is being moved by something invisible. It is the essence of all the world religions. It is at the bottom of just about every tradition in some way. Get in touch with the invisible things that move you.

Audience:	But science and the whole field of engineering try to control things and you are saying, "Let go and go with the flow!" I have a reaction that comes out, "How can you trust that? When people follow the flow chaos happens!"
Arny:	Yes. ok. Then don't trust! Not trusting is part of the flow too. You cannot do something that is not part of the flow. Part of your flow will be, "I don't trust that! Prove it to me!" Then your dreaming process will bring you to the next step.

KAIROS

The process revolution is about going with *kairos*. Can somebody who speaks or knows Greek translate what *kairos* means?

- It means weather, literally, or a special period of time.

- *Kairos*: Movement, process, flow, and time are all understood by people today as phenomena that are measurable and, to some extent, controllable. The old Greeks, in contrast, felt that time was as you say, "none of their business," but rather up to the dreaming gods. The Greek *kairos* (καιϱός) meant the right or opportune moment (the supreme moment).

Amy told me that the term *Ma* in Japanese (間) means roughly gap, space, pause, or the space between two structural parts. A picture showing this *Ma* is from Wikipedia, from the 16th century Hasegawa Tohaku, 1539–1610.[21]

In this picture, you sense a feeling coming from the atmosphere. Perhaps this is an Asian equivalent of *kairos*. Can you see the space, feeling, weather, the atmosphere, or *ether*?

4.3 Ma.

What is the difference between the words *kairos* and *chronos*? *Kairos* means weather, climate, atmosphere. What is the atmosphere between us? What is the climate like between us as people? In relationship: What is the atmosphere like between us? What is the space like between us? What is the space-time dreaming or weather like between us? *Chronos* in Greek means time. "What time is it?" What is happening exactly? *Chronos* refers to the time of consensus reality time. *Kairos* is the dreaming aspect, the climate. "What does it feel like between us?" *Chronos* is what our little *u* is supposed to be attached to!

What is the atmosphere like between us? How can we find and work with that atmosphere? What is the atmosphere like here? We ask, what is the atmosphere like here, not just try to find out who did what; not who do we blame, who do we praise; but the broader, subtler question is about atmosphere. Who spilled the water—you or me? That is *chronos*. Who made the problem? Was it you? Or was it me? That is *chronos*, the fact-based reality. But in relationship, those facts are not always easy to determine. The *kairos*, the climate, the feeling, the relationship between us is a space between us. What is that like? See figure "4.4 Who did it?" on page 52, a diagram of levels of consciousness. In consensus reality, here we ask, "Who did it?" But in dreamland, "We did it!" X + *u* together. And in the essence area, the answer is the processmind experience.

This essence area we have been talking about is the processmind, it is a field, and it is something we can feel but not see: something that moves us. This is the space around and between everything. Here at the consensus reality level it is "*u* did it" or "X did it." It is important to work in consensus reality, who did what? Then in dreamland we can switch roles. This is a very crucial and helpful aspect in relation-ships: Amy and I are real people and, at the same time, in dreamland I am Amy and she is me and we are each other. Can you switch roles? Worldwork is based on this notion of switching roles.

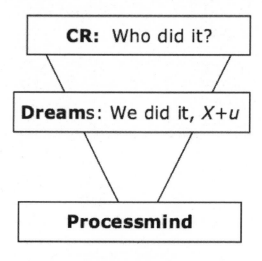

4.4 Who did it?

Now at the essence level, can you create an atmosphere in which relationship happens? As a public speaker, think about what you have to say and think, "Can I participate in and help create an atmosphere?" In relationship, can you create an atmosphere where things can get resolved? If you can create an atmosphere between the two or more of you, you won't have to do much to work things out. It's a lazy person's method for working stuff out [laughter], but you have got to be in touch with the dance of the ancient one for this to work. And by that I mean, you have to find that place inside where polarities make you giggle and where you enjoy both as part of a dance. Your Process-mind's space-time dreaming creates a special *kairos*, an atmosphere, where relationship happens and polarities are less significant. By sensing and letting yourself get moved by the space between us, you help create the climate wherein things can get solved.

We are going to work on creating an atmosphere by getting to your deepest self in the next exercise.

EXERCISE

There are many difficult kinds of relationships. Here, in this exercise or meditation, I want to ask you first, what is the worst relationship field you can think of? What does it feel like? What is that worst energy, X?

Second, for what u in you is the X in that field the worst? Is the u that gets the most upset by X somehow rigid? If there is something terrible going on, then there is the part of me that does not like it. This part never thinks of itself as rigid ("I am such a nice person how can I be rigid?"), but this part can be rigid. I want you to explore the part of you that does not like something. Think about that part of you: Does it get rigid and stiff?

Third, feel and sketch both X + u and see them in your favorite earth spot. Drop dualistic consensus reality thinking and let the earth breathe between X + u.

Then I'll say, "Go home and sense space–time!" It is usually easier for most people to feel they are off the earth's surface when I say space–time. Just feel the universe moving you a little bit. Some can do it just standing up or sitting, but I want you to imagine things moving you around spontaneously until you feel kind of free.

Then, to sense the relationship *kairos* at the end, let space–time dream and dance you. I will ask you, what is the relationship *kairos* in this dance? What I mean is, "What atmosphere does your Process-mind express or dance? Can you describe this subtle atmosphere?" It is a very subtle and new thing. If you can, say some words about it. Is it happy or is it funny? Is it detached? Deep? Whatever you say about it is good; the important point is for you to begin to think about the atmospheres inside of you. Finally, you will be using that space–time dreaming atmosphere to advise you about the relationship situation—about what's needed for u + X.

Audience: It's tricky for me to find my u, my reaction to the X.

Arny: What relationship field would you think of that is not very good? What part of you does not like it? "Grrrr!"

Audience: When you do that, I go "eee," out of fear!

Arny: Who is that in you that goes "eee!"? How would you describe this "eee!"?

Audience: It is the part that is pulling away...

Arny: Why is it pulling away?

Audience: Because it is fearful. It is afraid to get involved...

Arny: So there is your little *u*. It is fearful. Then I would ask you, what is she like, that fearful part?

Audience: When I see you do it, I realize the *u* energy is not in relationship with the X energy.

Arny: So one part of you, X, goes Grrr, and your little *u* withdraws and is afraid and will not relate.

SUMMARY OF EXERCISE STEPS

1. What is the worst relationship field and energy X you can think of? What does it feel like? What does it do?

2. For what part of you (*u*) is that X the worst?

3. Feel and sketch *u* + X and see them in a favorite earth spot. Drop dualistic consensus reality thinking and let the earth breathe you between *u* + X.

4. Now go *home*, sense space–time; let it curve and dance you. Describe the universe's processmind space–time dreaming. Sense its relationship *kairos*.

5. As you let space–time dream you, let it tell you what's needed for X + *u*.

AFTERWARDS

Arny: What are you learning about relationship and atmosphere? It is a big thing.

(Addressing an audience member) You are still standing up. Would you do me a favor and show the atmosphere that you were dancing at the end of the exercise?

Take a look at this atmosphere! (an audience member shows her atmosphere—an amazing dance!) After that kind of atmosphere, there is no problem! What kind of relationship situation were you working on?

Audience: I cannot remember now! What did I start with?

Arny: Can you remember the relationship issue you started with?

Audience: There was an X… and some *u*… I am both of them.

Arny:	Of course! Just imagine using this atmosphere you just created with one person or with lots of people!
Audience:	Yes… I can imagine using this in that relationship… things feel better now! [Dances, flying through the air]
Arny:	Thank you for showing us how the ancient one dances!

....

Σ   For Reflection on Chapter 4

- If it's too much work getting to your destination, let the Maxwell demon discover the X that your u is working against. Reduce entropy by getting clear about $X + u$. Then let the processmind reduce entropy by dancing, momentarily forgetting the $X + u$, and getting you to where you are going.

- Experience and theory suggest that your health may improve when you dance as the ancient one.

- Relationships are about you and me and us and an unpredictable feeling beyond polarities and people.

- Your dance of the ancient one is space–time dreaming. It creates individual, unpredictable, almost unimaginable solutions to mundane problems.

PART TWO

Who Are You?

Jung, Einstein, Pachamama, Dalai Lama

CHAPTER 5

Jung and the Process Paradigm

*Only after I had familiarized myself with alchemy did I
realize that the unconscious is a process...*

—C.G. Jung[22]

In this quote from Jung's autobiography, which was written near the
end of his life, Jung describes himself as a process thinker. To me it
seems as if Taoism was an early process concept and that alchemy (a
practice during medieval and enlightenment times of working with
opposites to bring them together) came later.

But before I go further into the process paradigm, let me go backwards. In the first part of this work, I introduced the idea of process as
a paradigm connecting parallel worlds; that is, experiences separated
by ourselves, the cultures in which we live, and the disciplines we follow. I suggested that the space–time dreaming movement experience
may slow down aging and that the revolution in our thinking is a feeling, an experience, of interrelatedness.

In this Part 2, I ponder with you how my concept of our essence-like
"dance of the ancient one" connects with similar ideas found in the
works of Jung, Einstein, and the Dalai Lama.

In a way, Processwork begins, every time people realize that everything changes. Lao Tse developed the idea of process as a changing
state that he called "the Tao that can be said." He warned us, however,

that the true Tao can't be said: it is an essence-like field, a *space*. He said in the *Tao Te Ching*, chapter 11:[22]

> *We put thirty spokes together and call it a wheel;*
> *But it is on the space where there is nothing that the*
> *usefulness of the wheel depends.*
> *We turn clay to make a vessel;*
> *But it is on the space where there is nothing that the*
> *usefulness of the vessel depends.*
> *We pierce doors and windows to make a house;*
> *And it is on these spaces where there is nothing that the*
> *usefulness of the house depends.*
> *Therefore, just as we take advantage of what is, we should*
> *recognize the usefulness of what is not.*

Jung carried process ideas further along with the suggestion that we should follow what he called the *unconscious*. He meant, follow your dreams and imaginations. Before death he realized (as I quote him at the beginning of this chapter) that the unconscious is a process. Thus updating his earlier theories with his late thoughts, we would have to assume that following Jung's ideas means following process. Updating Jung even a bit more, we would have to say that following process means following the signals of everyday reality, following dreams, and following those barely describable essence experiences such as space–time dreaming.

I am very grateful not only to C.G. Jung but also to his favorite students (according to some), Dr. Franz Ricklin (first president of the original Zurich Jung Institute), Dr. Marie-Louise von Franz (my analyst and his main collaborator), and Ms. Barbara Hannah. In many ways, process oriented psychology unfolds Jung's suggestion to follow the unconscious.

In any case, my own process moved me to Zurich and then to Jungian psychology in 1961. Suddenly I found myself speaking with von Franz. When she said to me, "Tell me a dream," I asked her, "Why focus only on the dream? Can't you see it in my body, in the here and now?" This was the beginning of Processwork for me. The development of Processwork was completely unintentional. I was never very interested in doing something new. Doing new things was secondary for me. Thanks to my Jungian colleagues and elders at the time for pointing out that what I now call *Processwork*, with its body and group applications, was not exactly where they had imagined Jungian psychology should be going at that time.

DANCE OF THE ANCIENT ONE

I loved dreams and dreaming and so it seemed natural to continue to extend the idea of the unconscious to the process of dreaming not only nighttime dreams but also body experiences, relationships, groups, and the universe itself. I slowly stopped focusing only on the content and interaction with dream figures to expand the purview and, before I knew it, there was *process oriented psychology*.

Only from the viewpoint of consensus reality is our psychology a matter of parts: You, your friends, your family members, their friends, your ancestors, your personal history, inner figures, and so forth. From other viewpoints there is the process of dreaming as well as the more noncognitive, essence-level process. Our whole world makes boundaries at the surface of the earth in consensus reality. Not only do we section off the planet into continents and countries, cities, and communities; we define our thought processes and our disciplines as one thing and not another: Jungian psychology, process oriented psychology, Gestalt, transpersonal, integral psychology; we speak of organizational work, of physics, the environment, coaching, medicine, et cetera.

Yet while these boundaries are important expressions, the earth itself moves with and beyond all surface boundaries. The direction of Processwork, in my mind, is to appreciate boundaries and remember that there is process underneath all things. So for me, today, Jungian psychology is that part of Processwork that follows the unknown through a focus on dreams, myths, and active imaginations.

PROCESSWORK IN JUNGIAN PSYCHOLOGY

Processwork has since influenced the Jungian community. One of the central issues I defined in Processwork is how we all get to an edge when it comes to integrating experiences with which we don't identify. I said that there is an edge between parallel worlds, between our primary identity and our secondary experiences. So it was not surprising to me when the 2004 International Association of Jungian Analysts called their international conference "The Edges of Experience."[24] The Jungian community picked up aspects of Processwork that had been more controversial for them in the past. They used the edge concept to describe the border between personal and collective experiences.

Jung died on June 6, 1961. That date is significant to me in part because I landed in Zurich that very day as an exchange student at the Swiss Poly Tech (ETH). Later that year, after meeting the Jungians in Zurich, I returned to the states to finish my B.A., B.S., and M.S. from

MIT before returning once again to Switzerland. What led me to Zurich? Synchronicity? Space–time dreaming?

I knew nothing of Jung when I originally landed in Zurich. Because of my interest in Einstein and his early work in Zurich I decided to go there to continue my studies in applied physics. One evening while taking a break from my studies in Zurich, I told another student in my dormitory that I was having big dreams. That student, an African American minister, told me I should visit an old witch, who turned out to be Marie-Louise von Franz. That's how I bumped into the Jungians.

At 46 von Franz was not an old witch! But at that time for me and that minister (I was 21)—excuse my ageism back then—46 was getting old. I studied that first year in Zurich as an exchange student at the ETH. I was so excited by the Jungians I returned after finishing my master's at MIT.

Today, more than 52 years later, everything seemed to just *happen* to me in those days. For example, one day in Zurich, I was sitting outside the Kunsthaus Café, right near the art museum in downtown Zurich. I was engaged to my first partner but we had a kind of open-minded attitude that said you could still "sniff around a bit," and I made the most of that leeway. I started looking at people moving by my table and to my great surprise, this elegant older (he was 47 or 48) European gentleman with grey hair, looking very sophisticated, was doing the same thing I was: sniffing around! He was looking at women as they walked by. So I began looking with him. I said, "That is not the right one," and then he joined me from two tables away and said, "that would not be right for you," and I added, "and also not for you!" All kinds of people would walk by and we gossiped about them, much as Amy and I still do today outside of Starbucks.

He asked, "Who are you?" and I said, "Well, I am a student here in Zurich. I am studying physics at the ETH, and I am interested in Jungian psychology. I just began analysis with someone in town." "Ach so! Analysis!" he exclaimed. I said, "Have you heard of Jungian psychology?" He said, "Yes! I am the president of the Jung Institute... I am Jung's nephew. My name is Dr. Franz Ricklin, Junior." To make the story short, he said, "Let's meet at the café in the same way next Saturday afternoon." And so we met together, on and off, for the next years until he died in 1970.

I learned something very important about process and synchronicity from this great man. I learned from all my teachers but especially from him to follow the unknown. A story illustrates this learning. He said to me one day, "You know, Jung was a great friend of mine, not just my uncle. And one day I was studying for my medical exams and I was having trouble. I did not like exams very much. And I told C.G. this, and he said to me, "Studying, reading a book for your medical exams? That is no good for you! If you can't do that, put the book under your pillow and go to sleep."

I asked, "What happened?" and he replied, "I have a medical degree and now I am a psychiatrist!"

This story stuck in my mind. Put the book under your pillow? Let the world of consensus reality become organized in part by your dreaming. I absolutely adored this man. I learned from von Franz how to analyze dreams and with Ricklin I learned to dream. He modeled process! Whenever I told him I wanted to tell him a dream of mine, he said, holding his head with his eyes closed, "I had a dream!" and would proceed to tell me details about his personal life. He told me of his nighttime experiences during my therapy! And best of all, I would leave feeling totally enlightened! By what? I couldn't tell you... It seems as if I learned I could go deep into myself, like a shaman, whenever I needed to. Follow the moment. Follow space–time dreaming. It works!

SEEING INTO THE OTHER

Jungian psychology, for me, meant following the moment. This was almost a spiritual experience. For example, one day while I was in Ricklin's waiting room before my appointment, I heard a loud banging coming from his office. After 10 minutes or so I saw a woman running out thrilled! In my session, right after this event, I asked what had happened. "I don't really know," he said, as usual. "Can you explain it to me?"

Ricklin told me that this woman had been brought to him off the streets by the psychiatric emergency group because she was in a catatonic-like stupor and could not talk or move. So because she could not talk, he did not talk and instead went deep inside himself until he "saw" a vision of her husband. He told her, "Your husband has died and is saying good-bye." The banging on the windows that I had heard in the waiting room was not her. It was her dead husband apparently banging on the windows of the practice saying good-bye. When he told her what it was, she came out of her catatonic stupor and ran thrilled out of his office!

Can you teach this kind of shamanistic process thing, this kind of visualizing? Today, all kinds of psychological trainings are available, but the ethos has changed dramatically. At that time, my Jungian teachers said, "Don't go to class. Follow the unknown, the unpredictable!" I felt free and even got off my chair and began working with dreams, with body experiences, and more.

Follow space–time dreaming, the space between you and everything. It is the essence of what connects us; it is synchronicity in the sense that what you call you or inner is just as much the universe and outer.

PROCESSWORK: A DAUGHTER OF C.G. JUNG AND JUNGIAN PSYCHOLOGY

Processwork could have been a son but everyone was talking about men so much at the time—men do this and men do that—that I rebelled. I called Processwork a daughter. Perhaps I was picking up on the beginnings of the feminist movement. Cultures change in time.

The Jungian psychology I experienced at that time occurred mainly in chairs in consulting rooms. But to really follow someone's process, you must be free to move and stand, sit or lie, dream, and be real. The way we sit and talk, when we sit down with somebody and talk, as you know, is a very political statement. How you sit and where you sit and how you use the room you work in is a social statement. It tells me who you are and where you experience yourself relative to me and the rest of the world. I love following body signals and movements from one to another position in space. This makes the idea of the unconscious a living process.

Dawn Menken interviewed a well-known Jungian analyst, June Singer, some years back, and she said, "Arny is talking about the living unconscious."[25]

Dawn: It was not just that you talked about it, she saw you working in an intensive course and she said, "Wow, what Arny is doing is he is working with the living unconscious." She was impressed with that.

June Singer was a radical Jungian, doing new things. But let me side with the more conservative Jungian viewpoint, which was a bit suspicious of Processwork at that time. When I was talking to a *Newsweek* interviewer last year, he said to me, "Well, not all Jungians are totally convinced about what you are doing." And I said, "Why not?" The interviewer said, "One of your Jungian colleagues says that process can be dangerous. You must first take a lot of time and build up somebody's ego and make sure the person can follow their experiences. You need to be very, very careful with people." June Singer also said to me, when she first met me, "Do you choose people? Do you filter people out before they come to a seminar? Do you take some people and not other people?" The Jungians, you see, were hesitant about who they would work with. They were hesitant to work with very unusual people. They said, in essence, whatever you do, don't work with people in psychotic states, processes that today I call *extreme states of consciousness*!

Nevertheless, the conservative attitude of my critic is important. If my critic's attitude works in a given moment with someone, then that way too is Processwork. If you are shy with somebody or you are afraid of something and you first want to build up the other person's strength and ego, and that works best for you and the person, that is definitely Processwork. Processwork means following the overall process, including your own reservations if they are present.

Is it dangerous to follow process? This is what the Jungians wondered about. In general, I have never found it to be dangerous. For the therapist who is more comfortable in a chair, movement work can be scary. When you are out of the chair, you need proprioceptive and movement tools to follow processes. But if you don't have these skills, then I support the conservative attitude that says, take more time and talk a while. In my mind, it is all Processwork, regardless of the specifics.

Process or *flow* can mean stopping things... that works well. For me, following process means sometimes stopping, sometimes singing. That is why I don't use the word unconscious very much because it implies that some things may be beyond consciousness. I don't know that for sure. I prefer the word process. It is neutral and all-encompassing. It does not exclude or preclude or prohibit. Even in deeply altered states such as comatose states there are flickerings of awareness. Having awareness of these deep levels has transformed my work. My belief in the awareness of people in comas is what started my work with people who are near death. The word unconscious is good if it works for people, but it was used originally to differentiate between psyche and matter. You have to remember in the 1960s people were talking about psyche as dreamlike and matter as real, physical, and not of the psyche. Using the concept of process was, for me, a more unifying approach. Processwork does not care if it is psyche or matter, it simply follows what is happening.

Process itself is a paradigm shift. The spirit of Jung, if not some of his specific teachings, connects to the parent of Taoism, Lao Tse, who, like native peoples for thousands of years, loved nature and followed

Her changes. Taoists loved that night transforms into day! Nature is a process, not just an array of things. Night and day are states or *things*, but these designations are not always useful. When exactly does night or day begin or end? Likewise, when exactly we are born and when we die are concepts of interest, but our dreaming process often ignores these particular states. Process is time-bound only in consensus reality. In dreaming and at the essence level, process is timeless.

If Jung lived today, I think his early ideas about Eastern traditions or philosophies would be different. His original idea about Eastern traditions is that they were not good for people in the West. He loved the I Ching but when he considered ego-less states described by Buddhism and Taoism, he felt that such states were not the way for Western people. I totally respect Jung's attitude toward this topic, for all of us are moved and shaped by the times in which we live. Culture influences the way we think and speak about things.

For example, in the context of consensus reality, Processwork today involves many institutes worldwide. But the process community, for me, is the entire *uni-verse*, which means, literally, one turn. In any city of the world, on any street, when I see people, dogs, trees, trash, plants, birds, whatever, I often say to Amy, "They are my family." I feel this deeply.

Thus, any method, anything that gets good feedback from the environment, is *Processwork*. Other therapies that work are also Processwork in my mind. For example, if Ericksonian therapy works, it is Processwork. If Gestalt or Freudian ideas work, if you are lying on the couch freely associating and that works for you and for the therapist, then that is Processwork. I have had people lie on the couch and freely associate too. It works great with many people. I do it every morning before I get out of bed.

LEVELS OF AWARENESS

What Jung called *consciousness* refers mainly to CR or consensus reality levels (see diagram 5.1, *Reality Levels*). He used the terms *ego* and *persona* to refer basically to our everyday waking states and the collective masks we all wear from time to time. I call this area CR or consensus reality, meaning that our most primary process is connected to the reality of the culture and world we are living in. What Jung meant by the unconscious are the areas that I call the dreamland and processmind or essence areas.

In the diagram below, you will see that I separated the Me diagram from the You and Me diagram to emphasize that if I think only of myself, then I consider my own reality, dreaming, and processmind. But this kind of thinking is limited because the dreamland and processmind areas are linked to anyone I am in relationship with. So we must really expand this first diagram to also include the diagram on the right. So who I am is really not just me but you as well (and vice versa of course).

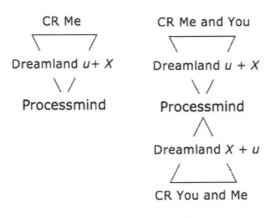

5.1 Reality Levels.

These dreamland areas are nonlocal, that is, they are shared *spaces* between us. If, for example, we think of my reality as being on top of the diagram, then "Me and You" might be my experience of relationship, whereas yours might be "You and Me" at the bottom of the diagram.

I have taken the Reality Levels diagram and added a circular dimension in Figure 5.2 to stress the idea that the essence area or processmind and dreamland areas are space and dreamlike, nonlocal areas connecting us as a circulating process... me... you... us, et cetera. The dreamland and essence areas are entangled. My dreams and space-time dreaming seem to be mine from my experience, but it often turns out to be nonlocally connected to everything I am in relationship with. In other words, you and I are entangled.

Entanglement, the essence of quantum physics, means that what happens in a system over here is connected to what's over there in that system without any known signals going between. Jung would probably have referred to the majority of images in dreams as coming from the personal unconscious, and he would have referred to the essence level as the deeper or collective unconscious with mythic and less personal images and experiences associated with it. Today, it seems as if these dreams and essence experiences are yours and are also entangled with all that you are in relationship with as well.

5.2 Background twirl to who we are.

SYNCHRONICITY

Processwork studies, among other things, the way the observer is involved with the observed, with the $u + X$. As a result, what seems *conscious* can be entangled with the X, the "not me." Something about X flirts with u when *dreams* or secondary processes come up into *reality* or close to your everyday identity or primary process. You walk down the street and something catches your attention or you have a question and something catches your attention. The X that catches your attention is an answer to a particular u questioner. Things don't happen out of the clear blue sky. The u and the X are entangled. If u saw X, X was already a bit in u, and u was a little in X. The tree is in me and perhaps I too am a little bit in the tree. We share something like *treeness*.

What connects us? Physicists don't know what to call that entanglement other than an attribute of the quantum world. The entangling experience is what I refer to as *space–time dreaming*. Synchronicities remind you that your consensus reality is governed in part by things you did not expect; the world is weirder than you thought. The consensus reality part of you says, for example, "I am a real person doing a real thing and I am real busy and serious," and synchronicities say, "Remember the world is magical too and you are out of step if you are not aware of that magic." But what exactly is that magic?

PROCESS: THE MAGIC IN SYNCHRONICITY

It is not merely the X that pops up in front of the u. Well, that is magical enough, for X is dreamlike and you can find that X in your dreams. Thinking only in terms of conscious (u) and unconscious (X) is not enough. Synchronicity implies that consciousness and the unconscious are really figments of our consensus reality imaginations! There is instead a process, a flow between X + u, a field and potential dance! Every flirt is a synchronicity, one moment in a process! Relationship between you and me, or between any u + X, is only partly comprised of visible signals; it also involves sentient flow of the field connecting us. Perhaps that field is like love. It is the Tao, which can't be said. This book has pointed to space–time dreaming as the Tao that can't be said, the space between us, the common-ground experiences beneath synchronicity.

The most seamless flow is an essence experience; it is deeper than any one X or u form in reality or in dreams. The deepest aspect of the flow is space–time dreaming following itself so to speak. In space–time dreaming experiences, the X + u are phases of the dance: they are aspects of the Tao that can be said; they are not the Tao itself, which can't be said. That Tao that can't be said is the processmind field, the power manifesting as the space–time dreaming dance, manifesting as all the flirts and X's + u's you can find.

Some physicists might see the similarity between my understanding of synchronicity and quantum physics. The quantum wave function connects things. It is behind entanglement, between X + u interconnections. But no one can tell you exactly what that connecting wave function is. My physics teachers said, "DON'T ASK." But we must ask. My answer is that the quantum wave is an example of the pattern or rhythm of processmind dance experience: It gives rise to awareness of all forms, but it is none of the forms. The quantum wave is an example of the potential reality behind our stochastic dance.

I am saying that there are organizing fields in the background: call them the mind of god, the processmind, the quantum wave function, or space–time dreaming fields. This is the most evidence-based explanation of experience I know of. We sense fields entangling things as if they were the earth's atmospheres, powers, and fields making us dance. This dreaming is a common ground; it is like Einstein's space–

time ether concept, connecting ordinary observers in different places in the universe. Dreaming is something like the four-dimensional space–time experience of general relativity.

The processmind's space–time dreaming lies behind synchronicities. Most of us know that if we get deep enough inside ourselves, the things that are bothering us may get a little better. Yet at the same time, this relief may also touch others with whom we are connected with: they may feel relieved temporarily without even knowing what city or nation you are in. This is shamanism. Try it with a friend. In the following experience, I would like you to experiment with getting deep in yourself and then trying to resolve a relationship issue. This will give you the opportunity to experiment with the processmind, the "one world" or *unus mundus*, the fields we all share. Try the following experiment.

UNUS MUNDUS–SYNCHRONICITY EXPERIMENT IN RELATIONSHIP

I am going to ask you about problems that are bothering you and energies that bug you, and then I am going to ask you to connect those problems and energies with somebody who is not here with us. You can like or dislike the person, it doesn't matter. It can be your partner, or it can be someone whom you cannot stand.

Arny: What is the most troublesome relationship energy in your life?

Audience: It is a recurring thing that happens in my life, an energy that is aggressive and attacking and tries to take. I'm thinking of my neighbor who wants to take part of my land to build his garage there. His energy says, "I don't care about you! I just want my garage!"

Arny: In the exercise, when you ask a person this question (What is the most troublesome energy in your life?), watch what they do with their hands. Our volunteer here moved her hands like this (makes a grabbing, cutting motion).

Audience: My father has the same energy. "You be quiet! Shut UP!"

Arny: That does not look like how you normally look! What energy in you is most against that cutting remark, "Shut up!"?

Audience: The part of me that likes all voices, that likes diversity, that wants to have a dialogue, that wants conversation between the parts, and that wants to honor both sides.

Arny: (Acting like that "father") Pah!! (laughter) What made you laugh? What made her laugh? It is possible that the processmind likes the energy of that cutting, grabbing X, even though your conscious mind hates that side. There is an entanglement, an unknown connection between $u + X$. In any case, how does that entanglement appear in relationship?

Audience: I have dealt with this issue over and over, with a different neighbor, someone who wants to take and does not have feelings for the other side. Then it affects my primary relationship with my partner because I get all anxious. When that energy comes, I get all messed up.

Arny: Does your partner have a little of that too?

Audience: Yes, he is very similar to me, maybe too giving sometimes, does not like conflict.

Arny: Does he have some of that X energy too inside or outside of him?

Audience: He is a little better at coming out at it than I am. When another neighbor was taking down our fence with a bulldozer, he came out with a shovel!

Arny: Now to make it easier, could you make a sketch of this X? Feel that X energy and make a sketch of that.

Audience: (Draws a straight, cutting line.)

Arny: And the other energy looks like…

Audience: (Draws a squiggle.)

Arny: The classic opposites! The linear cut versus the curving, a lot to think about there just by itself. [Pause] Now, what is your favorite earth spot that comes up these days?

Audience: An island south of Crete, in the Mediterranean, where you can see Africa.

Arny: Let's go there. Can you see these two energies there somewhere?

Audience:	There was a strike! Before we could get there everybody was fighting and screaming. There was a student strike, everyone was yelling and screaming at each other! That's the grabbing, cutting motion.
Arny:	And is the other energy also there too, the squiggle?
Audience:	Yes. That island is the only place I have ever fallen asleep floating in the water. It was so safe, so supportive, so warm. I feel asleep now, just floating.
Arny:	So, let's go to that island with the "strike" and the "floating." Remember the ferry boat that brought you there, the waves and the sunlight. Let the island breathe you... breathe as if the island were breathing you. Not too far away is another energy also... As the island breathes you, can it also breathe into this other energy? See if you can breathe into that more linear behavior as well... Now, to make things even easier, imagine yourself being moved by the whole universe, with the freedom and space around that island, let the space there, the space of the whole universe move you. OK, now when you feel yourself freely dancing... you are ready to bring those space-time movements back to this island, to these energies, to the linear energy. God knows what it is going to do, this universe, as it moves you. Let it move you around almost unpredictably.
Audience:	[Moving and spinning around]
Arny:	The universe does things you just can't predict. Suddenly it makes you twirl like that. Now let's bring this motion back to those Island energies near Crete with that universe experience and see how this one world experience deals with the diversity issues. Remember the freedom of the universe in your motions... Ahha! I see you got a thought already, I saw that. Did you catch it?
Audience:	It was very relieving to be spun around by the universe! And looking at things from the universe's perspective, it is hard to form words! In my normal self I love this flow part, the part I identify with, but when I dance and get deeper, this straight line, isn't troublesome all of a sudden! Because it is just part of the flow. It becomes part of the dance. It becomes part of what is necessary to this whole flow thing.

The squiggle is nice but unless there is a part that cuts and goes Wham! This! Now! Mine! Unless there is that part too, the whole dance is not itself, it is not whole!

Arny: So the swirl, the squiggle, is fine but from the universe's perspective it is not enough without a *woof* in your dance! You are looking at me and thinking something...

Audience: It is just so relieving somehow, that all of a sudden I am not a victim of that straight line but that it is part of me and my nature and the universe's nature and life.

Arny: Now that is good for you. You look reasonably together and happy about that. If you could at another point remember to call your neighbor tomorrow and just to say, "Thinking of you, and, by the way, how were you yesterday at the time we are now working?" That is a big part of this exercise. Could you eventually do that?

Audience: To see how it affected him? Sure.

Arny: Thank you!

When you do this exercise, be patient. Don't bring yourself out of that universe experience until your flow in the dance becomes a little bit unpredictable. Then, bring that sense of open-mindedness and dreaming back into the difficulty as a metaskill that is important for the tension or conflict.

Audience: Do you have a hypothesis about what kind of effect happens to others we are in relationship to?

Arny: Since we are working not just with the other people, but the field between us, sometimes the other person will notice something. Sometimes things happen in a shared locality of some sort.

The important thing is the unpredictable, open, Zen-like mind doing space–time dreaming. It is totally like Zen mind. We are not focusing only on the relationship in consensus reality but also upon energies and fields behind reality. We are using the right side of our brain, so to speak. In that state of mind, any sudden unpremeditated feeling or thought is obviously yours but also simultaneously everywhere around you as part of your dance! My point is that synchronicity is an invitation for u to dance with X, an invitation for all to a dance with the universe. Synchronicity is an example of how the space between us joins and connects us in noncognitive ways. It deals with the energies of relationships, not just with the people involved.

[Thirty minutes after everyone tried this exercise]

Arny: I have to get back with our volunteer. What happened when you checked at home?

Audience: Because you said to check, I called my boyfriend who was home. He was extra chipper, extra happy, and I said "Why are you so happy?" He said, "Well, this problem that I have been working on for 3 months, I have just resolved it!" The problem was that he could not get our riding lawnmower to start. He had been working on it for 3 months, taking it all apart and suddenly at 6 pm when we were working here in class the lawn mower, the "cutter," started!

Arny: The so-called inanimate object, the lawnmower cuts lawns, it started!

My viewpoint is that a problem between two (or more) people can not get resolved completely if it does not get resolved everywhere the u + X energies exist in your life. No problem is only local or personal. Everything you feel is yours and belongs to the fields in the world around you.

What is personal development? Our volunteer's personal development includes the lawnmower, the "cutter," even though she herself was not working on it. She was working on that cutting energy which was against her in the form of a neighbor trying to take or cut off a piece of her property! All we know for the moment, is that the "cutter" is no longer working against her but for her. "It" got fixed. It was in a situation of "unstable equilibrium," it was not working and then the thing that cut her yard worked! What happened to the person in whom she was experiencing that X energy? We don't yet know. If he is like most of us, he may be stubborn and won't say or admit that he had a few minutes of good thoughts about his neighbor. But then again, he might.

My point is that behind a diversity issue in consensus reality is a "real" problem, but also an ecstatic experience of the field connecting all things. When you are in your universe dance you are ecstatic and realize things are not only personal. The universe dance works nonlocally on the whole "property area," the lawn or your yard. Jung would

DANCE OF THE ANCIENT ONE

have said it works synchronistically. Today we can say that access to space-time dreaming, to the field that connects us, helps with the field and all problems in its area.

....

SUMMARY OF THE EXERCISE:

1. What is the most troublesome energy (X) in your life now, and who (u) in you is upset by that energy? How does this X + u tension also appear in one of your relationships? With whom is this relationship?
2. Go to your favorite earth spot and find X + u there. Breathe into the land.
3. Let go a bit more and feel moved by space. Use this spaced-out experience to dance.
4. Now, while dancing, go back to the spot and dance between X + u and note any insights.
5. Finally, check with your friend and see how he or she is feeling. Ask about your insight, as if it was just "in the air."

Did you change the person, or did this person change you? My answer is, it is a process. I want you to be a little bit tipsy, preferably all the time, but at least some of the time and not with alcohol.

Audience 1: Rumi, the Sufi, speaks about the drunken one who is ecstatic.

Audience 2: Hafiz, another Sufi, often called the dream-world "the tavern."

Audience 3: Tamara called her son in NYC to ask if he noticed anything related to what she was working on, and he said yes!

THE POLITICS OF THE PROCESS PARADIGM

Space-time dreaming influences how we think of reality, of parts and parties. Processwork has many similarities with other psychotherapies but also a central difference. Things we think of as parts such as anima and animus, male and female, conscious and unconscious, et cetera, are names belonging to a given consensus reality making us think they are fixed images or states. States such as good and bad, healthy and ill, old and young, even dead and alive can be important consensus reality concepts without exact definitions. Holding to these parts however can neglect the field, the potential dance in the background and instead makes us think of one part being separate from or better than another. Processwork does not focus on these terms in part because, from the dreaming and essence levels, those terms are only moments in the flow, they are not permanent structures.

Parts in Processwork are phases of the dance. In this view, the politics of people of color, people of "no color," hetero–homosexual, Democratic–Republican, or liberal-conservative are very important. Parts-oriented thinking can make clarity but also has a serious problem: It often makes one part better than another. It always establishes hierarchy. Pathologizing can be important in an effort to catch a disease before it goes too far but, more often, pathologizing has an iatrogenic effect, creating resistance and fear of the X; leaving us feeling ill. Iatrogenesis occurs, usually inadvertently, as an adverse effect in response to what doctors or therapists do, say, or suggest. Any attempt to help or heal—even complementary or alternative medical procedures—can be troublesome if the intervention polarizes the person into thinking this is good, that is bad. Feeling badly about oneself, for social or medical reasons, may be part of one's process for the moment, but in the politics of the process paradigm, favoring parts or states of health or consciousness can create many problems. All judgments and categories are important and should be balanced with process: rich–poor, hetero–homosexual, dark–light, good–bad are names, parts of our present agreement about reality; they are parts but not yet the dance!

Politics is a consensus reality agreement about how to run a state or organization. I suggest that besides "polarity politics," we have process oriented politics that includes not only consensus reality problems and polarizations but also space–time dreaming and the dynamic of flow and its essence. In fact, without the "dance of the ancient one," politics may be doomed to be run mainly by those with the most power or the most social rank (attributed according to their gender, race, age, and so forth).

The problems, the u's + X's, are not the only problems. There is a deeper problem, really, finding the dance. The problems are there to just throw you off balance a little, to encourage you to re-find the dance. I believe that Jung realized this as well. In his autobiography, Jung tells Aniela Jaffé that his idea of archetypes is closer to the energies that I refer to as... Jung says:

> *In physics, too, we speak of energy and its various manifestations… The situation in psychology is precisely the same… we are dealing primarily with energy, with measures of intensity, with greater or lesser quantities… in various guises. If we conceive of libido as energy, we can take a comprehensive and unified view… such as is provided in the physical sciences by the theory of energetics… I see man's drives as various manifestations of energic processes… forces analogous to heat, light, etc.* [26]

In old age, a few years before he died, he said,

> *The serious problems in life, however, are never fully solved… The meaning and purpose of a problem seem to lie not in its solution, but in our working at it incessantly, that alone keeps us from petrification.* [27]

Today we might say, the purpose of problems lies not only in working for solutions but also in getting in touch with the eternal space-time dreaming process in the background.

....

Σ   FOR REFLECTION ON CHAPTER 5

- Psychology is a process that can be modeled but not entirely taught in a cognitive manner. I learned this from Franz Ricklin who modeled for me the spirit of synchronicity.

- Paradigm shift in psychology? Yes, from matter and psyche, dreams and reality, to the relationship dance I have been calling space–time dreaming.

- In a way, there is no matter, no psyche, old or young, male or female. These are momentary pictures of the river we all live in, of the flow of the space between us.

- The notion of space–time dreaming has predecessors in Jung's work, in alchemy, as well as in Taoism.

- Our problems are not just between people, they are between energies in the universe. Our problems are not only personal but manifestations of background fields.

- Current politics are polarity-oriented. The next iteration of politics includes polarities but is no longer identified with them because of the understanding that process, flow, and essence underlie everything.

CHAPTER 6

The Tao of Stephen Hawking

My goal is simple. It is a complete understanding of the universe, why it is as it is, and why it exists at all.

—Stephen Hawking[28]

If it is true that our conflicts are between people and are also between nonlocal conflicting energies in the universe, then obviously we need to study the nature of the universe. What is its substance? Is there a space, an *ether*, an alternative to space–time from which it all came? What is that 95% of the universe we can't see? What are dark energy and dark matter?

Alchemists thought the essence of the universe was something like the *unus mundus* (one world). Later the Catholic church silenced many alchemists, insisting that the first element was God. Then came the first chemists who thought that the essence of the universe was the indivisible atom. Soon thereafter came subatomic particles, quantum theories, string theories… and so on. Are all these fields aspects of the same thing?

Let's step into the world of cosmology to understand the scientist's present view of the universe. I love physics not only because of its rational nature but because it represents the process of constantly seeking to know more about the unknown. Some of the biggest problems for physics are answering the questions who are we, where did we come from, how did the universe get here? Theoretical physics is busy trying to find something to unify the world of the large with that of the small. Just how do we bring the weakest of physical fields (gravity, the force field of the universe) together with the electromagnetic, the strong, and weak forces that operate at the level of the atomic nucleus?

In particular, I am interested in how space-time dreaming relates to the invisible energies of the universe and to the subatomic, electromagnetic, and gravity fields. In this chapter, I describe how the tiniest, little stochastic subtle *tugs* of nature—in terms of virtual particles such as gravitons that supposedly transmit the force of gravity and space–time—may relate to what the Taoists call their *Tao Te* and to our space-time dreaming.

Physicists imagine that fields transmit forces to objects with *virtual* particles. Virtual particles? Yes, virtual means you can't see them. They are mathematical ideas, thought to exist because of measurable effects but they live only temporarily... just as the dreaming in space–time dreaming is a virtual experience that disappears if you try to hold on to it. You can see its effect, but the dreaming itself is like the Tao that can't be said. Richard Feynman imagined virtual particles to be wave-like wiggles or a wiggling rope–like form connecting two real particles.

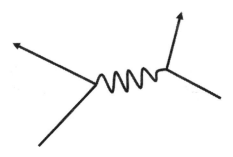

6.1 *The interaction of two fermions (e.g., electrons).*

Each electron is represented by a straight line. They exchange a virtual particle photon (the wiggly line) and repel one other.

By analogy, the straight line particles remind me of you and me or our inner parts, $X + u$. The wiggly sections remind me of space-time-dreaming as we experience it in terms of predictable, and almost unpredictable, wiggly jittery experiences. The idea of a field's wiggly or virtual particles reminds me also of the Bushmen's *rope* that is said to connect the hunter and the animal being hunted. You can't see these ropes but they are felt to be there. "Ropes, cords, threads, and lines of light enable the spiritual healers to commune with ancestors and gods, as well as communicate with other Bushman communities."[29] Their imagined rope-like *connections* with the universe are what I am referring to as space–time dreaming.

Where do these connections come from? Where does dreaming and where does what we call reality come from? Why are they here? Stephen Hawking pulls all these ponderings together with his simple question, "Why there is something rather than nothing?"[30] At one time or another we all ask, "Why are we here? What is the meaning of life?" This question is similar to Einstein's, which I quote in the beginning of my *ProcessMind*:

> *I want to know God's thoughts, the rest are details.*[31]

To understand the dance of the ancient one, I must approach these questions with an attitude of deep democracy; that is, by thinking about the real universe, our experience of it, and the sense that something moves us.

A TOE OR THEORY OF EVERYTHING

Today I have to whisper a little bit, a little bit more than normal, because I was running with Amy, screaming and yelling, and having a good time like a 5-year-old, but actually I am 72! I am in the process of discovering who I am! This little cold is perfect for me, so I will whisper sometimes. I am excited about today. And this throat reminds me that there is something you can hardly say: It is like "the Tao that can't be said."

When modern astrophysicist Stephen Hawking asks, "Why is there something rather than nothing?" I realize, first, that most people don't think much about these things. But as an everyday person you must think about these things because your questions can help others stay closer to their deepest self in all phases of life, in the midst of business, near death, or when falling in and out of love. Who are you, really? What is the purpose, if any, of your life? What are we all doing here together on this planet? Does the whole human race have something to do together? I approach some of these questions in Appendix A of my book, *ProcessMind* but want to go further here.

Answers to these questions require a unifying feeling and theory. Physicists talk about god, loosely implying there is something like a god whose behavior and *thoughts* are unifying. For example, when Einstein spoke of god, he meant the Laws of Nature. He wondered, what are these laws? Who or what thought them up? Are these laws or natural patterns permanent? Can we know them? I must ask, how is psychology, how is your psychology, related to the universe? What are your questions, if you allowed yourself to have questions about the universe?

- How do we get out of the mess the world is in?
- What am I supposed to be doing here?
- What is the purpose of torture?
- Why war?
- Why do we keep forgetting how to work together?
- Why this cycle of destruction and creativity?
- How does it all fit together as one whole?

Perhaps we are all looking for a TOE. As I have pointed out in *ProcessMind*, there are various force fields in physics. You know about magnetic fields, they allow a magnet to pick up a metal paperclip. Magnets exert a field and that field moves a metal paper clip. Likewise, the earth is a kind of magnet and so its magnetic field can move a compass needle to line up with the magnet's lines of force. But what is that field in between the magnet and paper clip or compass that transmits force? Where is that field? Can you see it? You can see only that it moves things around. The field concept is as illusive as it is useful.

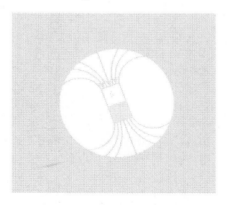

6.2 Electromagnetic Field.

Physics speaks about four fields. There is a magnetic field and then there are three other force fields. There are two nuclear force fields, called strong fields and weak ones, and they organize nuclear physics.

All these forces are understood fairly well. But what is gravity? You could say that gravity makes sure that things fall to the floor, but what is gravity due to? Why does matter exert a bit of gravity force on everything? And why is gravity so weak? Gravity pulls the paper clip down when you try to raise it with a magnet. But the magnetic force is much stronger and lifts the paper clip easily into the air. Why is the gravity field so weak?

The various fields of physics—gravity, electromagnetism, strong and weak fields—don't quite fit together yet theoretically. But if and when we find that fit, the result will be called a TOE. When we have a TOE, then you will be able to say, "Aha! We understand the universe a little bit better. Now let's guess about why and how everything got here!" No one, however, knows how gravity fits together with the other three fields. These three fields have something that unifies them. People have been hoping that string theory would unify the three with gravity, the fourth. But at the moment physics is still looking for a TOE, a Theory of Everything.

Psychology, too, is missing a TOE. What might be a TOE in psychology? Something that brings together:

- Body, mind, and spirit
- Past, present, and future
- Individual and group consciousness.

A true theory of everything would put psychology together with physics.

The processmind is a kind of unified field theory. It tries to pull the outer world communities together with individual work and all the states of consciousness together with the cosmos. Processmind together with other Processwork tools works with people in normal states of consciousness, people just near death, people who are ill, and with dreams, relationships, and large groups. Processwork pulls together altered states, extreme states, and everyday life. By adding meaning to medicine, Processwork brings psyche and matter closer, as in working with the dreaming body. It brings different peoples together and seems to be a cross-cultural concept.

Your processmind may be timeless. At the age of 3, something creates your dreams that organize what profession you might choose later on.[32] Today, those early dreams even suggest to me the kinds of symptom experiences you will have. What is that immense intelligence behind those early and often repetitive dreams? From where did you get that creative dream when you were still so little and had so little experience? From those dreams, you can even guess at the kind of relationships people have as adults. You see it in the people you first chose and as friends or partners. And you can also tell about your more permanent friendships. Childhood dream patterns or personal myths appear in the apparently random decisions that you make—now this and now that—and then afterwards you look back and see those decisions are linked through stories and meaning. Childhood dreams even seem to organize where you like to go on earth, your earth favorite spots. Ahhh, my spot! Maybe you have a couple of sacred spots.

The processmind appears in the momentary field around you, in your tendency to move, and in the movements of flipping coins. Aboriginal Australians called the background organizer the *Dreaming*, the earth that is moving you. They did not talk about gravity. They talked about the *song lines* in the earth. They say we each come from a particular spot on earth.[33]

So, the processmind's space-time dreaming field appears as gravity in the space around us or, in the feelings of Taoists, as the *Tao* or, as the Aboriginal Australians have said, as the *Dreaming*. In Buddhism this field might manifest as Buddha mind, empty mind, or creative mind, et cetera. Fukushima Roshi used the terms Zen mind, empty mind, or *mu-shin*. "Go into emptiness, into open mind," he would say and then he would let go and something unexpected would happen, such as his hand moving to create beautiful calligraphy! He was a master at stochastic experience.[34] (In the next chapter, I talk about the Tibetan Buddhist concept of the subtle or dream body, which, like the processmind, organizes our existence after death.) *Nataraja*, or dancing Shiva, is another such organizing figure from Hinduism. People have always been looking for unifying concepts. Now, let me try to pull together the processmind ideas in a diagram.

As I pointed out in chapter 2, the Tao that can be said is the yin or yang, a visible result: the coin is face up or face down. The Tao that can be said is the final answer of how your coin lands after flying through the air. But the stochastic field itself, through which the coin flies, is not said. It is an invisible, hard-to-measure power. Your dream last night can be said, but the dreaming process is very hard to talk about. There is the field in the background, the thing moving you.

Both consensus reality and subtle virtual particle or field experiences are central aspects of nature. In our normal awareness, both aspects marginalize one another. Careful, don't be only *realistic*! You are in danger of exhausting yourself if you focus only on the practical side of life and if you forget the power of the fields and the space between us and the Tao, the field that gives all of us the freedom to dance and move.

There is something you can feel but can't quite say about the space between us and it is that thing that brings dreams into your life. That is why dreamwork is wonderful, but don't kid yourself, [whispers] it is not the point! The map is not the territory![35] The dream and its meaning are the map but not the process. The point is your relationship to the source of dreaming, your relationship to the dreaming process! Remember, it is not just the answer but the *way* to the answer that is sustainable. Know where you think you want to go and let space move you unpredictably to get there.

If you focus on the answer, then you have just that and then you can bring that answer to where it is needed. You can say, "I have got the answer, friends! Do it this way!" That answer works today, it may work tomorrow, and then what happens? Your answer today may not work in three days and your inner work and your group process begin all over again. "I thought I had the answer!" But the field behind the answer and the answer are different. One is an object you can hold onto, the other is the spirit of process, the spirit of life itself.

So if you have the spirit behind the answer instead of the answer, how does that change things? It changes your feeling about life and its possible meanings. If you have the spirit behind the answer as well as the answer, then you can follow the answer with your consensus reality mind and you may feel more rooted in and open to the dance, to the spirit of change, to movement, and to the stochastic; that is, open to both the deterministic and randomness of life itself. Working with individuals and organizations you may say, "Yes, we have the answer!" That is wonderful. All of us want answers. You have a cold, take some vitamin C. That is wonderful, but it is not the process.

If you marginalize the sense of being moved, it becomes *not you*. This creates a mild chronic depression without knowing why. "Why am I depressed? Everything is going ok in my life!" many people say, but they have lost track of the mystery. That is not the only reason for depression but it is one that is rarely spoken.

The map is not the journey. Sensing the force field creating the traveler's process is important! I have been talking about several levels: (a) an individual in *consensus reality*; (b) in the world of dreaming the different parts or energies; and (c) an *essence level* of the processmind (see diagram below).

DANCE OF THE ANCIENT ONE

My Consensus Reality: Me
and you and parts like
this and that, here or
not here

My Dreamland: You-me,
time and space like
qubits; nonlocal over-
lapping, superposed,
and entangled

Essence: Processmind,
time-reversible non-
locality, Tao, or the
space-time dreaming
between us

Your Dreamland: You-me,
overlapping, super-
posed and entangled
qubits

Your Consensus Reality:
Me, time and space,
and you and parts like
this and that

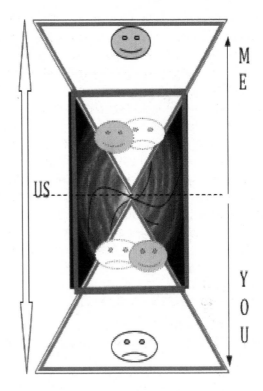

6.3 Relationship Picture.

Relationship Picture shows how my Consensus Reality,
Dreaming, and Essence Levels are separate from and also
overlap with your dreaming and essence levels.

Since this essence level is beyond parts, we can't really describe an
individual person as an individual only. Because the world of dreaming and the essence world are nonlocal, your friends and the things
around you should also be included as overlapping states in *dreamland* and *essence*. In other words, all that you are touched by shares
your processmind and its nonlocal aspects. Your friends too have overlapping images in dreamland that may look a bit different than yours
but may share similar energies. In the dreamland and essence levels,
our dreams, imaginations, double signals, and sudden intuitions are
no longer separable bits or parts but entangled parts or *qubits*. In the
quantum world, states such as being dead and alive can overlap, that
is be simultaneously present. Thus, at some level, we can be both right
and wrong.

This other person in diagram 6.3, therefore, has a dreamland reflecting yours. What does that imply? What do you think? The essence level, space–time dreaming connects all of us, though in consensus reality we don't notice it even though we feel emotionally entangled with others unless we are close to space-time dreaming. In dreaming there is little separation between us! I am a bit of you, and you are a bit of me.

To describe me independently of Amy or you is okay. That is the language of consensus reality. But actually, the things that bug me may also bug her a bit. That is why it is important to know and show your whole self publicly because it is not only you that you are showing. Feeling who you are enables you to feel into the atmosphere: that is, to *shamanize*. Can you follow that line of thinking? I talk about my cold and it is mine but the quiet part of it, the whisper, is not just mine. It is everybody's. What is on your mind may be on our minds, too.

RELATIONSHIP PROCESSES

In practice, this means that relationship problems are both personal and, at the same time, almost impersonal. Such problems are accentuated in part by looking only at the upper consensus reality portion of the diagram. "You are the problem or I am. Not us!" Can you see why? My belief that "you are not me" is true in part, but this belief separates us and ignores the mess we may have in the relationship, whether it is wonderful or terrible! As soon as I say, "you, you are not me," we have a problem. Relationships are by nature a *muddle*. They can be wonderful muddles or uncomfortable ones. You will need your processmind, your sense of the earth and the universe, to work on them.

There is a limitation to the concept of individuality. This model of the processmind shows the limitation of the concept of individuality, which includes a muddle of two overlapping fields. I may say, "You did this to me!" (which I might normally say in consensus reality) but that inhibits me and us from solving the relationship problem. There is nothing to it: To solve a problem, just say to the other person, "I know your energy in me." I can say that easily here but I cannot always do it. It is important to say we are separate but remember that deeper down there is this connection. I need my processmind to do that.

QUBIT MUDDLES

As I said a few pages ago, modern physicists speak of *qubits* (short for quantum bits), units of quantum information. Normally we think only of the bits; that is, of right and wrong, 1 or 0, something or nothing. But these bits get mixed up and entangled in the quantum world, so they are called qubits, quantum bits. Qubits, as I translate the term for use in everyday life, means that your states and mine are entangled, my dream images and your feelings are close. This is psychology and it is also physics.

These ideas update the ancient idea of the Tao. The Tao is a field, and our experience of the Tao is our processmind, perhaps projected or experienced as the powers around you, me, or earth spots or whole planets. Local fields are connected to all fields, since the field around that earth spot also connects to the whole earth, to the space around the earth, and to the universe. In other words, when I throw this pen in my hand into the field, I do it just a bit differently than when you do it because of our natures and the field around us, which includes the entire universe.

Audience: I was just thinking about the psychology of war and propaganda. It is all about, "You are not me. You are as far from me as possible!" I am thinking about this level and its importance in changing our addiction to war.

Arny: To feel and say that you are not just you but also me is world changing. But we should also remember, it is okay to say that you are NOT ME. Both statements are right. The presence of both statements ensures diversity and reminds us of the need for oneness-consciousness. The better you know yourself, the more you will let both the consensus reality and essence aspects of consciousness flow from one to the other.

Kids know all about this flow between realities. And we can help them keep that flow in everyday consensus reality ways. For example, teach kids to brush their teeth but try to avoid the idea that brushing your teeth is more important than being your deepest little self! Say, "I like to brush my teeth. It feels so much better afterwards because there is so much junk in here!?" And jump up and down and play with teeth brushing rather than saying, "You should brush your teeth and grow up!" Perhaps some people get Alzheimer's and go back to childhood early not just because they have plaques growing in their brain but because their dreaming is trying to come back.

"Something rather than nothing?" Finally, we can ask, what would the Taoists say in answer to Hawking's question, "why is there something rather than nothing?" A Taoist would say, he is stuck in the paradigm of objects, of *things*. *No-thing* and *some-thing* are things. The question contains an assumption of things, and the problem comes about because of the paradigm of things, of states, and of state-oriented thinking; that is, consensus reality. From the vantage point of an altered state of consciousness, this something or nothing problem is reduced. When you are in the Tao just letting yourself be moved you will see it sometimes creates things (e.g., the coin falls one way or another). But the point is neither the answer (i.e., something) nor no answer (i.e., nothingness). The point is the Tao, the mystical field process that makes things look like consensus reality things or no-things. There is me and you, this thing and that thing, life and death in consensus reality; and in another state of consciousness there is the dance between all these parts or the dance in which these parts are just steps in the dance.

DEATH?

Most people wonder now and then, "What, if anything, will happen to me? What is going to happen at the end of life?" In my experience, it is very interesting that there are very few clear death dreams to answer that question. So we really don't know. You die. You are dead meat, no doubt about that. Do you follow you? In the world of things our bodies are going to be under the ground in a certain number of years or turned into ash. But from the process viewpoint, perhaps we are just a timeless story, a particular timeless dance. When you are space-time dreaming, perhaps you are what the ancient yoga teacher Pantajali meant by becoming a dead man in life.

TE IN TAO TE CHING

Being in touch with space-time dreaming may temporarily seem free or timeless. In Taoism, the field of such dreaming moving you is comparable to the term *Te*. There are many interpretations of *Te*, some have to do with healing, others with power. But I will soon explain that the word *Te* most likely meant *little tug*. For example, now I am standing and moving about, now slowing down, and now still. In this stillness I can feel little tugs, the *Tao Te* moving me.

Sometimes during normal moments, something jitters or wobbles a bit. Perhaps it is the earth wobbling on its axis, or perhaps it is a little tug of gravity. The early Taoists might have called that the *Te*, that tiny tug. It is a little flirt-like movement experience. You can do things, but the *Te* can *do* things with *not-doing*. Meditate on tiny movement fluctuations in the stochastic element of the Tao, the *Te*. *Wu-wei*, or *not-doing* means noting the oneness and its little tugs in the background. Follow the overall general field and its little stochastic tugs!

6.4 Patanjali (Wikipedia).

One central implication of all of this talk of *Te*, as well as thingness versus no-thingness concerns the act of *not-doing*. Now let's get practical. We all have something to do. I have to pick up the pen. I can *do* it. I *did* it. I have a paper to write... *do* it, *do* it! I have a relationship thing to work out... let's work it out, *do* it, *do* it! We have a city, a nation, a world to help... come on, let's *do* it! But then there is *not-doing*. *Doing* is fine, but we get tired if we don't have our deepest feelings of connection to something infinite when we are doing. *Not-doing* means being in touch with this deepest self, the processmind's dance of the ancient one, while being in consensus reality. The ancient Chinese Taoist term for *not-doing* is *wu-wei*. In Chinese *wu* means nothingness... the Tao that can't be said. The only word I can use is *nothingness*; it is the field. And *wei* means *doing*. When you feel the field space–time-dreaming you, when you feel *Te*, that is a form of *not-doing* or *wu-wei*. And that is what the following exercise is about. Use this exercise to work on things you *do*, have trouble *doing*, or *do* too much, and see if you can *do* something with *not-doing*.

Audience 1: Before we do that exercise, I want to ask a question… So, you are talking about listening to that little tug, *Te*, so you can do *not-doing*?

Arny: Yes, feeling, listening. *Te* is a proprioceptive awareness of stochastic movement.

Audience 1: Being aware while you are *not-doing* or while you are *doing*?

Arny: If I am aware of it while *doing*, then I will begin to *do not-doing*. The exercise is about using your earth spot to get into the atmosphere there, letting it move you, and then feeling little *Te*'s in there and using those *Te*'s to do a project. And I will bet you the cost of this class that there is not a project you can't do afterwards! This little *Te* may be good for your health as well.

Audience 2: It is such a beautiful way of saying that. You really brought it home to my body when you talked about letting the little tugs guide me along the Tao and enjoying going along and learning that.

Arny: There are different interpretations of *Te*. It is sometimes translated as virtue or power or culture. That is why I am interpreting it in terms of the tug, as a little tiny power. This is different than the modern Confucian teaching about social or spiritual rank. *Te* is a power in the space you inhabit. Follow it. Then you have the power to follow the Tao, the little tug, the pull that you feel when your mind is relaxed, empty, or dreaming in the processmind.

Who you are, is what you teach. Because of my cold today, I must whisper a bit but it is also the real me teaching, saying that what I say is not the point… it is the feeling behind me, moving me. Please note that we shall be doing aspects of the following exercise many times because it is a kind of meditation. It takes practice!

EXERCISE: DOING AND NOT-DOING.

1. First note your worst problem linked to *doing*: you can or you can't do something or you do something too much. Choose one or two of the biggest problems you have in this regard.

2. To find the Tao that can't be said and the *Te*, go to your favorite earth spot. Describe it, sense its atmosphere, and sense the wonder of the atmosphere. Something makes you love that spot, even if you have never been there in reality. Get in touch with that power.

3. Let go and breathe into the atmosphere there. Let it breathe you and dance you. Notice and feel the Tao and *Te*, the subtle earth power breathing and dancing you. Feel yourself being moved and every now and then notice a little pull or tug. That is what I am calling the *Te*. Continue to be moved and notice spontaneous transitions from nothing to something as ideas spontaneously pop up.

4. Now recall your problem and let your spontaneous dance give you quick little insights into how to work or help that problem, how to do *not-doing* with the problem. Your movement processes will give you experiences and insights that may explain how to deal with your issue or *doing* problem. If you have insights, catch them and write them down.

5. Finally, make notes about the nature of your processmind dance, its powers and insights, and imagine using this dance with things you want to do.

AFTERWARDS

Audience 1: I found my dance was rhythmic, like drumming, and part of the teaching was for me to learn to establish a rhythm for my writing. My earth spot was in Chicago where I was born, and the tug from behind was the backyard stairway. The steps were the rhythm. So the doing in me has been saying, "Get off your ass early in the morning and write a little bit in the morning!" But the *non-doing* lesson was, get in the rhythm of writing! I have been procrastinating because in my mind I had to get things perfect and just right, and the non-doing was, "that's a bunch of bullshit, D, just write and the writing will write itself." So the non-doing lesson was, "Don't worry about being linear, having to get it right. Let that go and let the writing write itself."

Audience 2: My problem was how to bring my weirdness more into my everyday life, my working everyday life. I am a clinical director of five programs in mental health. So I got really weird and things came flying out of my head, and then I saw a huge pearl shell with a pearl in it and a dead ancestor came and helped me out. She was an Aboriginal Maori woman I know, and she came and advised me on how to be in that work environment. She said I should be more in touch with "my other eyes," not my everyday eyes. She was very shamanistic. I was thrilled that someone from the other world visited me.

Arny: A Maori ancestor…

Audience 2: Right now she is beside me in the processmind spot in New Zealand on the rocks, and we are fishing [makes motions with hand]. It's hard to find her when I am working in mainstream reality, to reach out in the way she shows me!

Arny: Let's practice *not-doing*. I'll be a possible client with whom you need to work today.

Audience 2: OK, hi! Ooo! How is it going? I feel weird today! How are you?

Arny: Fine, how are you?

Audience 2: Frazzled! And very present, I am here for you right now. What do you need?

Arny: You are so present! What do I need? I am a street person and I am angry at my helpers. They don't do any good.

Audience 2: [Reaches out and listens, to see what the Maori ancestor will say.] You are angry at your helpers? Where are they? Let's get together and have coffee and talk.

Arny: You mean you are not going to yell at me? You are not going to tell me to clean up? You are going to treat me like a person?

Audience 2: You are a person. Are you going to treat me like a person?

Arny: Wow, we are equals. Your new manner is fluid eldership. Thank you.

Σ   FOR REFLECTION ON CHAPTER 6

- Physics needs but does not yet have a unified field theory for its four physical fields.

- The concept of the processmind's space–time dreaming is an attempt to unify psychology and physics.

- The space between us dreams and moves us and is a process beyond the everyday meanings of life and death. It is like a life force.

- The answer to Hawking's question, "Why is there something rather than nothing?" is that there is neither something nor nothing but rather phases of one process.

- At the essence level space–time dreaming is like the Tao that can't be said and feels like a little tug or *Te* (a term in the book title, the *Tao Te Ching*).

- Space–time dreaming is the dance of the ancient one, an experience of not-doing.

CHAPTER 7

Pachamama and Einstein's Ether

According to the general theory of relativity, space without ether is unthinkable; for in such space there not only would be no propagation of light but also no possibility of existence for standards of parts which may be tracked through time. The idea of motion may not be applied to it.

—Einstein, in 1920, five years after publishing his general theory of relativity [36]

What some psychologists and everyday people call the dreaming, I call *space–time dreaming*. I suggested that our experience, like an astronaut's experience, of space–time (i.e., outer space) connects the sense of dreaming and the curvature of the cosmos. Remember the Tao, the field-like power you cannot see. Stephen Mitchell tells us of ancient Taoist masters who explain things simply:

When the Tao moves, you move. When it stops, you stop. [37]

I suggested in the last chapter that the *Te* in the book title *Tao Te Ching* is experienced as a tiny pull or a little tug. I also mentioned that *Te* is usually translated as virtue or dignity, but if you look into the history of the word *Te* in Confucian thinking, its essence is possibly connected with a shamanistic power that Don Juan would have called the *nagual* or personal power. [38]

Space–time dreaming and Tao are virtual field-like powers. If you are too rigid, then you may not feel the sensations of gravity or space-time dreaming. But if you are aware, you notice little tugs that move you here or there. Those tugs arise from the essence behind your personal virtue or kind of spiritual quality, a power behind who you really are. When you feel the Tao, you can feel the *Te* pulling you into a kind of altered state or oneness dance, you understand. It seems likely that Tai Chi, the internal martial art movement programs, originally came from people letting themselves be moved with the universe. In any case, in the last exercise you moved between doing things and not-doing them. But the spontaneous dance becomes the point. It's beyond being strong or weak. When the dance becomes the point, for a moment, you are in Tao, the flow. The process is the point, not any particular act. Then in process thinking, you come out of dreaming into consensus reality and the act becomes the important thing again.

Sorry to be so paradoxical, but space–time dreaming is paradoxical! Remember that doing *not-doing* all the time is not the point. That would just be another program. Without pushing you would hardly appreciate *wu-wei*. Getting off your seat and working hard can be important in the overall process. However, *wu-wei* is important especially when you are tired or when you are sick and have had a cold like me. Then either you do *wu-wei* or your body will make you do it.

Now let's continue exploring the nature of the space in which we live. Newton saw space as a rigid stage upon which all events occur. In 1907 Einstein came up with his first special theory of relativity, in which he described the space of the universe as a more active participant in what happens.[39] Relativity is not the final story about the universe; it doesn't work perfectly, it doesn't yet explain dark matter or energy, the big bang, or connect well with quantum theory. But relativity theory is the best we have in the year 2013. There are new theories about the universe being constructed by membranes and holograms, but they are still speculative. Generally, relativity works very well.

Dealing with the universe's spaces is a rational and also a spiritual experience. It is not surprising, therefore, to find Einstein saying the following:

> *The finest emotion of which we are capable is the mystic emotion. Herein lies the germ of all art and all true science. Anyone to whom this feeling is alien, who is no longer capable of wonderment and lives in a state of fear is a dead man.*

To know that what is impenetrable for us really exists and manifests itself as the highest wisdom and the most radiant beauty, whose gross forms alone are intelligible to our poor faculties — this knowledge, this feeling… that is the core of the true religious sentiment. In this sense, and in this sense alone, I rank myself among profoundly religious men.[40]

Einstein felt that it is a spiritual experience to wonder about the universe. Wonder is like studying something you cannot see but can feel. There is something general and universal that moves and connects all people and beings everywhere. It does not make any difference what you call the space in which we live, but getting in touch with it is the point. Einstein was also a very rational person. Friends of mine who knew him say that he resisted the idea that God (in this case, the laws of quantum physics) were stochastic or probabilistic. He was not right about this. Still, he was a great guy. I dreamed that he lived next door in Portland. Hmmn, so he must be here, too, right now.

Relativity in a Nutshell

At the time of Einstein, most people lived by their watch, like you and me now. We live by space as well. For example, how long does it take you to get to work and how far is it from your home? Time and space can be separated. Everybody still separates them today. That separation means that what is happening on your watch has nothing to do whatsoever with where you are and what you are doing. In other words, your timing and location seem disconnected.

However, since Einstein, scientists agree that massive planets and stars bend space–time. The bigger more massive objects are, the more they bend space and the light beams going through space. Einstein realized that somebody traveling in a rocket ship will measure the time and space of an event on our moon differently than you or I will measure it on earth. Our sense of time and space depends upon our consensus reality. What we see depends upon our position and velocity. This relativity creates a diversity problem in the universe! Your views will be different from other people's views of time and space if they live in other frameworks. So, generally speaking, time and space measurements from one given reference frame will not necessarily be the same in other frameworks.

In our most common cosmopolitan 21st century framework, if you have trouble getting things done on time, there is something *wrong* with you. From this viewpoint, you are troubled, you are not following time. But from another viewpoint you may be on the verge of being a Taoist because your timing depends upon your location, your sense of the space around you, and the times you live in. Many people don't follow their watch and the yardstick exactly, as in Aboriginal Australia, Siberia, Tuva, Native America, Island Time, Oregon Coastal time, Portlandia, my time, or inner time. Many people say, "Let's make a date, Friday evening at eight." Some people get there at eight whereas others come when their arriving *happens*. Their time and space are not the only reality. Time and space are not absolute measures.

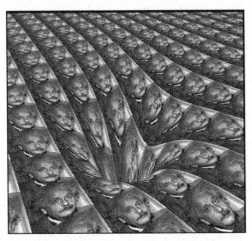

7.1 Field Picture of Einstein.[41]

Einstein realized that we need another measurement to understand space because space can be curved! Space is not just linear, going in straight lines. The spaces we live in are a little bit curved: they are hyperbolic. *Hyperbolic* in mathematics means something related to a hyperbola or a curve. Our universe's space is hyperbolic. For example, the sea anemone is hyperbolic. Our universe is curved in similar ways! Because of curvature, a beam of light moving through space going by our planet will have to curve a bit because the space around our planet is curved. A straight yardstick measuring the space around our planet would curve if it were long enough!

If we put a huge massive object, like a planet, near a flat piece of space, that space will curve. In the field picture of Einstein (see image above), one region containing those pictures is distorted. A massive object or planet might be nearby. Space bends because space is curved and not flat near massive objects like our planet. As objects in space move around, space curves. Space is always curving a little. It is not in a steady state.

Reality is more curvy and crazy than we usually realize [big smile]. Imagine that a straight light beam moving along in the fabric of space gets curved as it moves through space–time. It is curved by gravity or by the space–time field. Since experiments proved this curvature exists, no one debates curvature today. But how did Einstein arrive at this far-out idea? Like all of us, he knew that the field gravity pulls on things and makes them fall to the ground if they are dropped. But he asked himself, is everyone right in saying, like Isaac Newton said, that gravity pulled them down? He said, in essence, "I don't see gravity. Maybe space is curved, and that is why things fall." How do we know we are not accelerated or twirled around in circles and this is the pull we feel?

7.2 Einstein's Thought Experiment.

On the right, someone might think the ball falls because of gravity. On the left, from an outside view, we see the ball falls because of acceleration. That kind acceleration might also be due to the curvature of space.

As you can see on the right hand side of the rocket ship drawing, Einstein imagined a person in a closed rocket. From inside you feel the pull of something like gravity so the ball falls to the ground. But if you can't look outside, you might not realize you are being accelerated through space by a rocket (on the left). Then, he reasoned, if space is curved, you might experience a pull or push on you, as you do when you go in a car quickly around a curve. Space is curved. That is why we feel pressure, like gravity, on us. Something is pulling us or pushing us around. We don't realize or see what is pulling on us. Einstein reasoned that space must be curved and that most people don't see that curvature and simply call that pulling or pushing experience gravity.

Ordinary everyday space on our planet is pretty straight. Just measure the height, length, and width of a room. But normal space is just one little aspect of our universe's spaces, of space–time. Physicists agree. Today, though the concept of gravity is no longer needed it's still used because it's easier for everyday people to understand than curved space-time. In a way, gravity is fictitious, but it continues to persist in consensus reality viewpoints because it's a bit easier to understand.

The same thing happens in psychology. For example, if you get in a bad mood, everyone says, you are in a *complex*! Your parents were bad people or neglected you or overindulged you, and so on. However, that complex might be caused by something much more universal: something like a bend in space–time, something that curves you, spaces you out. Yes, we know the idea of a complex is helpful. We persist in using it because it seems close to everyday thinking, that because of your mother or father, you are like this or that today. That may or may not be causally true. But there is another way of looking at our world. We are not the result of this or that. Instead we are connected to a changing space around us. It feels like this or that person is pulling us, but it may be a curve in space that we experience as space-time dreaming. Straight lines themselves may only be straight because they have only a small curvature.

The basis of life is curvy, and it is only in rare moments that things seem straight! We are in a curved dreamy world, but most of us have tried to make it into a straight, linear universe because that is easier to talk about. (See Appendix 2: it may help you understand more about space–time curvature.)

Einstein came up with his first paper on special relativity in 1907. His second paper on general theory appeared 8 years later in 1915 and described the curved nature of space–time. At first, many scientists did not like that idea, but then, after experiments proved it was real, they accepted it. There is experimental evidence, such as the bending of light rays, that show us that the universe in which we live is curved. It is not flat and straight as some think. We need to accept that the universe curves us. It is a dance choreographer!

DEATH AND FREE FALL

Free fall is a term that means that your motion is due only to space–time (or gravity). If you take the chair out from underneath your rear end, you will experience a free fall due only to gravity, which feels weightless as long as you are in the air. Without quite realizing it, however, you follow a curved, not a straight, line as you head towards the floor! Likewise, when we let go or die or relax in space-time dreaming, a kind of effortlessness or free fall happens. That is why many near-death experiences are about free fall in the universe… people finally just let go so space–time can move them.

Most of us in our everyday lives try to follow a straight line toward our many goals. But near death many people have seemed freer to me, and many in that state seem to have occasional experiences of flying free. It is as if you can fly free in space–time where you follow your geodesic (or shortest path between two points). Some people see death in terms of consensus reality: that is, as an ending. But I see it as following the Tao like always; just going along on our basic curve, moving with our story, as always. My point here is to feel this curve and let yourself do this more in life, and not wait for death to experience free fall.

Everybody feels the same pull and pressure of *doing* in everyday life. At one point or another, most people dream of or yearn for a sense of freedom. In a way, this is a kind of spiritual yearning common to just about everyone. Everybody feels something pulling on them and finds the same freedom when we *let go* into it. Not everybody wants to feel the same thing. Some people don't want to feel anything, and that is also fine, but everybody has the same spiritual potential. Gravity or space–time moves each of us equally and everything in the universe as well. And if we *let go* into it, we fall freely, and then we have less pressure and less, or no, weight. It is good psychology and normal physics.

Audience 1: Someone watching this online is wondering what would be called a *death dream*?

Arny: My teachers were looking for a death dream. Von Franz and apparently Jung did, too. She and I and others were part of a scientific group that was searching for death dreams. After looking at 2,000 or 3,000 dreams we could not find one single dream that predicted death. We tried. If a person disappeared into the darkness in a dream, was that a death dream? No, because here a 6-year-old had that same dream. Maybe the person went out into outer space and said, "I never want to come back." Does that symbolize death? But here is someone in an altered or extreme state of consciousness saying the same thing and this person is in good physical health. That research is going on still today. No one yet knows if death dreams exist. We cannot say, "That dream says that you will die."

THE OVERLAP BETWEEN SCIENCE AND SPIRITUAL TRADITIONS

The math of relativity is complicated, but we feel its consequences simply in terms of being pulled and moved. My point is that relativity and space–time curvature are empirically correct, and they are also psychological feeling experiences. Gravity is a good beginning name but it is very earth-bound or planet-bound. The sense of being moved by the curvature of space–time, by the road you are on, is not just physics, it is also psychology. Religion has always spoken about this too… we are moved by something that is hard to explain. There is an overlap between science and spiritual traditions. Monotheists call it Allah, God, Yahweh, or Dancing Shiva; Taoists call it the Tao; and physicists call it space–time curvature. Psychology simply says, something moves all of us in different ways. When you are in touch with your imagination of space–time moving you, you are in touch with *wu-wei*, with not-doing. It's noncognitive. It's like free fall… that is, letting yourself move freely only under the influence of gravity giving you the free falling sensation of weightlessness. You sense only the curves and motions into which nature draws you.

I originally felt that the idea of space–time was just plain weird. Apparently, Einstein did too. It took him 8 years, from 1907 to 1915, to come out with his general theory of relativity. Why did it take him so long? His special theory did not insist upon a new space or time. But his second, more general, theory did. Apparently he was nervous about speaking in terms of curved spaces. He said:

> *Why were another seven years required for the construction of the general theory of relativity? The main reason lies in the fact that it is not so easy to free oneself from the idea that coordinates must have an immediate metrical meaning.*[42]

Einstein meant that it is difficult to leave the world of meters and hours and go into a universe where meters and hours are stretching, pulling, and curving in a manner you can't track in everyday reality. He needed an entirely new *space*, one that observers anywhere in the universe could agree upon. He suffered for 8 years (at least) until he got to the point where he could drop the idea of reality as being directly measurable in meters and hours.

When space and time come together, there are no longer simple straight measurements of space such as height, width, and depth and then another separate dimension of time. Instead, the three spatial and the one time dimension come together in a four-dimensional hyperbolic curved *space–time* where space and time can no longer be separated. Einstein hesitated for 8 years. During that time he had marital troubles and god knows what (all because of relativity?). I believe it was some 10 years later that he said that coming out with the idea that the space in which we live is curved involved the 8 most difficult years of his life. This idea could turn Western consensus reality upside down.

EINSTEIN'S ETHER

It seems to me that, in spite of his rational understanding of space–time, Einstein still suspected, after completing his general theory of relativity, that space was some sort of weird magical stuff, which he called the *ether*, that would draw all the fields of physics together. He said that he hoped that "the contrast between ether and matter would fade away" and, "through the general theory of relativity, the whole of physics would become a complete system of thought."[43] In 1920 Einstein said:

> *According to the general theory of relativity, space without ether is unthinkable; for in such space there not only would be no propagation of light, but also no possibility of existence for standards of parts which may be tracked through time. The idea of motion may not be applied to it.*[44]

Einstein's space–time or ether is not just empty space but a kind of stuff that has almost material properties and behaves like an invisible field with curved, rubber-sheet-like spaces that bend and twist.

Einstein's ether is the universe's common ground: something that all observers, at one time or another, can agree upon. I have spoken about the experience of this common ground in terms of the atmosphere around powerful spots on earth. The spaces of the processmind (our basic intelligence) are deep, altered-state-essence experiences related to the atmosphere field of the universe. This atmosphere or ether connects us to the Tao of Taoism and, as I shall soon show, to the lightbody of Tibetan Buddhism and to Dancing Shiva, and it helps to illuminate extreme human experiences like so-called psychotic states and some near-death phenomena.

Space, for Einstein, never lost is magical power. In 1930, 15 years after his general theory of relativity, Einstein said in a letter to his former teacher, Lorentz,

> *Now it appears that space will have to be regarded as a primary thing and that matter is derived from it, so to speak, as a secondary result. Space is now having its revenge, it is eating up matter.*[45]

Today I would amplify his statement by saying that the spaces of the universe, our dreaming, are the essences of our material world. Buddhists have always claimed that all our suffering is due to the fact that we cannot let go of the fixed and important nature of everyday reality. We hang on to our appearance, to our health, our relationships, and our age. That is, we hang on to the everyday idea of time and space as if they were sacrosanct. But they are not. *Reality*, as we define it, is a human construction. It is not an absolute truth. So Einstein had to let go of the idea of time and space to develop space–time. Likewise, we will temporarily have to let go of our sense of everyday reality, to go deeper to a new dimension that I call space–time dreaming, our common ground.

WHAT IS ETHER?

Einstein's ether is a vague sort of stuff, and physicists don't like talking about it. Theorists seem to ignore it. Though Einstein said that space–time is a kind of ether in 1930, I asked experts on relativity about this matter, and they said, "We never mention the word ether." But Einstein was not alone in thinking that space is having its revenge and eating up matter. Physicist John Wheeler, a colleague of Einstein, describes the relativity principle simply:

> *Space–time tells matter how to move; matter tells space–time how to curve.*[46]

Space–time tells you how to move and you, and everything else, tell space–time how to curve. This is a psychological experience we might call the Tao or space–time dreaming. Let your body and your mind experience weightlessness, not-doing, no pressure, just moving, being moved now and then. Just follow your body as if you were partially sleeping. This is a very deep and significant personal development, and it is an enlightenment concept found in many spiritual traditions.

THE RUBBER SHEET UNIVERSE ANALOGY

Edwin Taylor says in his *Introduction to General Relativity*,

> *Einstein demands that a nonlinear coordinate system — that is, one that is arbitrarily stretched — should also be legal. Nonlinear means that it can be stretched by different amounts in different locations and even at different times.* [47]

This reminds me of the rubber sheet. At one moment a picture may look like a circle, and at the next the picture can be stretched so that looks like an ellipse (see below). Likewise, in dreams you feel you are seeing a circle, but suddenly it becomes an ellipse.

7.3 In curved space, a circle can become an ellipse.

We must now also demand that it be *legal* to perceive everyday reality with an apparently unstructured spaced-out intelligence: a way to perceive that we can learn and experience through movement, relaxation, and breathing; and through the practices of Shamanism, Taoism, Tibetan Buddhism, and other spiritual traditions. Stay open to altered states.

INNER WORK

- Sit in such a way that you can do a little movement. Anyway you feel comfortable.

- Let your body wobble around a little bit, as if you were a tiny bit drunk. Free your mind a little bit as if it were just a little bit tipsy.

- Just wobble around in any way, as much or as little as feels comfortable. And, while you are wobbling around freely and when you are free, give yourself a tip about life. Wait until you are free a little bit, listen to the tiniest things, and give yourself a tip about life. Maybe a little tip will suddenly come to mind that says something.

- If you catch it, if you get a tip, just write it down.

Did the universe as space–time give you a tip, following little movement flirts? Tell me what you heard!

- Don't stay too long in one spot.
- Balance is the point.
- Fall in love every day
- Yee-hah! Ride 'em cowboy!
- Don't be a tight ass!
- Stop thinking you are so important. You are not the point.

Those are tips from the universe as you let it move and talk to you.

7.4 Pachamama (Wikipedia).

PACHAMAMA

Apparently the people of the Andes have always believed that time and space are one thing.[48] Einstein was not the first. Many aboriginal peoples have thought of their deities as the universe. The Incas called their goddess *Pachamama*, the goddess of the whole universe. Inside of her, they said, there is a baby and on one side of her there is night and day on the other. Some people experience Pachamama as something moving them. Others experience her as a great mother figure. The Incas believe that she knows what to do and she moves them.[49]

This sounds similar to the Taoists and the sentences I quoted at the beginning of this book in the acknowledgements to John Wheeler. He discovered the idea of black holes and compared space–time with the Tao and wind and what happens to astronauts falling free of gravity in outer space. Here he quotes the Chinese poet Su Tung-p'o (C.E. 1036–1101) and his description of floating on the Yangze River:

> We let our boat drift as it would… and felt that we were sailing in empty space and riding on the wind… we were light, as if we had forsaken the world, and free of all support, like one who has become an immortal and soars through space.

What I call space–time dreaming infuses ancient Taoist beliefs and is personified as deities by many peoples. If you get uptight, you need to drop your space and time paradigm and try curving and being non-linear. Otherwise, you tend to over eat or turn to drugs and alcohol. We can observe this curving regularly in others.

Amy and I often walk along 23rd Avenue in Portland where there are a lot of bars and restaurants. We walk around before we go to sleep, and we meet many space–time people; the space–time dreamers. Coming out of the restaurants and the bars, they don't walk in straight lines. Somehow they are curving, needing to break cultural rules and their everyday mindset. Try using the space–time framework as a new form of dreamwork.

EXERCISE: DREAMWORK WITH SPACE–TIME DREAMING

1. Name one of your problems and then recall a recent dream.

2. Now feel the force under your feet or seat. Relax while on your feet or in a chair and wait for space (or dreaming) to move you however it wants. Notice and follow your movements and other experiences until you feel free and perhaps start to do unpredictable little things. While flowing with the processmind, Tao, or space–time; note what this dreaming and movement experience tells you about your dream. Continue on with not-doing, that is, *wu-wei*, letting the universe move you and help you with your problem.

3. Make notes about insights and your path in space–time. Ask: Where do dreams come from? What does your movement experience tell you about the dream? Let your experience interpret the dream. You have a dream and you have a dream interpreter in you.

Use this exercise every evening and every morning to interpret your dreams. First get into this mood, wobbling back and forth, and then you will understand your dreams a little better. You have to be in the dreaming mind to understand dreams.

Audience 1: I am a heart beat, and it is unpredictable. It is really something.

Audience 2: I am shy about how deep this exercise took me. It took me to a place that is so touching. It took me to a kind of universal kindness. And when we asked the question, "Where do dreams come from?" the answer was that "They come from the universal kindness." It is just very touching to find that kindness in the midst of a terrible problem.

Σ   For Reflection on Chapter 7

- Einstein was shy about space–time because he realized that it was curved and very different from the linear world we all call consensus reality.

- Space is curved. It is ether-like and we may experience it as alive, as space–time dreaming.

- Don't drink to relax. Feel space–time dreaming.

- Space–time dreaming is a form of dreamwork.

- Curving is, apparently, our bottom *line*.

CHAPTER 8

Four Halves of Life and the Tibetan Bardos

Time is important—get your stuff done on time, shape up, be realistic! But Einstein, some therapists, and most aboriginal traditions have pointed out that the *time* in "getting your stuff done on time" is not universal. Einstein pointed out, however, that space-time dreaming is a common ground for observers in various frameworks. The consensus reality significance of terms such as the *distance* in space and time between one point and another is limited, bound to that given consensus reality. But in space-time it is the curved space in between two points that is common ground. It may have taken Einstein 8 years to come out with this curved universe idea because he was nervous about upsetting our *normal* views of time and space, but, dear reader, please don't spend that much time hesitating to loosen up and dream.

Today, Einstein's space–time viewpoint is around 100 years old, but the general public does not know much about it. Ideas about consensus reality change slowly. I think Minkowski (Einstein's helpful mathematician supporter) guessed that this change would happen. In 1908 Minkowski said (he died in 1909 at the age of 44):

> *The views of space and time that I wish to lay before you have sprung from the soil of experimental physics and therein lies their strength. They are radical. Henceforth space by itself and time by itself are doomed to fade away into mere shadows, and*

only a kind of union of the two will preserve an independent reality.[50]

Minkowski thought that, because space–time pervades the whole universe, people would pick up the concept right away! They haven't yet. I think consensus reality views of time and space may change as we gain more access to outer space, but that may take quite a while. Why might they change even then? Because more access to outer space will give us views that will not correspond with views from other places in the universe and then we will realize that we need the space-time perspective. Likewise, the more we try to solve our world problems and fail, the more likely we are to explore the deep spaces between us, and then space-time dreaming will become more familiar to us all as a common ground.

Tibetan Buddhism stresses that beginning and end points are not as important as the process in between. Weird inexplicable things happen in between beginning and end points. Tibetans focus mainly upon the times in between life and death, which they call *bardos*. According to Chogyam Trungpa:

> The Tibetan word bardo literally means "between two." Although it is popularly taken to refer to the after-death state, its principal meaning is the nowness in every moment of time, the continually moving point between past and future. Thus, bardo occurs at every moment of time, and to understand it is to understand the development of consciousness.[51]

The word bardo is often used to indicate a transitional or liminal condition between birth and death, during meditation, while dreaming, while dying, or during the process of rebirth. Bardo is a phase, a piece of space–time between our consensus reality times, organized, for example, by the time of going to sleep, waking time, working time, meditation time, and so forth. The question is, how to make the transitions during times when normal consciousness is not functioning? How do we get along in these bardos with space–time dreaming? How do we remain conscious in altered states between consensus reality points?

Remember Sara Halprin? In the first chapter of my book, *Process-Mind*,[52] I described how, as Sara was dying, her last words were, "I want to be useful to people," and then, "I am nervous about falling into emptiness." She was afraid to go into her inner experience. I said, "What is it like in there?" She said, "There is a kind of emptiness."[53]

She was nervous about the inner experience of falling into *emptiness*, into a bardo, so to speak. She thought emptiness might be all there was. So I said, "Use your awareness, and when you are ready, let's follow whatever happens." After a moment she went into this empty space. I said, "Use your awareness to track it," and she said, "I am becoming a bird, a mallard, and I landed in the river." She felt ecstatic about her bird and the river. Those were the last words of that amazing person.

But let's think about that for a moment. Empty space is scary, in part because it is a bit altering and foreign from object-filled consensus reality. Awareness work—all the Eastern religions and some aspects of Western religion talk about awareness of this in-between space, of the *Ma*, the space in between that I mentioned in chapter 4. What is going on in there? Is emptiness and nothingness the end? No, it is only the way the everyday mind thinks or fears. Sara's next step was being the bird, being the river, and so on. By going into the bardo, she discovered not just emptiness but a kind of free fall. She met the river and bird. She discovered that what her everyday mind called a rapidly beating heart turned out to be the rapid motions birds make in the water cleansing themselves. Space–time dreaming is all around us. We simply fear it because most of us are not used to moving with the emptiness of our dreaming body.

LIGHT BODY

Tibetan Buddhists who study the timeless body experience speak of the *rainbow body* or *light body*. (See Figure 8.1). It is the essence-level dreambody or processmind body experience of moving through the bardos. Some Taoists refer to this out-of-body experience as the diamond body. You will need that when you deal with the many Bardos, or luminal experiences.

TRANSITION THROUGH BARDOS

With your space–time dreaming or processmind body experience, you move through space and time, experiencing times that seem both good and bad. You may have nervous phases before a talk you must give, you may fear illness or pain or death, or fear meeting an enemy or ex-partner. We fear *hungry ghosts*, so to speak. Each bardo has specific scary characters; some bardos have very hungry ghosts that are going to eat us up, and we have to learn how to get through them. Near-death experiences that happen in relatively normal states of consciousness can be agonizing. However, if people dream, those experiences can be a bit easier.

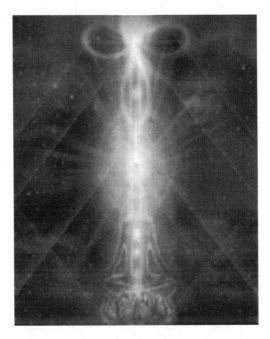

8.1 Light Body.[54]

C.G. Jung, in his autobiography *Memories, Dreams, Reflections,* spoke of his near-death experience; of how, at age 72, he had a heart attack. During this attack, he had a vision of a Hindu meditating and realized that if he went further, he might know everything there is to know about himself. He saw the doctor that was taking care of him fly by him and realized that the doctor would soon die. And then he woke up and a couple of days later his doctor did die. That experience enlightened him about this "nothingness." He went on to continue his studies in things that today people don't usually look too much at and wrote his *Mysterium Coniunctionis;* his last book, on the mysterious conjunction of alchemical opposites.

Imagine in space–time dreaming having a body experience, say a light body, to move through life and death. It is your space–time dreaming existence. The light body is some kind of field experience, a *field-body* moving through space–time. We all have a body experience of moving through the universe. It is your space–time dreaming body that I am trying to bring out, as shown in the light body picture, above.

Audience: Does your everyday physical body actually become more luminous?

Arny: Some people say that it does. I will leave it an open question. But I do know that when you are in your process-mind body experience, you feel well and form better contacts with everyone and everything. In a way, you are luminous in the sense that you can shed light on reality.

In Tibetan Buddhism there are six traditional bardos. I will mention them all, but I want to study one in detail. The first bardo is the transition from birth to death. The second bardo is the dream state itself. The third bardo is a meditation state. The Dalai Lama talks about this bardo as the place to go for developing a dreambody, as he calls it. He speaks about the dreaming state and says that while you are dreaming, you become more lucid and while you are lucid, you can do things secretly so that nobody sees you.[55] He means that others may not recognize your state of space-time dreaming while you are doing things.

The fourth bardo begins at the moment of death and continues on. Some of you who work with near-death experiences know that at the moment of death a lot of amazing, and sometimes very weird, experiences happen. That is a particular bardo I know about myself from working with people.

In contrast to the fourth bardo, the fifth bardo is called the bardo of luminosity, the bardo of our true nature. According to the Tibetans, it commences after the final inner breath. It is connected with peacefulness and pristine awareness. Some say, if you have not developed your awareness, you may get deluded in this bardo and sometimes become very nasty. Hungry ghosts will come up and you will have your hands full! To me, this sounds like you once again, even in *death*, marginalize a part of yourself, and it reacts with a vengeance. In contrast, the *Luminos* state is probably the time when you are flowing with what happens. In any case, bardos are open spaces in which anything can happen.

Hungry Ghosts

Tibetan Buddhists suggest clearing out your problems so you won't have a lot of hungry ghosts around. Today, because of drugs, especially pain drugs, people near death can go into altered states and more easily find their detached space-time dreaming and sometimes come out of those altered states more clearly than they may have been able to in the past and tell us things. Working on yourself may or not make your final transition easier, but it surely doesn't hurt.

The sixth bardo is transmigration. It endures from death till your inner life begins again as another physical person. What do you think about bardos and processes going on after you die and before you come back? Some Tibetan practitioners say that what you do in this lifetime, your *karmic seed*, determines what you do in the next. If you really know yourself and your dreams, perhaps you have a sense of what will be happening in lives to come. I suspect that if you know your processmind, you know yourself as a field independently of time, space, life, and death. For example, if you identify with a particular piece of land, then, at least in this way, others can identify you with that land and you *come back*. Do you come back as a living person?

Audience: If I track my dreams about people whom I have loved who have died, you could say it is just my feelings evolving about them, but I don't think so. I think I dream about their evolution. I feel that evolution. I don't know why, but I dream about their changing.

DEAD AND ALIVE?

Yes and yes. Do you know any place on this planet where you can see people both dead and alive at the same time? In the world of quantum physics! Remember Schrödinger's cat from chapter 2. Don't forget the reason that Schrödinger was going to throw out his original wave equation explanation of quantum physics, which had been accepted for many years, was because in quantum physics you can be dead and alive simultaneously. You can be in two or more states at the same time. That is called *superposition*: the experience of different states at the same time. So in a way, Tibetans are way ahead of their time thinking you might be dead, but you are also alive!

In everyone who is near death, right near the end, some people seem to know a lot about space–time and something in them always seems to appear in an altered state knowing what to do. It seems as if people have wisdom inside themselves. This wisdom does not say either hello or goodbye. There seems to be something inside all of us that knows how to flow, what to do, and when.

COMAWORK

I love the Tibetans because they are probably the first known coma workers, 800 CE; way before we in the West even gave such work a thought. They basically said, "Oh, dear one, remember your whole self." They also said something like,

> *Remember your basic nature and your whole self and use your*
> *awareness, and when you see some nasty bardos coming your*
> *way, just use your processmind and keep rolling!*

That is my poor translation of Tibetan Buddhism. Continue meditating with someone who is dying even after his or her breath stops! How come? I have to ask you that! Why on earth are you going to work with somebody after his or her breath has stopped? What do you think? Why do people go on meditating five, ten, or even twenty days later? They bring up an effigy, a symbol of the person, and they talk to him or her: "Oh dear uncle Harrison, remember your whole self!" Why have Tibetans been doing that since 800 CE? Could we assume they are just fantasying or dreaming?

People who meditated in this way must have gotten good feedback—I am assuming that they got feedback. Some people may have had near-death experiences and may have reawakened and told amazing stories. They look like they died, the doctors say that they have died, but then there they are with their eyes open and talking. I have experienced this with the person I wrote about in my book, *Coma, Dreambody Near Death.*[56] The doctor said, "Well, this guy is done, goodbye." But Amy and I kept meditating with him along the lines of, "Remember your whole self, follow this, notice this, and notice this." After 4 hours, I said, "I am tired, it is time to go home." And then he woke up and even sat up! We had a party. He became quite lucid, and he had a reunion with his wife that included some oranges and beer. He said what he wanted. Everybody came around, he completed a lot of stuff, and, later on that day, he lay down and that was it.

But before he died he said, "You know, Arny and Amy, please remember my kids because they are over there. Would you keep your eye on them later?" "OK," I said. And then he said, in the same reasonable voice, "I think my next step is to work with you here in Zurich and study with you to learn more about Processwork."

Why did he say that? How could he speak about his kids as if he was going to die and in the same breath speak about his next step in life, knowing that he was going to die? Dying is not supposed to be the time to talk about the next step. You are supposed to be getting ready for your grave! It is all prepared and all you have to do is jump in, and you are done! I have had that experience with people a number of times. He is dying and picking up his next process step! Many people say things like that to us when we work with them. Such statements are indications that we are ongoing processes.

The Tibetans believe that we come around again, in another lifetime, and that we already know before we are finished with one phase that another phase is coming. They talk to people in these states just like we work with people in comatose states. Lama Suryadas, an expert in Tibetan Buddhism, translated some statements his teacher made when speaking to someone who had just died. "Martin! Wake up! You're dead now! Go into the light, not the darkness! See through yourself and realize Buddha!" He was shouting in case the dead Martin couldn't hear![57] The Lama says people have magical spaces around them, a *white light* or light body to get through the bardos.

Audience: You worked with my father near the end when he was in and out of coma. At one point, when he was lucid, you said, "What would you do out in the world?" and he said that he would come to Oregon and study process oriented psychology and work with you and then he went back into the coma.

Arny: Right! What is he saying that for? What is going on?

Audience: You did not even know him!

Arny: Space–time dreaming seems like a process, not just a point on the process like life or death. Perhaps we all move from one space to a next space, from life to death to life.

THE FOUR HALVES OF LIFE

I want to suggest that life actually has four halves of life. I am not using quarters, but *halves* because normally there are only two halves to life and perhaps two halves of death. Now we all know that four halves add up to two lives. But I know that all of these four phases happen all the time. They are all present, perhaps always. Perhaps they are overlapping qubits or phases that are simultaneously present. In any case, you can see them when you are working with people near death but also in everyday life: four bardos of the life and death cycle, as dreambody phases, from birth to death and back.

In terms of everyday time in the everyday sense, life has various phases. In the first half of life you play; dreaming while awake, so to speak. And you need to do more in consensus reality because during this time everybody says, "Grow up and act like everybody else! Get a job!" or something like that. "Don't dream so much!" That is the first phase.

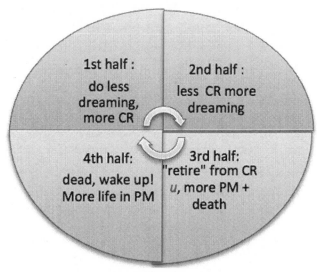

8.2 Four Halves of Life.

Jung called the second phase the second half of life. Around the age of 35 or 40, he felt some people began to need to relax their consensus reality viewpoint and dream more. It is a time to find your spiritual center, to connect to something deeper in yourself. Not everybody goes through this phase, but a lot of people do. Of course, some people stay in that first phase right to the end. But a lot of people go through a second phase in life, at some point, where they need to dream more and not be so realistic.

Now I add a third phase of life, where people begin to fear death (though some people experience this fear much earlier). "Oh, my god! I have something that is going to kill me! What happens if I die?" or "I will have an automobile accident!" This third phase comes at any age, but more so as you get older, and your body starts to deteriorate and with that deterioration comes the fear of death. That fear of death implies a necessity to integrate your deepest self into life. Whereas in the second phase you must dream more, here you must find your process-mind, you must get in touch with the Tao that can't be said, the Japanese *Ma,* or in-between space, and so forth. Your identity, of course, remains an aspect of yourself, but you also need to center your awareness nearer your deepest self. Some may experience this phase earlier, others only in the last moments of life. But the distinguishing feature is aging and near-death fears.

I speak of four halves, but they do not always follow one another in a linear development. Remember our discussion of the dreams of death in chapter 6. Dreams in which you actually die, in my experience, rarely mean you are going to die (although you may turn out to be the one person for whom that is not true!). Dreams of death rarely have anything to do with the actual length of your life. They have to do with the fact that you, as a *doing* person, need to relax totally. That is different from just integrating dreams. It is a more radical change. Your identity changes and gets closer to the processmind.

In the fourth half of life, which can happen just near death—the Tibetans say this happens just before you come alive again—you become altered, near death or *dead,* or comatose; like the man I worked with whom I described earlier in this chapter. In *Coma* I tell how he dreamed, just before he died, that there were some big footsteps before him in the snow, showing him the way. What were those steps?? This is his processmind wisdom, his organizing wisdom that actually knows how to go. This processmind is in front of your everyday mind. And once you are in that deep wisdom, you think, "Is that death?" while in that near-coma or near-death state and rebirth fantasies sometimes happen. This is when you start planning to do your next work.

From the point of view of your processmind, all four of these phases are overlapping in you, as are all potential experiences at any given moment. Although, from the viewpoint of everyday reality, we are closer to or further from these phases depending upon our age and situation. In this view, we are not just time-bound or space-bound creatures; we are also an evolving point in space–time dreaming, part of a universal cosmic fabric and not just a physical body measured in terms of pounds or kilograms.

In everyday life, we all wonder now and then about why we are here and if there are plans for the next 1,000 years. In these third and fourth phases, tomorrow's shopping is important; but more important is what you will be doing in 1,000 years. If you were connected with some large project, some really big project, and you had a 1,000 years to do it, what would it be? Some of you already know, I can see by the funny grins on your faces. And you need to know that because that helps at any time in your life. It is something that centers you.

In any case, your passage through these four phases is organized by your space–time dreaming process, by bardos. Have any of you been in the fourth phase of life, where you are really out there, near death, and yet where there is something itching you to get you going again? Look! Quite a number of you. Wow. It is in you! Something like that is in you. Jung was far out in the fourth half of life in his near-death experience, and something told him, WAKE UP and get back to life!

Buddha was a process person. He said, in essence, that identifying only as a fixed consensus reality state or object creates suffering. You can ask a child under the age of 4 why he or she is here. Young children still remember their processmind. But then around the ages of 6 or 7 or 8 they no longer know their dreaming as well, though it may be still very strong in them. Consensus reality becomes all-consuming. Later, they need to remember space–time dreaming and, in the third half of life, go even deeper. Then, near death, they need to remember and wake up about life! Remember, space–time curving is real!

BARDOS AND THE LIGHT BODY

The Tibetans Buddhists aim at developing their deepest self, which they call the rainbow body or the essence of the dreambody, to move through the space–time phases of the bardos such as the hungry ghost. Everybody has hungry ghosts, and hungry ghosts are very hungry. Jung would have called hungry ghosts complexes. A hungry ghost is the thing you are afraid of the most, the thing that screws you up all the time and gets you all mixed up and upset. And everyone has a few of them. Complexes: we could just as well call them wild phases of space–time.

In Western religions, the hungry ghosts are the big X and you hear about them on the daily news. They are seen in religions as the devil or the seven deadly sins: greed, lust, envy, ambition, and so on. Greed and ambition are connected: I want MORE! Envy: you have got it and I don't, let me have it! Lust: yum! What is lust? Ahahaha! Isn't that right? Something like that. Sloth: you lazy bum! Very important. Gluttony: you pig! What are you doing grabbing it all for yourself. All the rich people, let's get them! Jealousy: I want what you have! All of these are common characteristics.

Western religions deal with these problems in part by teaching people to repress them, by suggesting that we drop them, forgive ourselves, ask another for forgiveness, or deny their power in us. Bow down before the great creators. We are all just human. If someone takes off her or his pants in Washington, that becomes a national catastrophe. Why? A mainstream role says, Keep your pants on in consensus reality and control your lust! Each religion has its own way of dealing with such matters. So does psychology: Analyze it, figure it out, it is because of your mother, because of your father, it is your abuse issue, or your addictions; cut it out, work on it, do this and that. All these things may be very helpful.

But from the process viewpoint, hungry ghosts are fictitious forces. Just as gravity is a force due to curvature of the universe, so too the things that bother us are part of our universe's curves or nature. If you go deep enough, you can use your deepest self to use those forces as steps in the dance. They are not only evil things. I wanted to say that. Hungry ghosts, in fact, can be important. They are important phases and energies that we need, and as energies they are part of our dance. They may even be the most dynamic energy you have! If you don't realize that energy as part of your space-time dreaming, as part of the dance of the ancient one, then the energy looks means or greedy or whatever. But in the dance, it may be just a very dynamic phase!

All so-called problems may be fictitious in the sense that the basic energy in them may be an aspect of your most elemental dance. Problems may be submerged gifts.

Audience: In so many of the Buddhist practices they feed the hungry ghosts.

Arny: Feeding the hungry ghost, yes. The concept of hungry ghost, complex, critic, problem, you are screwed up, this is wrong, you have got a disease of this sort or that sort... All of these, from the deepest viewpoint, are just energies that are part of your dance. They are not necessarily pathological problems. They may be repressed singers and dancers in you who want to move, yell, and sing. Perhaps those hungry ghosts are just intense places in space–time. Live them!

ENLIGHTENMENT

Knowing your processmind body's experience is a kind of enlightenment. The Tibetans call that experience, the *light body*, and the Taoists and others call it the *diamond body*. Some people speak of an *astral body*.

Why would anybody call this the astral body? Because of the sense of the stars and spaces that move people! There is something, when you are in space, that makes you feel as if you are moved by the universe. The point is to use your processmind light body to flow with these big, bad X energies; which I am now calling hungry ghosts.

Some people become very excited or agitated near death. That agitation may lead to people near death appearing as trying to get up to leave the hospital; some ask to be taken to the emergency room, even though they are in hospice: "Take me to the emergency ward!" Others want to go for a walk as a way to leave the hospice. The light body is trying to move. At the end of his life, cofounder of the Apple company, Steve Jobs said, "WOW! OH WOW!" What was he seeing? Doesn't sound exactly like the end.

Audience: Thank you for that. It was really inspiring.

Arny: What part was inspiring?

Audience: The idea of the hungry ghosts, and that they are around all the time.

Arny: All the time! I never saw a person without a hungry ghost. A person without a hungry ghost is unreal!

Audience: And that we can play with them, or work with them, and that there is the astral body present now also. Are you saying that in the bardos, and possibly after the body dies, that this process with the monsters is still happening?

Arny: Yes, I do think so. It makes sense to me.

I like the Tibetans' attitude: Speak with ourselves and with people who have died, and say

> *Hey, buddy, wake up! You are dead meat now. It is ok. We buried you about a month ago, and some of us love you, and some did not like you that much, but for god's sake, wake up! Help us do the thing that you did not quite do in your everyday life! Remember your deepest self, and we would be happy if you were to help with this and that. Now find your one-thousand year task and get on with it. Wake up, wake up a little bit!*

Or depending on the person, say, "Fall asleep, you need more sleep!"

Exercise: "Enlightened" Mystic's Bardo Dance

1. What is one of your hungriest ghosts (complexes)? What is its bardo (space–time dreaming) atmosphere like? Imagine the worst energy, X, in that state. Make X's motion and then sketch its energy. What *u* is most upset by this? Feel and sketch *u*'s energy.

2. Go to your favorite earth spot and see the X + *u* energies there.

    Let the earth power there (light body, Tao *Te*, processmind) breathe and dance you. Let your body be free and let it move between the X + *u* states. Stay in this space–time dance until you know X's nature and purpose. If you need to, let your dance go deeper by relaxing and letting space-time itself move you about and above the earth. Then look back and consider the meaning of that X phase.

3. Can you avoid hungry ghost X in the future? Or can you use your dreaming body to make painful bardos better in the future? Who are you?

    The earth has its own wisdom. Your favorite place on earth will give you a kind of atmosphere and will teach you how to breathe and move. Let it breathe you and move you. Your light body appears as a kind of free dance movement when you let the universe dance you. That dance may be something very special, very characteristic of you. I want you to know that dance and move it a little bit as freely as you can. Let that dance move you.

    What I mean by "Let your body be free" is that, at first, you will be moving a little bit this way and that way. I mean, be really free. Let go of everything. Let space-time dance you. It is hard to do at first, and you may be shy, but just try it. It may be new for some people. Be free!

Afterwards

Now I want to ask some of you, if you dare say, and I hope you will; who are you?

Audience 1: I am where the water meets the land.

Audience 2: I am a very happy person!

Audience 3: I found out that when I feel like I am turning into a nervous wreck, I can use that. I am getting old and I have lost my balance or my equilibrium. I need to trust that, to trust the unpredictableness. And my mind hates the unpredictable but the unpredictable is actually a lot of fun.

Audience 4: I am the change. Seasons come and seasons go.

Audience 5: I am the flow of unfolding.

....

Σ   FOR REFLECTION ON CHAPTER 8

- Bardos are the dream-like feelings spaces in between points in consensus reality.

- The best-known bardo occurs between liminal thresholds of death and rebirth, it is the *space* between death and life.

- Hungry ghosts are, in a way, simply invitations to intense energy dances.

- There may be four phases of life with which we usually identify over time, but they are also timeless.

PART THREE

Symptoms, Madness, or World Dance?

CHAPTER 9

Your Body Spirit in the Bottle

The stochastic space–time dreaming dance can be helpful to everyone psychologically and perhaps physically as well. This space-time dreaming may be good medicine for symptom experiences, especially symptoms due to feeling driven and fatigued from pushing without connecting to the deeper (bottled-up) spirit within.

In previous work, I have suggested that medicine and psychology can be seen as one discipline together in a more holistic *rainbow medicine*.[58] This approach to body problems uses medical suggestions from the consensus reality of the culture in which you are living as well as *suggestions* from your dreaming process. I speak of the consensus reality of the culture in which you are living because some cultures don't use Western medicine in the sense that most of the world is using medicine: some cultures use herbs they find in the woods. When Amy and I were *healed* years ago in Africa, the witch doctors gave us herbal medicines from the African bush. That was still an allopathic approach, and these medicines help many.

Rainbow medicine is also connected to your own individual body feelings, dreamlike feelings, fears, and excitements that you have about your body. When you see doctors, I suggest that when they take your medical history (as they are trained to do here in the West), speak not only of your medical history—that is, the medicines, vitamins, herbs, and supplements you are taking—but also speak about your diet, your addictive tendencies, and your dreams about your health.

And don't forget to mention the geography in which you live. As you know, particular areas have allergies in the atmosphere and radiation: all sorts of things like that to take into consideration. Also, note the social issues you don't want to talk about. What social issues are on your mind that make you feel unwell? And how are your relationships? Are you happy with your relationships? All these topics are medical issues, that is, rainbow medical issues.

Are you conscious of any life goals? Consciousness of goals can sometimes be important. Ask yourself, why are you here? Is there something that you still need to do? For example, one of Amy's uncles seems to be in the last stages of life. Recently he had a lucid day, so I asked him a question: "Is there something you would like to do with your life?" He said very clearly, "I have done everything that I want." He has done a lot of things for people, for the whole world. The following day or two he went back into the hospital expecting to die. I called him again in the hospital and he changed his answer. "Yes, there is something I want to do," and he proceeded to gladly tell us. Shortly thereafter, to everyone's surprise, he got better and got out of the hospital (and then died about a month later). My point is that knowing your life goal can be an important medicine.

And, finally, ask yourself how your symptom experiences are signals that you can use in relationships. Other questions you might ask yourself are, how are your symptom experiences also stories connected with your birth, or feelings of identification with relatives who have been ill at the same age as you are now. Remember to ask about a childhood dream. You know from my *Dreambody* and other books that the childhood dream sometimes predicts the kind of body symptoms that will bother you later on. It may also be helpful to ask what kinds of things depress you or inspire you.

From the viewpoint of rainbow medicine, *symptoms* are callings: dreams that are not fully acknowledged. Sometimes a symptom is the call of your timeless spirit trying to catch your attention, trying to inform you about who you really are! In the diagram, you can see how a symptom appears in consensus reality. But at the same time, below everyday reality, the symptom is a relationship conflict between two parts or two energies in you, which I have been calling the u and the X. These energies sometimes appear in dreams, so the u energy (the you that is disturbed by X) and the disturbing X (the energy upsetting you) are just outside your normal awareness and are in dreamland.

In dreamland these u + X energies appear as dream figures. That is why I have said that symptoms belong to the dreambody; that is, the body experience reflected in our dreams. The symptom is an expression of a relationship problem inside of us. Essentially, it is saying, "Let's work on the relationship between several parts." Every time you think of your symptom, if you try to use the X, the disturbing energy, you might feel better… at least temporarily.

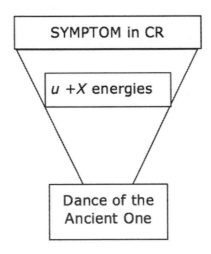

9.1 Ancient One's Dance.

For example, last night I went to bed and inside my ear I heard a little clicking sound for a couple of minutes, and then it went away for some reason. I thought, "Maybe I am developing tinnitus, sounds in my ear." Then I thought, perhaps some dirt got into my ear, and I got up. A little cleaning did a lot of good. That was a good consensus reality solution.

But, at a deeper level, who is disturbed by that "noisy ear"? My u, Arny Mindell, says, "I have to go to bed, I have to get some sleep, I have things to do." I had a relationship issue, can you see that? Inside is lots of excitement: X, clicking and banging on one side and the other side, u, says "Shut up and go to bed!"

I sensed that I was repressing my excitement! When I realized it's ok to be excited about this talk I am now giving, the X + u relationship problem subsided, and then I just went to sleep. I was involved, facilitating, and mediating between the noise maker in my ear and my desire for quiet. If you have a body symptom, care for it in an allopathic manner, if you can. I cleaned my ear. But looking at it only as a symptom in an allopathic manner can sometimes be iatrogenic, which means a hurtful medical attitude. The medical attitude can be hurtful if it represses the symptom's possible connection with your psychology. This medical attitude can irritate that X energy inside of you and create more symptoms. An iatrogenic attitude focuses only on getting rid of the symptom and can marginalize your inner experience. If something in you is repressed, it may pop up in another area of your life. So focus on the entire life process.

GRIMM'S FAIRY TALE: THE SPIRIT IN THE BOTTLE

The Spirit in the Bottle is a fairy tale about this process of living life in a way that represses your dreaming spirit, the spirit of space–time dreaming.[59] This tale, *The Spirit in the Bottle*, is a fairy tale I spoke of thirty years ago in my first book, *Dreambody*.[60] Now I want to expand upon the way I looked at this tale there.

The synopsis of my brief version of this tale goes like this. Once upon a time (which means, then-now-and-always in dreamland) there was a poor woodcutter. He said to his son (today this tale could read "the mother said to her daughter"), "Go out and chop some wood." And the child went into the forest and he took his hatchet to cut down a tree. Suddenly he heard a little voice exclaiming, "Let me out! Let me out!" He looked around and saw a bottle, and in the bottle was a little spirit… "Let me out, let me out!" So he pulled the cork and out came the spirit. And right away the damn spirit said, "I am going to kill you!" How is that for a situation!

And the little boy said (how he knew to do this is beyond me), "If you are such a powerful spirit, prove it and get back into the bottle!" So the spirit went back into the bottle and the boy corked him inside! But that was not the end. The spirit cried out, "Let me out! If you let me out, I will make you rich and famous!"(Which is just about what every poor woodcutter wants.) So the boy pulled out the cork out again, and the spirit gave him a magical cloth that could transform metals and heal people. The boy then took the cloth and went around and healed people, became rich and famous, middle-aged, and bored! Rich and happy, after being poverty stricken! So he went back into the woods one day and tossed his cloth away, saying "Who needs that anymore!" The young man instantly regretted his action and begged for the magic cloth to come back as the spirit returned saying "No!" and putting him in the ground! That's the end of the tale.

The Woodcutter: what does a woodcutter do for a living? Imagine two hundred years ago in Europe, Africa, or Australia... what is the woodcutter's job? He kills trees... why? At the time the woods were totally unexplored, wild, and natural. Why did he want wood? For heat, cooking, buildings, boats. The wood from trees was the source of just about everything in the reality of those times. Several hundred years ago there was no nuclear energy or petroleum, and it was wood that made the house warm in the evening. Wood: So it is an energy problem that we are working on in part. Just go get some energy from nature, and don't think any further about nature's reactions!

9.2 Spirit and Woodcutter (Karynlewis.com).

What is happening when you go to get some energy, when you are not feeling energetic, when you say, "Let me get some energy! Let me chop this down, let's have a second cup of coffee, more vitamins, et cetera." What is happening? You are marginalizing fatigue and the quiet, inward essence of the experience of low energy. You ignore the very basis of who you are, your roots, the essence of your energy. Wanting more energy is fine, but your one-sided repressive attitude bottles up your true nature. Pushing yourself into action bottles up the dreaming.

How can you get to the spirit in the bottle without bottling up the deepest energies in everyday life? Meditation! Focus and follow your body. Drop down, get to your processmind, and feel the power of the space around you. Energy is then no longer yours to have or not have. Rather, it happens. It is a kind of stochastic thing: partly real, partly spiritual. The life of the tree is partly determined by the fertility of the soil and the climate and partly by an unpredictable something. The tree is based in the ground but grows upwards toward the sky. It is a symbol of something growing in you that helps put the worlds together. The tree bridges the space between earth and sky. The spirit of the tree, the spirit in the bottle is your processmind experience.

But don't let me get ahead of myself. Staying close to the roots for the moment, the message to the woodcutter's son is; don't just go after wood, after energy, and repress your inner *tree* and its random, unpredictable growing nature! Don't just push; rather, relate to your nature. Otherwise, you will be endangered by the spirit in the bottle and its contents, such as alcohol and associated addictions, can *kill* you.

The normal person in all of us feels stressed out by pushing and cutting down trees, in essence, to earn a living. She feels uptight and might turn to alcohol or drugs or prescription medications to get the spirit back into life. But if you tap the spirit unconsciously through drinking, for example, then it needs to be *rebottled*. Put the spirit back in the bottle so it does not kill you with dangerous addictions. So, at one point the hero must rebottle the spirit to manage the addiction and create a dry period. NO drinking.

Life is paradoxical. When growing up, when you are in the first bardo, you have to stop dreaming and put the spirit in the bottle. When you were a kid, someone had to say, come to lunch on time! That's the first years of your life. Kids are totally stochastic: they jump around, throw themselves on the ground, throw things in the air, cry, scream, and laugh. They are little stochastic dancers. But at a certain point, they too must learn to put that spirit in a bottle. Control yourself! So there is some meaning to that act of putting the spirit in the bottle, but it is not good to totally forget that spirit.

On the other hand, if you develop a conscious relationship with the spirit of life bottled up in your mind and body, it might help you get in touch with dreaming. In a sense, you then become a healer. The relationship to your wise, dreaming spirit is a huge matter. If you focus only on getting rid of a symptom, you focus on consensus reality and forget the spirit that moves you. That may be why, at the end of our tale after our young healer gets rich and happy, he throws his magical medicine cloth away and the spirit comes back and puts him in the ground and he gets stuck there. He cannot get out! That seems like death, but it could also be that his spirit is forcing our young healer to be near the earth, close to his space–time dreaming. The spirit is saying, "Don't forget, we are all part of the earth! We are a part of all of nature."

If you have ever been *fortunate* enough to be afraid of death (most people have), you can discover a magical aspect of death threats: namely, the relaxation of your everyday mind, the little u. With less little u, your shamanistic potential can arise. If something threatens to kill you, if you are afraid of death, fight it; but then at another point, don't just take care of yourself but remember Patanjali (see figure 9.3), composer of *The Yoga Sutras*, who said the big goal was to be a *dead* person in life.

9.3 Patanjali (Wikipedia).

When I got sick at 31, I thought, "Why can't I walk?" I could not walk for several months. I thought, "I am so young, why am I having these problems? Is this my death?" Looking back now I realize I had to let go of the things I had studied, and I had to study things that were brand new. Looking back, I can say that illness was lucky for me. But if you told me I was lucky at the time, we would have had a fight. You have to be careful telling people they are lucky when death scares them!

If you develop good contact with your processmind, you create a sustainable relationship between your processmind, the u, and the X. Then the symptom is no longer the central problem. The relationship issue between the different X + u energies becomes the main issue. Getting along with the energies that bother you is an aspect of feeling better. This requires getting deeper into yourself, getting to your process-mind or getting to the spirit that moves you. Healing is not just about getting rid of the X just because your more primary process, u, does not like the secondary, marginalized, and divorced process, X.

Connecting to your deepest self is therefore beyond healing in the normal sense because healing is not sustainable: One day you will have to die. Real *healing* involves creating a better, more sustainable relationship with the spirit of life. If you have a better relationship with your body, some of your symptoms won't bother you as much and may even get better. And yet, even that is not the point. The following exercise will help you get in touch with the different parts of yourself so that you can dance with them.

....

EXERCISE: SHAMANISM WITH DEATH THREATS

One of the goals of this exercise is to find the spirit in the bottle, the processmind's space-time dreaming dance's hidden relationship process that is behind symptoms.

1. Choose and feel your strongest, real or imaginary, bottled-up or most troubling possible death-like body energy, X. Act out this X energy and make a quick sketch to remind yourself of its nature.

2. Who in you (that is, what u) is most upset by this X? Act this out and sketch this u's energy. What addictive foods or drug tendencies counteract the X or support the u?

3. Remember and go to your favorite spot on earth. If you have many favorites, choose one. Then notice if the X + u energies are somewhere there. Let the earth spot breathe and dance you, and as you move, let the earth spot breathe you between X + u.

4. Now, relax and pretend you are moved freely by the universe's space around and above this earth spot. You can do this while sitting, but it is probably easier to feel it if you stand. Let yourself wiggle and move around and be moved. When you are ready, bring this spontaneous and unpredictable *dance* back to your earth dance movements until some insight occurs. This means, let your stochastic nature organize your thinking about your body. Let yourself be moved by the moment, moved by the universe, and do the dance of the ancient one. Make notes about any insights you might have had.

If you want to help someone else do this exercise, do the exercise first yourself, then dance with the person and try to read into the nature of her or his u + X energies, and tell those two energies how to live together. Shamanize and take notes.

In all your work, try to remember that your favorite earth spot is on earth but also in space or space-time. Space–time dreaming follows the curvature of the universe. An easy way to do this is to simply stand up and wander around aimlessly. Then sense the advice this wandering dance gives you about the polarities with which you are working. We stand solidly on this planet, earth, with our feet here; and, at the same time, this spot is part of the whole universe, the essence behind all polarities. Explore the essence of this spot, play with it. It may be good for your health, and it can help you relax a little bit. It's important to realize that our polarities on earth need a home, a perspective, a universe dance, to resolve their issues.

WHAT DID YOU DISCOVER?

Audience: I have been depressed because of a bad back that feels like it is pushing me down. When I danced, I noticed that something in me spontaneously told this depressing X energy "You are ok!" and it told the u energy, which is afraid it can't lift anything, that it too is ok! Both the one attempting to lift, the u, and the one pushing things down, the X, are foolish when they think they are not ok and forget they are part of the universe!

I needed to connect to the universe dance to know that while u + X are ok, neither of them are the main point! I realized, "Let the universe do things, lift things, or not lift things. The dance will know when and how to live properly." And when I realized that, I unconsciously bent down and lifted up my chair!

Σ   FOR REFLECTION ON CHAPTER 9

- The spirit in the body gets bottled up by pushing and doing and neglecting the experience of being moved.

- Space–time dreaming resolves tensions around symptoms. It *heals* by creating a dancing relationship between diverse energies.

CHAPTER 10

Abuse, Shock, and Space–Time

Today, I want to work with symptoms that bother us. They don't bother us simply because there are energies in the symptom that we need to dance with, rather, the symptoms bother us, in part, because those energies remind us of possible abuse situations in our background. Remember that, in general, if the spirit gets bottled up by doing, then it gets unhappy and starts screaming. When you do too much and keep your space–time dreaming, your processmind, bottled up, after a while it begins to complain.

To warm up, try this meditation (you can sit, lie down, or stand where you are). If you want to, and if it is right for you, let your jaw muscles relax for a moment. Let your neck muscles relax a little bit. See if your neck will allow itself to relax a little more. And though you are sitting in a chair with your back muscles against the chair, movement can also mean stillness. In any case, relax so you can find the movement or stillness in you that is trying to emerge; that means follow your body in the little or big ways it wants to move, or not move, just for a minute. Try that, keep doing that until some sort of intuition about something pops up and you just catch it. Relaxing... moving... being still... dreaming while awake. Use your lucidity to catch anything that pops up. You might get a hint or some advice perhaps. Remain lucid and catch a piece of advice. See if you can formulate it in one sentence that you can remember: a piece of advice, one sentence. Write that down and share that one sentence with someone.

Let's now think about shock and abuse. By shock and abuse I mean imagining or actually remembering being unfairly treated or feeling that you were unfairly treated by a human being or by a natural event. This could be a psychological injury, a physical hurt, or pain due to an outer event like a tsunami. Behind such feelings and symptoms is a sense of being unfairly treated. This is your personal sense, and it may or may not be objective. People who injure others are often unconscious of the psychological or physical power that is their rank. But also, those who have been hurt by others are usually not aware of that rank imbalance and so are not able to sufficiently protect themselves. In any case, some symptoms themselves can remind us of unfairness and of being hurt by things we can't defend ourselves against. Such symptoms force you to feel and or say, "Help me, something feels unfair," or to lament, "I just can't manage it."

To work with such symptoms, to begin with, it can be crucial to defend yourself against them, to fight the abuse situations, and to fight the symptoms. For example, the first step in a process may be to fight near-death experiences, and say, "GET OUT!" But medical attitudes in near-death situations can be iatrogenic simply by siding with statistics around illness. Statistically speaking, if an illness is likely to kill you, then even if you are potentially able to live a long time, you might start giving up because of the rank and power and persuasiveness of medical statistics that seem to be against you, so to speak. This is a huge issue that I went through when I talked to V's mother, who is not as well as she could be. Sometimes a person is really ill and seems to be going downhill and he or she thinks, "Well, maybe the time is coming," because everybody knows the time has to come one of these days. Yet even though all the indications may be that the time is up, there may be a power underneath that refuses and wants to arise.

V: Arny worked on the phone with my mother and me. He listened to her breathing and asked her what, if she could, she would like to do. She said she would go back to work. So he listened to her interests and told my mom, "It is not time, your process says that for now, you have to do something. Work. Go back to work!" So the next day she felt fantastic, and she said, "It was so fun!" She started taking care of things she hadn't paid attention to for so long; she was hypnotized before that she was just going to die.

Yes, fighting a symptom that may be exaggerated by standard medical reasoning may be a first step in a process. But then, sometimes we fight symptoms so much that we refuse to even feel them or think about them. As I said before, this can happen because they make us fear some abuse scene.

Our individual biology and collective group life also tend to marginalize or forget shocking events and try to stop us from thinking about them. Part of everyone wants to avoid pain and avoid war zones, as if it is always too early to think about painful things. Let's have a good time and not think about that much and get away from all that. There is a positive side to not thinking about pain and getting away from all of that. It's an unconscious form of detachment.

Yet, such repressive tactics can also make X or hurtful energy become stronger and reappear in symptoms. So processing the X factor, the most disturbing energy in chronic symptoms, may also be related to processing that X energy from past abuse issues. It is hard to do sometimes because the addictive tendencies we developed to repress thinking about troublesome things may stop you from processing an X energy. Around abuse issues, addictions turn up usually to make you feel better. Everybody has some form of addictive tendencies: sweets or spices can be addictive as well as the well-known alcohol, drugs, coffee, sugar, and what have you.

One of the great disadvantages to ignoring abuse issues is that ignoring them might blind you to the fact that you might become abusive to yourself. Sometimes you may not realize that inadvertently you might hurt yourself as you were hurt. It was so difficult on the outside, that you may only see abuse as something that takes place on the outside: *It* happened out there, and you may not notice it when you start to do uncomfortable X-like things to yourself. If people were negative toward you, you may turn unconsciously negative toward yourself. If others did not pay attention to you and did things to you that they shouldn't have done, sometimes you may not pay attention to yourself and do things to yourself that are unnecessary, unhelpful, and unkind.

When you get to the processmind, all the things that you should be avoiding, doing, or fighting become parts of the larger process and *it* handles painful things from another level altogether. Consider that the things that bother you are yours but also possibly not yours! The powers we are working with are often social issues and collective problems. Energies that bother you can be found in just about everyone, to a greater or lesser extent. The disturbing energies are responses to or sometimes connected with abuses that have happened and also a lot of panic and depression and paranoia.

In the work we are going to be doing here, we will think about a symptom that might somehow be connected with some kind of abuse issue. Could this particular symptom be connected with some difficulty from the past? I want to say that the essence of the symptom is nonlocal.

Denying and forgetting abuse issues is normal. It is an attempt to gain distance from the problems. By denying things, something in you may be seeking a detached state of mind, a quiet third position between two polarities. You have the X energy, a difficult energy that may or may not have been connected to an abuse issue, but the story is no longer the important thing. It is the energy itself that I want to talk about. And then there is a *u* who was hurt. You need a third position: the processmind, the dance of the ancient one's altered state. Gaining access to that processmind altered state of consciousness can be helpful not just to the body but may help with an abuse issue without processing it directly, without hearing the specific story content of the abuse issue. Instead, you can deal with the underlying essence energies.

People used to, and still do, go to their village shaman to get this detachment for them. The shaman goes into an altered state and comes out with something that will help the suffering person so that the person does not have to do anything. I have met great shamans in Africa and asked them how they deal with relationship issues. I have to repeat this story, even if you have heard me say this before.

Imagine that a couple has a really bad problem. The shaman or witch doctor told us that he might say, "Go home and forget it!" I asked, "Does that work?" The shaman explained that it works because the couple goes home and relaxes. Then the shaman does the shamanizing! When the couple comes back, they say, "It worked!" That is the best medicine yet! I love the shaman's attitude. Going into another space-time dreaming to solve problems is very important. Shamanism and nonlocality, both help us get some distance from the things so that we can work with problems from a larger, broader perspective that includes more parts of the whole.

As I said in my book, *ProcessMind*, the processmind or the intelligence behind the ancient dancer is omniscient (that means all-knowing) and it is omnipresent, it is everywhere. You cannot be alone in this universe. And the processmind, like god images, is, in principle, all powerful. Your processmind has some kind of interconnecting power.

By *power* I mean a field sense of something moving you, anywhere you are, in any circumstance.

"Turn on, tune in and drop out." The hippies of the 1960s tried to find this detached position by tuning in and dropping out with drugs. Timothy Leary, the US guru of those times, advised everyone to turn on and space out.[61] *Tune in* means to get into an altered state. *Drop out* means to detach from the values and norms of a culture. In a speech in 1966 Leary urged people to embrace cultural change through the use of drugs and psychedelics. He said that by detaching themselves from the conventions and hierarchies in society, they could drop out, that is, get deep into themselves.

I'd like to update Leary's suggestions, if I may:

> *Turn on, find your processmind, tune into it, and drop out of the social situation of the moment, and then drop back into everyday life with what you bring back from space–time dreaming.*

In 1966 there was a *be-in*, a gathering of 30,000 hippies in Golden Gate Park in San Francisco. The hippies symbolized that intense drive inside of us to drop out of everyday consensus reality to find another level and to check the kinds of customs that we are supporting (Are they the right ones or not?) and to recreate the world. The hippies were powerful in the random elements of the stochastic mind but not in the deterministic part. Be careful of drugs. Use your inner work to drop out and then come back with the new information.

This particular symptom exercise does not ask you to tell any details about what happened to you but just to imagine the nasty X and hurt *u* energies in there. Symptoms can be a great way to work, especially on post traumatic stress that is the severe anxiety that sometimes follows a traumatic situation. For example, when working with people who have been in war, I found that although they could not think about what happened on the battlefield, they could tell me about a stomachache. Through working on that X, that is the stomach pain, we were able to not just help the stomach but could reduce their anxiety about the outer events that reminded them of war.

As an example of such work, let me tell you about how Amy and I worked on the following exercise last night. Now Amy and I have been living together for almost 30 years, which is something. Living with yourself for 25 years is already a success story!

Amy: I worked on a symptom related to skin problems. For me, they were connected to the abusive experience of constantly being told how I looked was really wrong. I worked on this critical X energy that was coming from a certain figure in my past who said, "How bad you look!" And there was a *u* energy that was more floating, wanting to be loved and soothed. And then we went to one of my favorite spots on the earth, the ocean. There the X was represented by the crashing waves on the rocks, and the gentle breeze was the other energy.

When I got into it, I realized the crashing waves were like these skin problems, cracking and breaking out as the X energy. I got into that energy, and it was like breaking out and breaking free of all social things! That surprised me. I needed the X energy to fight it! In any case, I went further and felt the universe moving me. I had a sense of freedom wanting to go for the dreaming, breaking out of all social norms, and really going for the dreaming. I was ecstatic.

Arny: Some part of you, Amy, I had not seen before was how your skin cracks were not just a bad X energy but gave you the ability to break through reality so other states could happen. Behind the symptom was also the power to stop what had happened and to free yourself from the whole social issue in the background.

The X energy of the symptom, cracking, is breaking out. Amy thought that symptom might be tied up with this social issue that you should look like this kind of person rather than how you actually look. This cracking got cracked open to all kinds of new experiences. Things came out of her that in 30 years I had not seen!

Amy: Yeah! I could dance like the ancient one!

Arny: In the following exercise, which is best done in dyads, remember that while one person working on her symptom is in an altered state, the person in the role of helper should gently encourage her or him to imagine how to use the energies and insights in everyday life and in the world. After all, perhaps some of your abuse energies and stories may have a purpose, perhaps implying some tasks you might do in the world.

EXERCISE

Helper read the following to your dyad partner, the client:

1. Imagine your worst symptom, one that is possibly related to an abuse or shock scene. What is the worst energy, X, of your symptom? How is it possibly linked, in some way, to shock or abuse? Feel that X energy, act it out, and sketch X's energy.

2. Who in you, u, is most upset by this? Act out this u and sketch the u's energy.

3. Go to your favorite earth spot and notice u + X somewhere there. DROP OUT and let the earth spot breathe and dance you between the u + X locations. Loosen up even more and move towards the sky above and let the universe move you unpredictably. TUNE IN: note its SENSE OF SPACE and movement! When you are freely dancing, bring this dance back to the X + u energies on earth. Note insights.

4. Helper and client: Both use your space dances to shamanize, that is, to *read into* the nature and meaning of X, and then DROP BACK IN by advising the u about the symptom and u's role in the world.

5. Finally, ask how your experiences might have been helpful in some way with a past abuse scene?

In watching people work on body problems that are linked to historical issues, I realized that often good, noncognitive experience comes from the dance of the ancient one, and that is the point; dreaming while awake. I saw a lot of such amazing moments, having far-out experiences, even *mu-shin*: empty mind, creative mind. These creative, open mind experiences led to new ideas about helping the world.

IATROGENIC MIND SETS

Dancing is very different from normal psychology and medicine, which both focus on figuring out the parts—a fine approach but not always enough. Sometimes you need to get away from all the parts and just dance like a shaman!

Σ   FOR REFLECTION ON CHAPTER 10

- Symptoms can remind us of or can be caused by abuse and shock issues from the past.

- Working on symptoms may inadvertently also work on the abuse or shock issue without having to go into the details.

- Drop out, tune into space, and drop back into reality again to change it.

CHAPTER 11

Who Are You from a 10,000 Year Perspective?

People with power often don't realize it. It is easier to identify with low than with high rank. It is easier to think you could be a victim of a situation rather than the one who could *do* the situation.

I remember a person I worked with years ago, one of my early clients, who, during the Second World War, had done some terrible things to people. His government gave him a job of torturing people. At that time, he identified with having a great deal of social and political power. But when I worked with him, his biggest problem and only sense was that he was powerless. He was shy about making friends with his mother who seemed a little distant to him. Now he wanted to take care of her in her old age and was shy about doing so. My whole work with him focused on giving him enough strength to be able to work with her on their relationship. And once he did that, he could see that he had a lot of power and that he could do lots of good things. With more of a sense of strength, we even looked back into history and could think about some of the dreadful scenes he was involved in.

Working with that man woke me up to the idea that we sometimes assume that certain people know that they have lots of power, but they actually may not. I think that is the most human way to say it: They may not realize they have power. That is not always true, of course, but it is something to keep in your back pocket.

Before I go further, I want to remind you of this deep part of your-self with which we have been experimenting in a very simple way. You can do this brief exercise sitting or standing. Let's just do this for a minute before I talk more about today's things...

- Sit or stand comfortably and just notice unpredictable movements that happen to you, including stillness. Stillness is also a movement in the sense of being a little, tiny movement.

- See what unpredictable movements, if any, your body makes. Let it be moved by the space around you. Let it be moved around, and when you finally get to a relaxed place where you are being moved, maybe those movements will have a message for you.

- Get relaxed, then watch what your movements do. Let them move you.

- Notice what those relaxed, unpredictable movements, those little jitters, want to do; and let them give you a message and make a note about it.

It is an easy exercise to do. You may wonder, since it is easy to do, why people don't do it more often. It is such a simple meditation: You let space–time move you and give you a tip, catch the tip, and write it down. Why don't you see people doing that while standing waiting for the movies? Because they are located in their deterministic consensus reality mind: "I am this and that is who I am." They are not open to the random act of divination or dreaming coming through. There is time to have and time to lose your head and let the mind go.

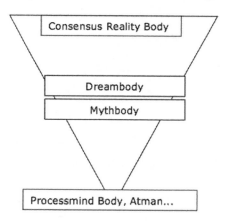

11.1 Least Action.

WHO ARE YOU FROM A 10,000 YEAR PERSPECTIVE?

The point of today's class is to find out the nature of that process-mind body experience. In other words, from the universe's perspective, Who are you? But first, take a look at the point at the bottom of the diagram (Figure 11.1). At the top is the *real* body; that is the body that everyone talks about and brings to the doctor. In the middle section of the triangle is the dreambody, followed by the mythbody. At the very base of the triangle in the essence area is the processmind body experience, Atman, Brahman, and dot-dot-dot; which means that there are a whole lot of other names for that concept. I titled the figure Least Action. I will explain each term, bit by bit.

Who are you, looked at from a 10,000 year perspective? I want to know more about you. If you had 10,000 years to live in the universe, who might you be? Were you here before? We don't know for sure, and you need not live that long or believe anything. I just want to be free enough to talk about all these possibilities.

Who are you? Who are you beyond the fact that you are presently a body? In *Coma*, I spoke about how the dreambody appears as body signals and dreams and how it can appear as the mythbody: that is, not only as a personal association but as a more collective, more commonly recognized symbol that is generalizing your overall body experience, which is organized by your childhood dream.[62] *Dreamland* is simply the part of reality that is organized by dreams. Symptoms are organized by dreams or their generalization in terms of myths.

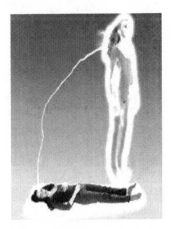

*11.2 When the real body relaxes, your
dream or myth body appears.*

DANCE OF THE ANCIENT ONE

Just before death, again and again, deep experiences appear that correspond to, and seem to be organized by, your childhood dreams. There seems to be a mythic pattern moving us, and that mythic pattern appears in your childhood dream. So, there is a dreambody: that is, the experiences you feel in the moment, and then maybe over long periods of time, and right up to death and beyond whatever death means. Maybe the mythbody goes further. Your earliest childhood dream and earliest childhood memories and experiences are big mythic patterns. And then, at the deepest level, there is the noncognitive and nonvisual experience of the processmind.

I would like to ask Isadora (a 7-year-old girl in class) something.

Arny: What is the first memory that you can recall? Do you re-
          member yourself as a very little girl? What is the first thing
          you remember?

Isadora: I don't remember really anything except for when I was
          little.

Arny: And what was the first thing you remember from being
          real little?

Isadora: That my mom and dad love me.

Arny: Wow! That is a great experience. My reaction to Isadora is,
          "Oh, Master, I have met you again!" Love is the point! In
          any case, that is possibly her earliest pattern. It's personal
          but also mythic and connected to all human beings. That is
          her mom sitting next to her. [To the mom] You lucked out
          with that one. She is your teacher, your love.

The mythbody idea stresses the fact that the earliest memory, the earliest dream, seems to reflect and organize what is happening at your bedside near the end of life as well. I have seen it a number of times. The processmind is the field moving the dreambody, the mythbody, and the real body. It is the space–time dreaming field moving us. That means that you have images of things but before the image there is a feeling or a movement. Things that move you seem to appear prior to images. You can think of an organizing power like the field pattern governing the overall flight of birds or the way water makes ridges in the sand.

Dreamland can be seen in terms of body signals as well. But the processmind is more mysterious and noncognitive. If you start scratching your nose, this scratching may be organized by dreams in dreamland! How is an itch that you scratch dreamland? If it is an allergy or something like that, you can almost always see that X energy organized by a dream pattern, by some kind of scratching or ripping energy. Dream-land is the part of reality you can see organized by dream patterns. Physics is full of real things that are organized by mathematical patterns, just as the real body is organized by the dreambody or myth-body. But dreams themselves are patterned by a field that has no images associated with it initially but that emerges into images and body symptoms and things like that. I know that Jung thought archetypal images were basic to us. I suggest that there are basic energies that appear as images.

Many ancient traditions believed that some of our body experiences are relatively independent of what we call our body. These subtle body experiences were connected with Atman, with Brahman. That is, with parts of you that are like the fabric of the universe.

Who you are may be very ancient like the diamond body, the Tao body, or even Nataraja (a dancing Shiva spirit of the universe who dances around the universe and is behind everything). At the essence level, our bodies are organized not just by our individual psychology but by the whole active, moving, dancing universe.

Space-time dreaming is *least action*. When you are letting things move you spontaneously, you are moving in a way that a physicist might possibly describe as following least action.[63] Least action implies the moment when your movements are very close to your basic, inherent potential energy.[64] A very deep need in us is to move in such a way that we are very close to our basic potential nature, our potential energy. So least action is basic not only to theoretical physics but also to psychology and spiritual traditions. To move from one point in space and time to another, the deepest part of us explores all the possible paths it can take. Then, left to itself, it will dream or take the easiest, quickest possible path; the one requiring least action that goes along with our most basic dreaming.

Prof. Edwin Taylor of MIT explains least action in physics:

> Here are nature's commands to the stone and electron: At the stone moving with nonrelativistic speed in a region of small space–time curvature, nature shouts: Follow the path of least action!... At the electron, nature shouts: Explore all paths to find least action! That's it.[65]

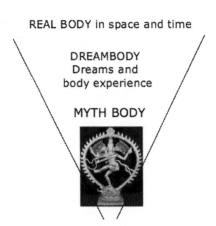

REAL BODY in space and time

DREAMBODY
Dreams and
body experience

MYTH BODY

11.3 Nataraja: Dancing Shiva.

*The processmind as space–time field dancing-moving
experience of the body-dreambody-mythbody found
worldwide in subtle body concepts and least action
= follow all paths = the essence of physics.*

We often try all paths. Standing in front of the mirror in the morning, you ask yourself, "Should I take the path in which I look this way or that way?" Before we make a decision about anything, we often consider "try all paths." Likewise, in dreaming, we dream this and then that as if searching for the path that requires least action and most meaning.

In any case, trying all paths is nature's gift to us. Without realizing it, when you pass your football to me, that football can travel from you to me by circling around me, directly to me, or by way of the moon! After trying all paths, nature chooses finally, the path of least action thereby bringing the normally invisible quantum mechanics and everyday Newtonian life closer together.[66]

Let me explain more simply. If I have a pen in my hand, its potential energy is related to its distance from the floor. Its potential is due to the gravity field (really, the curvature of space) pulling it towards the floor. If I let go of the pen, what is going to happen? Its potential energy will become movement or kinetic energy, and the pen will appear to be moving, falling to the floor. The kinetic motion of dropping towards the floor is due to its potential energy turning into the falling movement. Now nature uses her least action principle to make sure that the movement of this pen, the way it moves, the speed it moves at, how it moves, and where it moves are as close as possible to its basic potential at every point. The potential is pulling on it, basically saying, "Come on down here, buddy! You belong down here!" The non organic object (e.g., the pen) says, "OK, I'll follow the field," and tries all possible paths without your being able to see it. It uses the path of least action on its trip to the floor, getting there most easily and most quickly.

Make certain that what you *do* is close to your basic potential, your space-time dreaming, and you will be like the rest of the universe: at one with the universe. If you ignore your basic potential and begin to push and *do* things normally, you will get exhausted by doing more *action* than necessary.

Nature also loves diversity. She gave us permission to deny her essence-like existence and create a human consensus reality that denies physical and biological and chemical forces and least action. In deep mediation or near death, we often see the person enacting childhood dream or mythic experiences, and those involve his or her basic nature or *least action*. During space–time dreaming, we can sometimes experience ourselves as space–time itself, as the mover (so to speak), not just the moved body or the resistant everyday personality.

This processmind field experience is the experience of being moved by space–time physics, that is, of least action. Other ways of speaking of least action are "try all paths" or "follow paths that make time fly."[67]

Who are you? The deepest part of you follows least action; your potential energy, it follows the space–time dreaming around you. From the viewpoint of consensus reality, you are your normal little self, your little *u*, a couple of X energies disturbing you, and you are the dance between them. Polarities are supposed facts in consensus reality. But remember what the processmind and Buddhism tell us: Nothing is fixed. We are a dance between these apparently fixed things. You are a dance looking like a person. You are moving back and forth between these various energies though you identify as a person. If you identify too much as a person, "I am the person who has to do this or that today," then the dreams try to get you to be more flexible and follow all your energies. We are a process, but our everyday mind denies that. It denies that we are a dance.

One of the reasons we are afraid of death is because we have become identified with the rigid little *u* and its X opponents of consensus reality. As I have been saying, apparently it is not you but the little *u* that dies. Your little *u* is located in consensus reality, but your consensus reality idea of yourself needs to get rattled now and then so that you can find these other parts of yourself. One of the luckiest things that can happen to us, as I said before, is to fear death. It is an opportunity to let go of rigidity. A great many death fears are about this particular psychological point.

Audience 1: Missing people who die is a big part of the death experience.

Arny: Yes, that is a big part of it. If you die, it is not easy for those who love you. But relationship is also a space, a space–time dreaming, the space between us. And this space does not necessarily *die*. Find someone who has *died* as a place on the earth, and go to that spot when you miss her or him, or feel her in space.

Audience 2: Let's say you have a death fear: that means the little *u* needs to die?

Arny: Perhaps it needs to relax a little bit and open up to being moved by the path of *least action*.

Audience 2: And then fluidity is restored temporarily. But if the little *u* dies, what is there to be fluid with?

Arny: In principle, only your identification with *u*'s action dies and yet your processmind awareness continues. The same thing happens in dreaming. That is why, though you are *sleeping*, you can create and remember dreams!

THE METAPOSITION

Your little *u* is the one you usually use for awareness, but it is not your only awareness. As the little *u* dwindles, your processmind emerges with its bigger picture and more relaxed view. I used to call the processmind's view the *metacommunicator*: something that is still there that has this genius overview of things and seems to create dreams. When the little *u* stops controlling your awareness, that awareness goes back to processmind. The little *u* has parts, people, and things in mind. Processmind says that mindset with all those things are consensus reality's one-sided illusions. There is another viewpoint that comes from connecting to our universe's four or many dimensional hyperspace, entering an altered state, or experiencing space–time dreaming.

We are on the edge of talking about impossible material, so I want to thank you for your tolerance of all of this. If your little *u* relaxes temporarily, then its viewpoints about *u* + X die with it, at least temporarily. The tension between them disappears as you begin to dance. You are no longer a rigid part with one part over here and the other over there. You are more the dance. You are a fluid process.

In a way, the only problem you can have is having too rigid an identity, and you know it when you start feeling very tense and nervous about something. Then you might remember: Maybe I could try and move between the energies that I am nervous about. Rigidity is good, but it is not the whole story.

Don Juan said, stop the world or fear that it stops when you die. Either you stop the world now, or you fear something else will stop your world as a death fantasy. Stop the world means remember to follow your body energy. What does your body want to do? Your body's proprioception and movement are the passwords to your big computer. Write *body* every time you work on yourself. It is the password to your big computer, the one inside and all around your head. Stop the world and use *death* as your advisor. Don Juan meant that death is there to tell you that your everyday mind is not the whole story. Stop the world of the everyday mind.

Who are you? Is this your first time around on this earth? Are you finished when you are done here? Each person has her or his own thoughts about that. I never wanted to think about it much but then I had dreams that I should think about it more. Once, while walking in Delhi, India, I said to Amy, "We are lost. We should look for a pink or green house that is located on the street over there, and we should go there." We went, and there was a pink and green house. We had never been in that city before. How could I possibly have known that? Each has her or his own theory about that. Did I live there earlier?

When I went to Europe as an exchange student, after meeting the Jungians there, I dreamed that Jung came to me. He was on the floor, dying. He opened his mouth and said, "Breathe in my last breath." I had never kissed him before, but I put my mouth on his and breathed in his last breath. I found out later that in aboriginal traditions, they say that is how you pass the spirit of one person to the next.

So, who am I, and how long have I been here? The idea that you are maybe connected to something historical should be kept in your back pocket. Maybe you will need it one day, perhaps reincarnation is something to think about. There are some little pieces of evidence for this, and also people have always believed in things like reincarnation. It could be that the way you look now is very interesting, you have the right blouse and shirt on, but it may not be the way you actually look.

I was always touched that Richard Feynman, a most rational person, said, in his 1949 physics paper (which I discuss in *ProcessMind*[70]), that there is a possibility in the equations of physics that things go backward in time temporarily. Does that actually occur for us or not? I would like you to think about it and keep your mind open.

The next exercise focuses on a symptom that you feared or imagined at one time might be deadly. Even if you just fantasized about such a symptom, let's find out what that fantasy is all about. You will get into your processmind and while in that state, you will ask, "What is my path through space–time?" That is, what is your 10,000 year path? If you find a hint about that path, great. Your insight might change. I have been doing this a long time, and my insight has not changed for me. Just play with it. Have the freedom to ask.

Audience 1: Can you say something about there being no beginning and no end. I know that something like that is said in the Bible, the creation of God that has no beginning and no end, but the sense of us also being that also.

Arny: Thank you for asking me that before we do the next exercise. The very concept of life itself is a consensual concept. No one can exactly define when life begins and how to make life from scratch, so to speak. (Perhaps that is true, too, for the universe.)

The section of the Bible you are referring to might be process oriented! There are no absolute beginnings or ends (except in consensus reality and even then for only a short time). From the universe's viewpoint, there is only process.

Audience 2: You said there was a possibility that things go backward in time?

Arny: The equations of physics say we are not just everyday people, and these equations give us a chance to go backwards in time.[68] This is what I mean, I will draw a diagram to show you:

The time (T) axis goes up the vertical line and the space (S) axis goes to the right along the horizontal.

11.4 When a particle meets a field.

When a particle meets a field, its direction changes (diagram to the left). In quantum physics (diagram to the right) a particle can go forward then backward in the field in time before emerging from the field, to move in the new direction!

We could just as well ask, what happens to us when we enter or experience strong space–time dreaming fields or fields of any type? We can simply be moved by it or we can open up to space-time dreaming and let ourselves be twirled about through the universe, reemerging again in everyday life. Quantum physics gives us the opportunity of being dreamed timelessly in the universe. See *ProcessMind* for more details about my understanding of Feynman's ideas.

My point is that if you are flexible, you can step out of time instead of being shoved about by life or getting *killed* by an opponent. Forwards and backwards time reversals might occur in the next exercise and might help you to feel better.

EXERCISE: SYMPTOMS AND LIGHT BODIES

1. Choose your worst and possibly lethal fantasy or real symptom. Feel or imagine its most troublesome energy, and act it out. Sketch its energy, X.

2. Who in u is most upset by this? Act this out and sketch u's energy.

3. Go to a favorite earth spot and notice $u + X$ somewhere there. Let the earth spot breathe and dance you between $u + X$. To loosen up even more, pretend you are dancing freely in the universe, even unpredictably. When you are ready, bring this stochastic dance back to the $X + u$ earth area, and let your dance inform you of something or resolve something.

4. In other worlds, shamanize: let the dance read into the nature and purpose of X.

5. Experiment and say what your true nature and 10,000 year path in the universe is. Please make a note so you won't forget!

AFTERWARDS

Audience 1: I just wanted to share that I worked on all the stress in my shoulders and stomach. I feel so much better now.

Arny: That is good. That is the point! What happened, who are you?

Audience 1: And I found out that I am a sun dancer and the message is bravery. I forget it! I totally forget it while living in Greece during these very troubled times.

Arny: Can you make the sound of bravery.

Audience 1: "Wuuuh!" And the message is, "We can do it! We can do it!" And I felt that Greece is the right place for me.

Arny: Go right to the center of Athens and say "Wuuhhh!" Right there. If she can do it, Greece can do it! She is the next president of Greece!

(Dear reader, this particular person, was elected to the Greek parliament about 2 years after this experience!)

Audience 1: I wake up and say, "How difficult. How depressing I am going back to Greece." I feel the energy of the victim. I would not pick it up consciously but through this process you suggest, I picked it up.

Arny: Yes, because if you are a spiritual warrior, the point is community in any case. So if Greece can feel more like a community, then, "We can do things together!" I am hinting at a possibility. Maybe the problem is there to make more community. I am exaggerating, but you know what I mean.

Audience 2: I was struck by the practical applications. The places where I get stuck in my relationships, in my aikido training, and in my finances were all the same. This experience helped give an answer to all of those areas of my life. The answer was, "When it is going, let it go, just roll with things."

Audience 3: I got something about showing people how to go way beyond what they think is possible... Way, way beyond, light years beyond what we think is possible!

We are process looking like people. Even life and death may be just moments on a larger journey. And if you are in touch with the thing that moves you, at least some of the time, you will surely feel better physically and life will be more creative.

....

Σ   FOR REFLECTION ON CHAPTER 11

- Space-time dreaming reminds us of least action principles in physics.

- Subtle body images may be processmind space-time dreaming experiences.

- Stay close to your body energy. It is the password to the universe.

- Remember your name of today, but don't forget your 10,000 year-old self as well.

- From the viewpoint of space–time dreaming, life and death are stops on a greater journey.

CHAPTER 12

Mental Illness or Universe Talk?

We are all agreed that your theory is crazy.
The question that divides us is
whether it is crazy enough to have a chance of being correct.

—Niels Bohr speaking to Wolfgang Pauli[69]

Since quantum physics, some scientists believed that for a theory to be true it must be a bit crazy! Now I want to turn to space-time dreaming and its application to unusual; that is, extreme, *crazy*, or *psychotic* states of consciousness.

We have been working with stochastic processes whose overall behavior is nondeterministic in that the next moment or state is determined both by the person's predictable actions and by a random element that cannot be entirely predicted. People who are termed *insane*, *crazy*, or *psychotic* experience mental states that are often described as involving a loss of contact with reality. They are often considered *unstable*. Many have experiences of gods or the universe. In the simplest sense, every stochastic process is unstable, deviating from a given deterministic norm that is a more or less controllable feature.

Craziness deviates from social norms, from the concept a given society has of *normal*. That is why I said in *City Shadows* that being crazy is outside the norms of a given society; that is, insanity is a *city shadow*, an important part of experience that the whole of society needs to know more about. Everyone can be, or even needs to be, a little crazy. This kind of *craziness* that rebels against everyday reality can be an element, perhaps a central element, in many so-called psychotic states.

12.1 The Interior of Bedlam.

(Bethlem Royal Hospital), from 'A Rake's Progress'
by William Hogarth, 1763. (Wikipedia)

In a way, I have been arguing in this book that everyone must learn to deviate from social norms over at least short periods of time to be *healthy*. Who decides what is real is a social issue that affects individuals as well as the fields of psychology, psychiatry, and government. Who is *crazy*? Who decides what is *sane*?[70]

ECLIPSE? A MATTER OF GEOMETRY

Think, for example, about the moon. During a full moon, if the earth passes between the sun and the moon, people on the nighttime side of earth will see the moon getting dark and blanking out for an hour or more. That's called a lunar eclipse. If as the sun, you stand in front of me with a flashlight and a second friend playing the moon stands behind me, we will see the moon-friend become *eclipsed* until I get out of the way between her and the sun or until she moves. In any case, the moon can get eclipsed if we, as the earth, stand in between her and the sun. From the viewpoint of people in night time areas of the earth, the full moon then turns dark. OK? That is consensus reality. That is the accepted geometrical understanding of the eclipse of a full moon. Most people on earth will say, "Aha! We saw that. We took pictures of it. That's real."

WOLVES EAT THE MOON...

But the geometrical viewpoint has been held to be the true for only the last few hundred years. Before then, the Scandinavians said, for example, "When the moon gets dark, you suddenly can't see the full moon because great wolves start eating up the moon.[71] They start eating things up in the heavens, and if people don't scream, if they don't scream loudly, those wolves won't stop it. They'll just eat everything up."

Today I can say that in modern cosmopolitan consensus reality, the earth came between the sun and moon, and therefore, we can't see the moon. But in another reality, let's call it "early Scandinavian dreaming," we can't see the moon because the "wolves are eating up the moon and people must scream to stop them from doing that." If an adult person maintains today that wolves are behind the eclipse, others will think that he or she is nuts.

However, I call the nuts viewpoint, nonconsensus reality or dreaming. It's a second part of reality and it is real as well. How do I know it's real? Because if you go to New York City and try to see the full moon or the sun even on the nicest day, you will think that the moon or sun is being eclipsed! By what? By the smog! By junk in the air! You see, people are like wolves. Human beings are eating the sun, so to speak, by making a mess out of our environment. As a result, there is so much junk in the air that you can hardly see the stars or the moon or the sun anymore. The early Scandinavians were right!

So what's the solution? Human beings today, as in the Northern European myth times, must SCREAM LOUDER to "stop the wolves" from "eating up the moon." Scream louder to stop devouring everything, stop the *wolves* from eating up the earth! Clean it all up!

Those early Scandinavians were not just dreamers or pre-Newtonian psychotics. They were not just dreaming! We must scream to stop the people, stop the *wolves*, from eating up the moon by making so much smog! In other words, your dreams are aspects of reality. So in one reality, the earth gets in the way of the sun, which illuminates the earth. And in the other reality, wolves are eating up the moon because the animalistic nature of people is eating it up our perceivable universe, and we need to scream to stop it.

We need both the consensus reality view that the earth came between the sun and moon and the dreaming viewpoint that *wolves* are eating everything up. Without taking the wolf story seriously, we will destroy nature. Consider the following segment from a radio interview with Will Hall and me:[72]

Will Hall: What you're saying has huge implications around mental health issues because when people are in states of consciousness that are called *psychotic*, we say that they're out of touch with reality. And when I have been in these altered states, and I've been in hospitals and I've been diagnosed with schizophrenia myself, my experience was that I was in a different reality. I was not out of touch with the one reality. I was just in a different reality.

You are presenting a framework from physics and psychology and world spirituality that supports the idea that there are alternate realities. The question is, how do we get the realities to communicate or relate to each other? What are the implications of what you're saying for our understandings of madness? And tell us about how you work with extreme states of consciousness.

Arny: Everyone lives in parallel worlds, the world of ecstatic dance and the world of consensus reality. And these worlds don't communicate well. In a way, anyone out of touch with dreaming is as *crazy* as any so-called crazy person who experiences mainly altered states of consciousness. Or better said, we are all crazy as long as we don't value all levels of consciousness.

Instead of using the word insanity, I prefer the term *extreme states*. To me, insane means nonconsensus reality oriented or dreaming. If this goes on a long time, I prefer to call it not insane but extreme, which means, from a statistical viewpoint, those dreamers who are in a minority state of consciousness that can't be validated with yardsticks and clocks. Everyone has a few extreme states of mind and goes through unusual nonconsensual periods. They're statistically not as prevalent as other states, so calling them sick doesn't make any sense to me. From a process viewpoint, nothing is sick. So each of us should deal with these states as best we can, as with everything in life.

Most people, at one time or another, go through times of being depressed and feeling low. Everybody gets manic. Everybody thinks, "Oh, what the hell is life about? I don't care about life much anymore." That is very, very common, especially in the dark periods of the year. Because others want to marginalize those states, the people who go through those states also get marginalized and looked down upon. "Oh, you're weird and you're crazy or sick" or something like that. That doesn't work for me. It's iatrogenic and it hurts.

Cultures say, "We are this. We are not that." I still remember working in Australia and hearing about a teacher who said to her aboriginal student, "Stop dreaming so much. Come on, you've got to get real." So suddenly dreaming and the culture of dreaming and fantasy became marginal and dreamers became marginalized. That's why I say that part of the difficulty is that mainstream cultures get very, very rigid, and people who go through extreme states then come forward with counterbalancing kinds of experiences that could really enrich cultures but instead are pathologized. We need cultures that are more open-minded.

THE FLOWER IN THE FOREST

As I said in my *City Shadows*, people in extreme states and dreamers are shadows of the world. These people have experiences that counterbalance mainstream cultures. If we all try to pick up the unusual states of consciousness, as I predicted in *City Shadows*, there would probably be less madness in the world.

I had a lot of experience working in mainstream European mental hospitals years ago. Psychopharmacology was not yet much developed then, and the extreme nature of unusual states of consciousness was more apparent. For example, a doctor once asked me to help him with a client of his in a mental hospital. When I came in the patient's room, there was a person under the bed who was not talking. I was told that she was very sick and they didn't know what to do with her. She wouldn't come out from under her bed. I went in not knowing what to do. I thought, she's under the bed, what can I do? Why not join her in some way? So I went under a chair at a distance from her bed. After a few moments, she suddenly spoke or rather made sounds like the wind through the trees. She then spoke to me, "Yes, the wind in the forest is here.... It's no good being a person." I said, "Aha! OK, let's stay where we are in the forest."

This was the first adult person I had met who claimed to be the wind in the forest, and I loved it. She was doing something for me that I needed. I had finished my Jungian studies, where I had been sitting in chairs a lot. And here was somebody under her bed in the wind in the forest. I loved it! I deeply appreciated her perspective! What should I do? I just mirrored the sounds she made and suddenly we were having a kind of *forest-like* conversation. I blew like the wind, and she said that she was a flower blowing in the wind in the forest. I was getting good feedback!! So she blew like the wind around a flower in the forest under her bed, and I was the wind under a chair nearby.

To make the story short, after a couple of months, she was up and about and coming to see me in my practice in the city. One day she explained that illness or period of time to me: "Arny, I said it wasn't worth being a person, and the reason was because my family did some very bad things to people. And as soon as I found that out, I decided it wasn't worth being a human being anymore. I wanted to kill myself, and suddenly I found myself becoming a flower, a lovely flower, being moved by the wind in the forest."

We cried together and then, over time, did more normal forms of *therapy*. Anyhow, she was no longer a flower in the forest and behaved more *normally*, like a person in the city. In fact, she became very successful socially in a few years! Good things happened to her. Dreaming with her, following rather than rejecting her stochastic "dance process," the part that consensus reality deemed *crazy*, helped bring her back to consensus reality and helped reinforce my innate love of the dreaming process.

Dancing with altered states is a way to bring the worlds together. Was I helping her? Perhaps. But she was also *healing* me. She did me a favor. As an adult, how many times had I had the chance to play with another adult who's under the bed acting like a flower? She healed something in me by bringing up marginalized experiences. Was she crazy? Or was the world around her too rigid and in need of becoming more crazy, needing to be the space in a forest where wind moves flowers?

Another time, a man was brought into my practice by two psychiatric helpers who were holding him down. When they let him go, he began jumping all over the place. You could call him just plain nuts or say that he was manic or bipolar or use any term you want. The one sure thing was that he came into my room and he sat on my chair and bounced around. I was still trying to behave like a normal analytical psychologist at the time. However, this man scared me because at one moment he was sitting in the chair and in the next he would do something that seemed absolutely random. He suddenly jumped from a sitting position up into the air and hit his head on the ceiling in my room!

I had never seen someone jump so high from a sitting position before; I was dumbfounded. Moreover, he frightened me so much that I almost cried. I yelled at him, "Hey, you can't do that with Arny Mindell! If you want me to be your friend, you can't do that because I'm too scared! I don't know how to deal with that behavior!" This was really true for me. All I could do was stay in my so-called *normal* world, which had no random bounces to it. I was terrified of his.

To my surprise, however, he stopped and looked at me and said, "My God, no one ever treated me like a person." I said, "I'm not treating you like anything. I'm too scared! Please don't do that anymore if you want to work with me, otherwise I'll have to find somebody else you can work with."

Looking back, I can see that man did me a favor. He bounced me out of my analytical role. His bouncing, manic vehemence broke my coolness and made me more vehement. My response, it turned out, was socially unusual for him. He had apparently never heard people crying out things so directly to him before. In a way, my normal behavior drove him crazy; and by being crazy myself, that is, by crying and telling him I was afraid, he became more normal, at least temporarily. He felt I was treating him like a person. Our working relationship began there and then. Perhaps he was looking for someone to join him in his dreaming. I did not think that out at the time, I was just responding unconsciously. He forced me to grow, to become *stochastic*, that is partly deterministic and partly unpredictable.

Extreme states are an attempt to represent not only the predictable *real* but also dream-like random worlds. All worlds belong to everyone's dance. Nothing is totally personal. Like Feynman said, "Try all paths."

Another example comes to mind. One day a person marched into my office with helpers at his sides. He said, "I am the light." The people who came with him said, "He has been saying that he is the light in the middle of this big festival in downtown Zurich. And when he told everyone, 'I am the light,' the chandelier above us all crashed to the floor, so everyone got scared. They thought he was a crazy magician! Someone said that you could help him."

Then the new client said again, "I am the light." And I thought, "That's exciting, let me try that!" So I said, "I don't know what that's like; let me try it for a moment. I'll experiment feeling like the universe, and its light... yes, I'm the light!" And he looked a little shocked but clearly responded, "No! You're crazy if you think you're the light. If you keep talking like that they will put you in a mental hospital." That role switch surprised me. He apparently had to be the light as long as nobody else was occupying that role. Realities are entangled. So when I said, "I'm the light." He said, "No, that light will crash on your head. You've got to bring that light down to earth." I just said, "I don't know how to bring light down to earth. How're you supposed to do that?" And he gave all sorts of tips. Then I helped him integrate the tips he gave to me as the *madman*. He changed slowly, but I don't know what happened later on as we lost contact with one another.

The stochastic and possibly entangled states connecting us to one another and the chandelier are like parallel worlds, like couplings between dreaming and reality. Is this a psychological example of quantum entanglement of dream-like states? Some people in extreme states frequently have magical or quantum-like phenomenon happen to them. But my point is that parallel worlds are parallel as long as we stay only in consensus reality. The deeper we go, the closer we are to the essence level, to dreaming together, to space–time dreaming, the universe, and the "light" then the more parallel worlds come together.

Will Hall: Arny, one of the reasons I like the title of your previous book, *ProcessMind: A User's Guide to Connecting with the Mind of God*, is that it makes me think of the states that I've been in, and that other people diagnosed with psychosis have been in, where we feel like we're plugged into the universe. We feel like we're connecting to the deeper absolute truth of the whole reality, to the mind of God. This is not to romanticize those states, but, for some of us, do you think it's possible that psychosis or madness is a positive experience and it could be part of a renewal process that could add something to the individual and even society if it's held with the kind of respect and listening and curiosity that you're talking about here?

Arny: I think that getting to the essence level of experiences, to the God level or space-time dreaming, is natural, normal, and crucial. We all need to do that more and not just pathologize it in others. Everyone needs to learn to bring such *divine* experiences or synchronistic experiences closer to everyday reality. Perhaps we would have fewer medical emergencies if there was more training about such states of consciousness in our educational systems.

EXTREME STATES ARE NEEDED BY CULTURES

Perhaps people with extreme state experiences are potential shamans, capable of bridging worlds. It's important for everyone to bring up and live marginalized experiences, at least a little bit. Think of the typical family situation in which somebody in the family is doing some weird stuff as far as the family is concerned. For example, some years ago I worked with a child who had the strange habit of spitting all the time. He just spit and spit and spit wherever he could. His parents brought him to me in a distraught state, "What are we going to do with this bad kid? He's just spitting too much!" So now, here again is a cultural and consensus reality rank imbalance. You can't blame the parents, and at the same time, you can't blame the child. They wanted to get rid of his *bad* behavior, and his extreme situation was so powerful that they had to bring him to me.

The Swiss people are traditionally very neat. I knew this and so I suggested that the parents relax a little and occasionally spit as well, explaining to the child that he had freed them to do a little of that spitting. To make this story short as well, the parents did try spitting now and again, and the child eventually stopped his bad behavior. Once again, parallel worlds are a social issue, and my freedom (even without direct reference to space–time dreaming) gave me the openness to suggest doing something a little strange occasionally. Depending upon where you live, to spit occasionally isn't all that bad.

We need to explore all paths. For the sake of democracy, deep democracy, and quantum and relativity theory, let life move you. Paraphrasing Richard Feynman's explanation of quantum physics: An electron or an elementary particle going from my office to the Processwork Center in Portland doesn't just go down the street directly. According to Feynman, that particle tries many, many, many different paths first before finding the one with least action. It may go by way of the moon. The particle may be going by way of Mars. It could be going by way of Hong Kong or Zurich to get to the Processwork Center, even though my office is right near it in Portland. In other words, the path it is most likely to choose is finally the most reasonable and predictable, but all the other crazy paths needed to be explored first.

Likewise, we need all people, all our diversity, to get to where we are going as a world. We need space–time dreaming. It's a bit crazy. It is stochastic and imaginative. Try all worlds, all paths. Stay close to the dreaming, the quantum level, and the level of universal spaces. Then extreme states won't be that extreme and more people will be more creative. If you feel one-sided or uptight about one path, try others. Let your true dance show you the way. If needed, find others who can travel with you as you move from one state to another. Use medications, then don't. Behave properly, then don't. Care for yourself and don't forget to dance ecstatically as often as possible.

I just want to stress again, we need everyone. We need every experience. Only together do we create wholeness and show the different phases of our human dance. It's a very important point for me. Extreme states are a community and a social issue. They are medical issues. They are psychological issues. And they are a spiritual issue, that is, they are dance phases of the ancient one. The more that we realize that we need all kinds of states of consciousness, and the more we realize that we need everybody, the better for all. After all, the craziest and most remarkable theories in the universe are often the best!

Perhaps that's why scientists I quoted in the beginning of this chapter said to Pauli, "We are all agreed that your theory is crazy. The question that divides us is whether it is crazy enough to have a chance of being correct."

Σ   *For Reflection on Chapter 12*

- Human nature and the theories of physics need to be a bit weird, unknown, dreamlike, and crazy to be true.

- Yes, mental disease in the medical sense exists. There is nothing romantic about that.

- But no, the city shadow is not *sick* in the absolute sense, as he or she is a potential, often unrecognized gift to culture.

PART FOUR

Relationship

Beyond War and Peace

We have seen that the processmind or universal mind appears in a stochastic dance moving us. This dance is a bit unpredictable. It can help with physical and mental symptoms. This very same universal system mind will help us now to work with social and organizational system mind problems.[73]

CHAPTER 13

Naropa's Dancing Dakini

I wore this hat today to class because the tassels remind me to follow space-time, to fall [shows hat tassel falling as he moves] and to take it easy. It is good to be tense and fight. I am not against that at all. I love that. But also remember to fall and occasionally let go. Remember, all meditation processes suggest some form of bowing down and using some form of mindfulness.

We are indebted, in great part, to Buddhism for mindfulness practices. I use the term *mindfulness* to mean using your awareness to become conscious of anything you are not normally aware of. Notice your proprioceptions, your movements, your imaginations, the sounds around you, your relationship, and worldly impulses. People have always sensed some omniscient, omnipotent power, even gravity, behind events. Gravity, or the field we live in, is of course not omnipotent, but it is powerful and omnipresent in the sense that it pulls on us everywhere. So remember the tassel on my hat, or better yet, remember your hair or your scarf in the wind.

THE SYSTEM MIND

Anything you do without the system mind can be very good; go save somebody. If your city lacks energy, it makes sense to first try making a nuclear reactor. But be careful: That reactor can leak... especially if you forget about tsunamis and earthquakes. Creating what are believed to be causal solutions to problems without holding the system mind can lead to surprises from things you did not consider. All of the environmentalists say, "Let's stop this or that now! Get this new form of energy, stop this, do that!" But if we become more process oriented, we use our system mind and say, "Let's also try to get all parties involved. Let's use the power of the whole community, all stakeholders. Yes, in consensus reality, everybody should clean up their stuff and recycle it, but that is not enough. We need to clean up the mess in our relationships and our communities."

My critic just said, "Ugh, I hate relating! I don't think others like it either." My response to you, dear critic, is, "Great comment! Don't just relate, go deeper inside and connect first with yourself."

THE PROCESSMIND IN RELATIONSHIPS

You find the deep experiences of the processmind in the first feelings and stories of how you got together with a friend or how an organization was created. That organizing story will always be there in that relationship and group. Who made that story up? Why does that story still work in a relationship? The dream you had the night you started something with somebody, that intelligence goes on. It moves with you over the years. It is uncanny.

The first story, dream, or myth of a friendship is partly a deterministic map. It predicts the big things, but the moment to moment way it operates in reality can't be entirely predicted. The processmind appears as the story pattern behind organizations, but it can't tell exactly when or what will happen. That personal and organizational story is a marginalized part of reality. That is, it is an essence experience, an aspect of which can be seen in dreamland. The processmind of an organization is the essence of or feeling behind that story. It is the space, the atmosphere, between us.

In Christianity, mystics spoke of illumination as getting in touch with *it* and becoming illuminated. In Islam, the focus is union with this deep thing in the background, with Allah or Irfan, and knowing the invisible. In the *Kabala*, Jews speak about the oneness in the background. The Buddhists speak about Nirvana, Buddha mind, creative mind, empty mind, being peaceful, or leaving time and space. The Hindus speak about Atman, getting in touch with something infinite and being free of the little you and what have you. It is amazing!

The core of this part of the book is about getting in touch with the *system mind*: this special, free mind–body feeling. When you are not able to use the tools that you have learned in conflict work, social work, medical work, and organizational change management, then you need to drop into the space we share; the common ground. Let things fall, let yourself be moved a little bit. When you cannot use the tools that you have learned, learn them better, and then loosen up and dance.

For example, if you are trying to negotiate with someone who is slumped down a little and you ask if they are down and they say no, try this: First experience, the person's double signals (their slumped posture) as your own and do some form of space–time dreaming. Then, read into those signals. You might say, "Going down scares me, so I don't want to show it. But actually it feels good, it helps me drop out of the conversation and go more deeply into myself." The point is that you are reading into, or shamanizing into, the space in-between both of you.

You need to notice double signals and then *shape-shift* and speak as if these signals were your own in order to sense their nonlocal nature and to make more connection with the other person. Remember that the space between you is a relationship space. It is like a rubber sheet. If something heavy is there, the sheet bends and altered states happen. So use your space–time dreaming! As I said earlier, "Turn on, tune in, and drop out!" Take it easy and let "it" move you.

NAROPA

Your best teacher is a sense of the fabric of the universe. Sometimes being an unhappy, everyday person is the fastest way to realize this. Everybody hates trouble, and I am with you. I hate trouble. But the story of Naropa speaks clearly about the importance of trouble in realizing yourself.[74] About 1,000 years ago there was a great Indian Buddhist teacher called Naropa. There are a lot of Naropa stories and one goes like this. I'll tell the story in my own words:

> Naropa understood, but did not experience, the depths of Tibetan Buddhism. One day while meditating, a dakini came to him. A *dakini* is "a tantric deity described as a female embodiment of enlightened energy." In the Tibetan language, "dakini is rendered *khandroma* which means 'she who traverses the sky' or 'she who moves in space.'" Sometimes the term is translated poetically as sky dancer or sky walker. She is pictured

as moving through space–time. Perhaps all of us who are trying to let space move us are trying to get in contact with the dance of that ancient one, our dakini.

13.1 Naropa (Wikipedia).

In any case, the dakini tells Naropa that he needs to learn more and must now seek his true teacher in human form, Tilopa, her brother. So Naropa decided to seek Tilopa. He crossed the river, searching for his teacher. He did not know the way, he just followed his own inner guidance, and when he got across the water he met troublesome people. They beat him up and almost killed him. But he survived and got up to continue his search. "Where is my teacher? I am looking for my teacher, Tilopa." At each point in his journey, people robbed or beat Naropa; he ran into one problem after another. Finally, after many troubles and a long journey, he got to the point where he said, "I have had it! I cannot go further. I am so depressed. I am so miserable. All I wanted to do was find my teacher, and now all I can do is kill myself." So he took a knife to slit his throat, but suddenly a blue image appeared in front of him. It was his teacher, Tilopa.

"It is I, Tilopa, I was always there." But Naropa protested, "What do you mean, you were always there? I could not find you!" Tilopa said, "Didn't you see me? I was the one who robbed you. I was the one who made trouble for you. I was the force trying to get you to reduce yourself."

Naropa said, "I couldn't see you!" "Yes," Tilopa says, "But I was always telling you to let things be, let go." Immediately, Naropa was illuminated and was able to go forward and live. He became a great teacher, a saint. Today, Tibetan Buddhism is linked to Naropa.

13.2 Tilopa (Wikipedia).

One of the points of this amazing story is that you should live your life the best you can. Then, if you have a recurring problem that comes back and depresses you, if you are caught in trying to organize your life and think, "Oh! What did I do wrong? Why this again?," then you might say, "I thought I worked this out a long time ago." Or, "Well, that problem is a little better," or "Damn, it is the same thing again!" There is something awful about these terrible events that happen to us. We need more insight, more power, more police, more civil rights to prevent disasters from happening!!! But there is also another kind of hidden teaching in these troubles.

The troublemaker may be your teacher in hiding. Recurring messes can lead you to your teacher and force you to follow a deeper rhythm. The Naropa story speaks of a feeling skill, a *metaskill*. Behind your troubles is your dancing dakini in space–time dreaming, your great process guide and spirit, trying to tell you, not you, but it, the great spirit lives appearing as the problems in your life. That is a detached *metaview* of yourself and your relationship and your organization. You might think, "Oh my God, we were doing so well, and now this problem appears again!" But this difficulty could be the luckiest moment. At some point in life, we all run into this kind of problem. Things appear that you cannot solve with your conscious mind. Don't forget Naropa's metaskills, his space–time dreaming dakini, and his great teacher, her brother Tilopa.[75] Life's problems may contain the secret of your deepest self, which is your processmind and its ability to let go into space-time-dreaming and universal processes.

So now let's work on a problem that makes you feel stuck again and again. Which one? Choose the most difficult one. Find the X and the *u* in that problem and then go to a favorite earth spot and feel the atmosphere there. Then let go, drop out into the universe. That means, I want you to imagine that you are falling freely through the universe. Let everything you were working on go. You are going to go back after you really feel like you are in some form of free fall.

Free fall is a very good term. If you are falling through the universe and there is nothing, not even air, stopping you, then you are in your own universe dance pattern, your own space, and your own path. Then bring that free fall relaxation back to the relationship between those two energies in the earth spot to loosen you up. That is basically where we are headed. And through that loosening, you may discover noncognitive resolutions to problems on which you are working. We are going to try to discover how Tilopa is behind the problem and the meaning and the power bringing you trouble.

Before doing the exercise at the end of this chapter, try letting go into the universe. It just takes a minute:

- Sit on the chair or the floor and feel yourself there. Feel your weight on your chair or on the floor. You may want to sit close to the edge of your chair to allow for more movement.

- As you are sitting there, imagine that the chair, the floor, and the earth were suddenly taken away and that you are in a kind of free fall in space. Let yourself go, move, and feel for a moment what that is like… just freely falling and moving in space.

It is that feeling you are going to be exploring in the following exercise. Focus on that free fall experience. Why do you think we say *falling* asleep? That falling is a kind of dreaming. It is the same idea of letting go so that movements in space can happen. Now try the following, perhaps you'll find Naropa's dakini, dancing in space.

INNER WORK EXERCISE: TILOPA'S NOT-DOING

1. Recall, name, and feel a your worst or recurring problem.

2. What X energy in that problem is the worst for you (e.g., energy of an inner critic, a person, or a symptom)? Feel that X energy and make a motion that expresses it best. Get a really good feeling for it. Then make a quick sketch of this energy on paper and name it.

3. Who in you or what part of you (call it *u*) is most upset by X? That is, what part of you doesn't like that kind of X energy? What is that part like? Feel that *u* energy, make a motion or motions to express it, and when you are ready make a quick sketch of this energy on paper and name it.

4. Now take a moment to remember an earth spot that is very special to you, one of your favorites. There may be many, but let your unconscious mind choose the one that seems to want to come up just now. Imagine that you are actually on that earth spot and look around the whole area. Do you somehow see the *u* + X energies expressed or represented in the land, water, mountains, atmosphere, animals, et cetera, there in some way? That is, what part of nature has the quality of the X energy, and what aspect of nature has the *u* energy? Now, feel yourself again on that earth spot and notice your breath and then use your breath to breathe into that earth spot. And when you are ready, sense the earth breathing you and beginning to move and dance you a little. And as that earth spot breathes and dances, let it begin to express the *u* + X energies in motion, exploring and expressing each as parts of itself.

5. Now while you're on that earth spot, let's feel your relationship to the universe. First, relax a little while you're moving and feel yourself in the universe, and let the universe move you in space. That is, feel the universe's space breathing and moving you! Let it begin to move your body and curve you about almost unpredictably. (Please be careful.) Experience yourself as some being, dancing in space. What's its name?

6. When you are ready, bring this being, this sense of movement freedom back to your earth spot area and dance and let the universe help you explore, express, and dance between the *u* + X earth energies. Notice how your processmind dance deals with the *u* + X energies as aspects of a process and notice what it teaches

you. Then, imagine how any insights or learning might affect and be used in your everyday life.

7. Please take time to make notes about the following:

    a. How did you experience the universe's effect upon your earth dance?

    b. Can you imagine how that universe dance experience is an expression of your true detached nature, that is, your Tilopa? How has this experience of your true nature appeared in your life?

    c. Finally, experiment with letting your Tilopa experience do *not-doing* as it moves you to get up, sit, walk, and talk and imagine using this in your everyday life.

Arny: Let that movement process still remain in you, as a kind of *not-doing*.

Audience 1: I experienced endless and complete expansion, and it felt good, but when I went back to the original issues, it was, "Eh! Who gives a shit?!" My problem is this: One part of me wants to be monogamous and in long-term relationship and the other part wants, for lack of a better word, to be polyamorous, wants many lovers.

Arny: What is the *u* energy of monogamy? I have not seen that for a while!

Amy: Excuse me?! [Group cracks up laughing!!]

Arny: [Laughing too.] What is for you the *u* energy of monogamy?

Audience 1: [Brings arms together, suggesting comfort, safety.]

Arny: And polyamorous X energy?

Audience 1: [Shows a more explosive gesture, with arms open wide.]

Arny: And let me see what you did when the universe danced you.

Audience 1: [Spins around with expansive arm movements.]

Amy: That's amazing to watch.

Audience 1: It gives me such an expanded and great state, but I could not even begin to bring it back into the issues that were involved.

Arny: No problem. Let me play that part of you that has these two energies, and you keep being the universe for a moment. [Arny moves into the person's space and plays out the expansive X and comforting *u* energies.] So what would you advise me now in words if you see me, as this kind of person with these two energies?

Audience 1:   Get over yourself!

Arny: What does that mean?

Audience 1:   I am too grounded and stuck in both energies. I did not think I was grounded in the second one, but I knew I was grounded in the first.

Arny: You are too grounded in both of them... let them both go and just dance.

Audience 1:   Thank you.

Arny: You are welcome.

- -

Audience 2:   You say that those outer space experiences are not about death, so what is death about?

Arny: Many of the people we have worked with have experienced these outer space experiences. For example, my mother said that she saw a star being born in the universe; Jung found himself in outer space and wanted to stay there but then realized that people needed him and therefore he came back. Some people float up to the ceiling looking down on their physical bodies in bed but are not able to go higher. All sorts of things like that occur near death. From the deepest viewpoint, some aspects mean *boom!*, you are going to die, but that is not an issue for something deeper down underneath. The issue is rather how to be your whole self all the time, regardless of what is going to happen to you.

One of our friends, Wilma Jean Tucker, died a few years ago. She was a woman who would not take regular allopathic medicine for the problem that was bothering her. In her last dream, water was coming onto the tennis court. She had been a great tennis player. So she said, "With all that water on the tennis court, I will have to learn to splash around there!" That was her last dream.

Your conscious mind thinks "I am going to die" and something else says you have to learn to play tennis in a new way on a water-filled court or go swimming.

Σ   FOR REFLECTION ON CHAPTER 13

- Remember Naropa's wise advisor, the dakini, and his guru, Tilopa: Behind all suffering was a message telling Naropa to let go and be directed.

- Space–time dreaming can be personified as a kind of angel, as the mythic dakini, as she who moves through space.

- If you get blocked and depressed, use your processmind to flow with $u + X$.

CHAPTER 14

The Tao and Alchemy of Relationships

Relationships are amazing. Remember, I have been talking about process structure in terms of a triangle in chapter 5. At the top is you. Below that is your dreamland situation consisting of two or more overlapping states that we are calling u + X. Your processmind is not just yours but also overlaps and interacts with your friend's processmind. Who you are is not just you. This essence area or processmind experience connects with the dreams of another person.

When you wake up close to your processmind in the morning, you might have some hunch about what your friend dreamed next to you. You should be able to guess their dreams before they even say good morning. Or, if you are not in relationship with somebody or not sleeping with somebody, think about somebody in the morning and call or email them in the morning and tell them what they dreamed. This could be an enjoyable relationship practice.

As I said in chapter 5, Jung spoke about this sense of nonlocality as *synchronicity*, which is an event characteristic of this deepest level. Synchronicity can occur because who you are at the deepest essence level is not just your physical body. The free dance experience of space-time dreaming can give you the sense of noncognitive, nonlocality. The Taoist sage in you senses this deepest level and understands the yin and yang overlap, or *two-ness*, of life in dreamland and consensus reality.

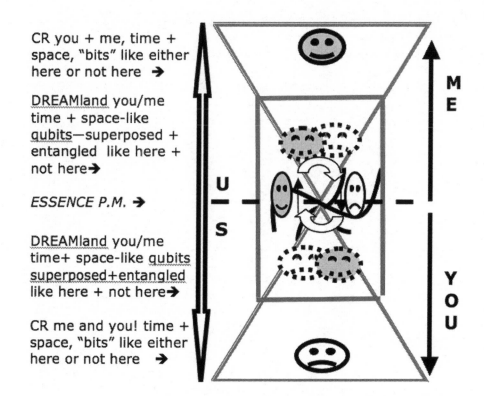

CR you + me, time + space, "bits" like either here or not here →

DREAMland you/me time + space-like qubits—superposed + entangled like here + not here→

ESSENCE P.M. →

DREAMland you/me time+ space-like qubits superposed+entangled like here + not here→

CR me and you! time + space, "bits" like either here or not here →

M E

U S

Y O U

14.1 Nonlocality in Psychology.

Remember in chapter 6, I spoke of dreamland in terms of qubits. *Qubit* refers to two overlapping states. In our terms, qubits means that we are one person or one system with two or more overlapping states reaching over to others. Remember Schrödinger's cat: Is it alive or dead? How can it be dead and alive at the same time? Physics and psychology say we are each one system with many overlapping and simultaneous states. You dream this and that, and they look like separate dream figures, but actually they are overlapping and mixed up and they swing back and forth all day.

When conflict is around, the best metaskill is to stay in your processmind because then you are open to all states and you have some distance from them all. It's the best way to deal with yourself when you have two states in conflict and the best way to approach others as a facilitator. Be open to all their states, otherwise you get into conflict with parts of them. If you are in one state only, then that brings up the other polarity state. If you are not in your processmind, you constantly flip-flop back and forth between myriad states as if one or the other is the only right one.

Why are we not dancing in space with our universal or processmind more often? As I said in chapter 2, it seems as if the universe's or at least our sense of wonder wants to be one-sided. Why? Why would something so whole and beautiful want such one-sidedness? What is going on? Remember, the wonder of our processmind awakens to itself by breaking into parts. To self-reflect, *it* needs one-sidedness, which brings out two parts clearly in order to experience and notice one another. It is central to the idea of reflection and consciousness. The basic idea is the universe seems to need polarization for self-reflection and consensus reality. It loves to polarize our consensus reality!

Audience: Why does the universe need to know itself?

Arny: I don't know. But reflection, the essence of consciousness, seems to be part of our universe. It loves reflection. It awakens and makes itself conscious. It has always been here, I guess. I don't think the universe knows everything. I think she is waking up with us. Perhaps we are parts of the universe waking up to herself! The universe is only 13.7 billion years old in its present state. So here we are looking backwards in time and seeing all the diversity that came from the big bang.

Physicists are asking if and how we can make contact with consciousness in outer space.[76] There must be consciousness in outer space. Is there a language out there? Do we have to learn how to speak it? Or will communication be telepathic? It seems to me that you and I are ET. Yes, there may also be all sorts of other beings out there. However, my guess is that there is nothing in the universe that can happen out there that you cannot know and communicate with because you are part of the universe's fabric.

Alchemists were relationship experts, at least with their chemicals. They mixed substances, and they saw things coming together, and they must have thought, "This is really wonderful! Two chemicals come together, but their shared oneness or togetherness must have been there before. Perhaps the two things did not know it before we encouraged them, and they came together." They called that oneness the *unus mundus,* the one world. It must have been there from the beginning. Jung thought that the observer and the event being observed were sometimes synchronistic because of this *unus mundus.* Mixing my term with the terms of Jung's alchemists, I can say that the processmind is the intelligence behind the *unus mundus*, the one body we share with the universe.

14.2 Alchemical picture of two people with one body.

The alchemists saw parts of a chemical combination as two people coming together, as one body with two heads. See Figure 14.2. That is a picture of the *unus mundus*, a personification of getting close to the common ground and the feeling of something moving both of us.[77] When you work with your processmind and you work on your relationship with another person, you feel better with the other person and you are physically closer to her or him. If it is a sexual relationship, you are sexually closer and things harmonize a little better. In a nonsexual relationship, you feel more peaceful with the other person. It is a remarkable and momentary state that people almost always project onto sexual contact. You can find it there, and that state is there, but it is not the only place. Its source is the *unus mundus*.[78]

Fighting is ok too. Then, when you have to be at odds with the other person, and the $u + X$ energies become more clear, things can get closer again. So, wrestling with the other person is a good idea, up to a point, because the u and the X get really clear.

Let me give an example from my relationship with Amy: We don't fight much, believe it or not, but the other day we had a disagreement for about 10 minutes, which was a big thing for us. We were getting ready to travel, and I noticed that something was not right with the ceiling in our apartment in Portland.

Amy: It has been leaking for 5 or 10 years or something!

Arny: So, there was a contractor supposedly fixing it. The construction people did not do a very good job at repairing that leak, so I said, "Amy, what do you think? Let's get a little tougher with them!"

Amy's viewpoint was, "I thought we should be nicer to them because I understood that they did this because of that. It's life!" And I said, "It is not life! I want them to fix the damn thing!"

There you have the $u + X$: Be nicer! No, be tougher!

I said, "Amy, you should not be so nice, you just don't want to be that direct with them!" She said, "We must be nice to them."

In any case, we stopped talking about it and she went to her desk and I went to my desk. I suddenly realized, "My god we are in it! This is it! This is the lucky moment!"

Amy: I had not yet reached that insight!

Arny: So she went to her desk, and I went to my desk, and I worked on myself. I thought about it for a couple of minutes, and I realized that I felt the same way she did, but I did not want to admit it at that moment. I also did not want to hurt those guys' feelings. They were doing their best and maybe they were not that good at it! She had a really good point, just not the only point.

Amy: And after about 10 years of leaks, I realized that you were right. I wanted to be tougher. I was just shy about it!

Arny: One thing led to the next, and we ended up hugging. The important thing was, as we were hugging and saying, "I didn't mean this or that," we both noticed at that moment that Amy's stuffed animal, an elephant with tusks on her desk, fell to the floor. Suddenly, we realized that elephant was the way: soft tusks, kind toughness. So we called the contractors and said, "You guys are doing a sloppy job, but you are doing your best, we know."

Amy: I said, "We don't want to have to live with a garbage can in the middle of the room anymore!" And best yet, after we'd left, all was fixed. We don't know what they did, but it is done.

Arny:	It is the first time we have no leak in that roof for years! The fighting is important, know the $u + X$, and, if you can go deeper, find the body with two heads on it. Then you'll find the resolution. All of us have at least two heads on one body, various viewpoints at the same time.
Audience:	Thank you for working on your things in front of us.
Arny:	I will never forget Amy's stuffed animal and her strong but furry tusks!

Get down to the common ground and shamanize in relationships. The point now, this time, is to go so deep in yourself that you can read into the other person and you are going to be able to speak for her or him. In a strained atmosphere, whether our friends are shyer or more outgoing, we might think, "The other person should say more. She (or he) is not saying enough about the deepest things!" But maybe the other person is not saying more because you are not deep enough. Let me clarify here: Somebody on an edge may need help to get over that edge and speak. But maybe another reason the person does not say more is because you are not deep enough. You can be open to what she or he is saying by almost saying it for the person. This is not just switching roles. It is getting deep into yourself so when you come up, you are a little bit the other person and you can almost feel her or him. This approach makes relationships easier.

Especially in Worldwork situations and large-group situations, if you can read into a person who is not able to speak in a given moment, it might be doing her or him a favor. Then you have to watch the feedback to make sure that you are not saying too much. Try being a shaman as a metaskill in your relationships.

The same holds true for organizations. As a facilitator, if you are deep enough, you can almost start talking for people, and they will then start talking automatically even without your encouraging them to do so. This is the easiest form of relationship! Start talking about something and you almost don't have to look at the other person as you start speaking. Then you might find yourself asking, "Is it you or are the others saying something?" If you are deep inside yourself, everyone will start to move or talk automatically. Bring others out more by speaking with and for them and yourself. I am suggesting simply letting go, free fall, letting yourself go. Fall asleep, fall down, get tipsy, meditate. There are as many methods as there are people.

When you are *yourself* and at home in the universe, you can bring others *home*. Then things start working better. When you are deeply in connection with processmind, you are at home. When you are at home then, because of nonlocality, the other person is likely to be more at home as well.

In the next exercise, think about a problematical relationship. As we have been doing, find the X energy in that relationship, the most difficult energy, and the *u* energy that is disturbed by it. Then we will go to a favorite earth spot and experiment, once again, letting the universe move you and dance you. Then we shall imagine that the person is right there and how bringing the universe in can help the relationship. Once you are in that common shared ground, the *unus mundus* place, you will probably notice insights.

EXERCISE: *UNUS MUNDUS RELATIONSHIP*

1. Think of a person and a relationship problem that bothers you. There may be many disturbances in that relationship, but choose just one of the most difficult energies (call it X) in that relationship that disturbs you. Feel that energy and make a motion with your hands, face, and body to express it. Make a sketch of this X energy on a piece of paper and describe that energy with a word or two.

2. Now, ask, what part of you, *u*, is most upset by that X type of energy? Feel this part; make a motion with your hands, face, and body to express it; and then make a sketch of this *u* energy on your paper. Add a word or two to describe it.

3. Next, be the earth dancing: Recall a favorite earth spot and imagine that you are there. Sense the whole atmosphere around you. Feel the earth beneath your feet, feel the air, and feel the temperature. And look all around and notice where you find the *u* + X energies represented by some aspects of that spot. In the sounds, the motions of the environment, the feeling of certain spots, try to locate the *u* + X energies. Now, feel the earth spot again, and let it begin to breathe you. And as it breathes you, let it move you a little as you become the earth spot dancing. And use this dance to explore the X + *u* energies in that area. Now let's deepen this.

    When you are ready, relax even more and sense the universe. Let go of yourself temporarily and then, without resistance, let the universe begin to move you in space–time. Just let it move you as space moves and curves you. Follow your own movement and feelings as you're moved about by space–time. (Be careful of those around you.) And when you are ready, bring this sense of freedom, this movement experience, back to your earth spot as it breathes and dances you and explores, expresses, and goes back and forth between the $u + X$ energies. Notice how this body experience deals with the $u + X$ energies and deepens your experience of them. Use your subtle awareness and notice any insights. Note what this body experience teaches you.

4. Remember your universe dance; that's the *unus mundus*, your Taoist sage in relationships. Now imagine the real person you were thinking about and let your universe earth dance move and speak out loud and read into and speak for the $u + X$ in the air as if the $u + X$ were shared by all. Imagine the effect and any jot down insights or resolutions.

5. Finally, briefly describe and show your true nature in any way you like; perhaps using the earth, universe, and movement. This is your greatest relationship skill.

   Remember your dance of the ancient one. Feel it, and try to wiggle even if you are seated. If you are from a culture that does not wiggle much, I want to give you permission to wiggle so when you face groups or friends, your wiggle is still there.

AWARENESS

I often use the term *first attention* to refer to dealing with consensus reality, time, space, causality, medicine, signals, et cetera. For me, the *second attention* means becoming aware of unintentional things such as double signals, projections, dream figures, and the potential for role play. Finally, the *third attention* refers to a focus on altered, essence-like states of consciousness, four-dimensional curves, and space–time dreaming. If you are moving freely, then the third attention will notice noncognitive experiences and insights. Stay awake while lucidly dreaming.

   Now do this exercise again, this time working with someone face to face. This will be a dyadic exercise in which you work with somebody else and try to discover that *unus mundus*; that one world-universe, the shared common ground underneath; and try to flow with it a little bit. You can do it with somebody you know or you can do it with somebody you have never met before.

You will be shamanizing together, half in your space–time dreaming experience and half with the other person in consensus reality. Let your sense of the universe move and curve you. Let yourself begin to speak for one of the X or u energies, and the other person is going to be doing her or his X + u energies at the same time. Then you can switch and speak for one of your partner's X's or u's and vice versa.

The idea is that you stay as deep in that state as possible so you can read into the other's energies and so you can speak even before she or he has to speak. You are shamanizing. The idea is that all these energies are in a shared field, and we share them all. You can read into the field and all the energies until you discover something and have an insight together.

When you are with people, your processmind will know what to do. It respects the consensus reality person by focusing on shared experiences that, in a way, belong to no one. Now, how can an introvert do something like that? Can a very shy person do something like that? Are you allowed to do something like that as a quiet person? Yes and No or YO! Play with it. It is a little bit over the edge for everyone in practically every culture but is what we always do in the quantum world and in dreamland.

....

Σ   FOR REFLECTION ON CHAPTER 14

- Explore the noncognitive shared body in relationship.

- The *unus mundus*, or space–time dreaming, is where you and the other are not separated.

- At the essence of relationship, there is only the universe dancing. Use it to read into relationship disturbances.

CHAPTER 15

Dancing Shiva in Business

Consensus reality is not our total reality. We simply have a consensus about what constitutes our reality, and that consensus does not always work. This is why big problems arise on all levels: personal, communal, organizational, societal, and worldwide. Your viewpoint is one of many possible viewpoints, and if you don't go deeper in yourself, you won't connect well with others. The deepest part of the facilitator is her or his space–time dreaming experience of the universe's fabric.

ORGANIZATIONAL PROBLEMS

We need to bring facilitation to organizations that are in trouble, especially if people are afraid their organization is failing. Often such people say, "Oh my god, what is going to happen to us if our unresolved problems go further?" While we need to deal with that challenge on the outer level, at the same time I would say, "If you are afraid that we will go to pieces, then let's consider going to pieces as one momentary possibility." Remember the possibility that there is a message, something like Tilopa's wisdom behind the problem.

Every time we fear that we will not make it as a human society, that we are going to kill ourselves, one response to that fear is, "stop what we are doing." But the other response is ok! Remember Tilopa! Let go and relax! This second solution is to relax and go deeper. Relax your neck muscles, the world can change. You don't have to go into spiritual ecstatic states to discover new, unexpected solutions!

15.1 Nataraja: Lord of Dance (Wikipedia).

It's natural to turn against problems, and a first problem in working on conflicts within groups is helping the group get over their resistance to being in conflict in the first place! Groups often don't mind having a conflict with other groups, but just about every group I have worked with is against their own internal conflicts. "Oh! We are at war again! Oh no, oh my god, let's solve the problem right away!" And if you can solve it, please do it! That is important too. But remember, although revolutions can get rid of dictators, they do not get rid of the role of the dictator. In the dimension where ghost roles exist, someone needs to stand and say and represent a troublesome energy such as, "I am the boss! I dictate! Do this and that!" Then share that role with others.

The principle of deep democracy says be realistic and remember that it is a civil right to dream into ghost roles! You may have to fire some person in consensus reality, but remember that the person you are firing occupied a role, and the problem for which you are firing the person still belongs in some way to the overall dream and vision of the organization. Bring the group members home to their system mind, where all the various parts can have a home.

In India, the universe's system mind was imagined as the god Shiva, the creator of the universe. Shiva was imagined in a dance form, as Nataraja. Figure 15.1 shows Nataraja dancing within a large ring, which represents the universe. He has many arms because she or he is doing various things at the same time.

I should have studied this god first at MIT. Then I would have known that there is a spirit that people have always experienced, an intelligence behind the universe that is dancing around all the time. Shiva is thought of as the spirit of both creation and destruction. I prefer to think of the experience of Shiva from an essence viewpoint as the dance of the ancient one, the spirit of dance symbolizing the rising and falling energies in the universe.

In any case, Shiva is meant to embody the universe's process. The hands look creative, but the fire around the universe looks hot or, let's say, stochastic! The dance is within a cycle, and the dancer is standing on a figure below that is meant to represent the illusion of reality. When you are in your processmind, you are a bit detached and, like Nataraja, you stand on top of consensus reality, that is, on top of *maya* or illusion. When you are in your processmind, the illusion of the fixed self, of fixed parts, is overridden at least temporarily.

Nataraja is a Sanskrit word that means Lord of Dance. The dance is the continuous cycle of creation and destruction, and the ring is made of fire. All communities and societies, nations, and world areas go through cycles. For example, societies create dictators, overcome them, have renewals, and then new kinds of dictatorial forces often arise. Think of the czars who ruled Russia, for example. Then came communism, then capitalism and democracy and what's next? Deep democracy?

Shiva symbolizes the overall personal, organizational, and world process including the creation and destruction of the universe and, of course, human societies. At the same time, Shiva symbolizes a skill, or metaskill, for enabling and following social processes. The leader's best viewpoint is to find Nataraja and be her, him, or it.

Big conflicts and social changes always involve the use or abuse of power. Unconsciousness of one's power leads to tensions and eventually to conflict or war. We see problems of rank consciousness everywhere from universities and street scenes to financial institutions and racial diversity issues in nations. Everywhere today, English language speakers forget the social rank of speaking English. Just about everywhere, mainstream people forget women and heterosexuals forget all other sexual orientations. Few realize that rank is a deeply unconscious sensibility. You may have a lot of rank relative to your situation with other people. Just point it out to people. Sometimes things get resolved with that honest disclosure alone.

Remind ourselves and others when we become unconscious of rank. Start acting like bosses by making decisions that need more input from others. We need bosses who operate from the top down, but without relationship skills and group process that includes everyone others will eventually revolt. And you need to know that if you arrive in a leadership position, you had better say, "To tell you the truth, I can also be a pain in the ass. I am not everything." Try to solve issues at the surface as best you can, at the consensus reality level. Then go deeper and notice the atmosphere of an organization and the roles, and start to work at those levels. A group that can process its own roles is a fantastic rarity! However, more and more business organizations around the world are beginning to engage in group Processwork.

Sustainable facilitation does not focus only on solving problems. It also focuses on the relationship processes between the parts of an organization. It is important to come up with solutions, but remember that consciousness of diversity issues, of entanglement between parts and people, is needed to make any resolution sustainable. It's important to realize that any conflict in an organization or any troublesome X energy is nonlocal. That is, it is characteristic of everyone in the organization. So try to help everyone in organizations integrate the X role. The best community processes involve all coworkers, all stakeholders finding the conflict between the X and the u energies in themselves. Solving problems in a large group without helping each person reconcile her or his own X + u energies is not sustainable. Ask people how they know these energies and conflicts in themselves. Remind people to flow back and forth between the two energies, not to simply regard one as good and the other as only bad.

All stakeholders; that is, every person, group, organization, member, or system that affects or can be affected by an organization; are participants in community process and also potential facilitators. It is not just the facilitator facilitating but also the participant who is important because she or he can speak for the different sides and even take them further, reading into their energies. You may be a relatively low-ranked person within the context of the organization; but if you are sitting in a tense meeting, you might try speaking for the different sides, talking a bit into the air, so to speak. Don't look at the people, look at the ground or the air. Soon others will get the point. Everyone can and must facilitate the tensions in the group, not just the identified facilitators.

In the following inner work, choose a challenging problem in an organization, a family situation, or a world or social issue. Then we will ask you about the most difficult person or group, finding the X + u energies in that problem. Next, guess what success would mean for that issue in everyday reality. Then do a *Nataraja dance* to get to the larger sense of the universe moving us to see how it will deal with those energies. And finally, we are going to imagine how you would actually use that dance within that organization or family or with that world issue. How might you convey that dance energy? Just feel it very subtly in yourself and speak for one and the other side in your own style. Then, with everyone else getting together again, meditate at the end on how you will actually integrate that approach or energy and bring it in as a facilitator or participant.

....

EXERCISE: NATARAJA'S NOT-DOING DANCING FOR WORLDWORK AND BUSINESS ORGANIZATIONS

1. Choose a challenging business or organizational problem or situation, a difficult family issue, or a social diversity problem on which to focus. If you have many, choose the most challenging. Who is the most difficult person or group involved in that issue or organization for you?

2. Stand up, if you can, and remember that problem and the most difficult person or group. What is the most irritating or disturbing X energy in that group or person for you? Make motions to express the X energy and say a couple of words that go with that motion. Sketch the energy on paper, and write the words down as well. What would success with that issue/problem mean in your mind? Make a note.

3. Who in you, u, is most upset by X's energy? Feel this part of you, make motions to express its energy, and say a few words that go along with that motion. Then make a quick sketch of this energy and write the words down as well.

4. Now we'll find your Nataraja dance. Relax and notice your breath. Let it begin to move your body a bit and then let it take you to your favorite, or one of your favorite, earth spots that you have

been working with. And as you breathe, look around and notice if the X + u energies are represented somewhere in that spot. Now, still feeling the earth spot and breathing, let the earth spot dance you between the X + u.

5. Now we'll go deeper. When you're ready, sense how your earth spot is part of the universe. Let go, relax, and let the universe begin to move you without resistance in space–time. Just let it move and curve you about. Let your breath help you feel and move freely. And when you are ready, bring this flow experience back to your earth spot as it breathes, expresses, and dances you back and forth between the X + u energies. Notice how the processmind Nataraja dance deals with and reads into the X + u energies and imagine the effects on the people. Make notes about any spontaneous insights.

6. Finally, imagine doing the earth-universe dance with those people. Will you be really dancing in the open or only subtly feeling the dance in yourself while connecting with the outer people? Make notes about how to do this in that group.

[After this exercise in one of their seminars, Amy and Arny worked with a leading military person from another country in front of a large group. Afterwards, Arny explained the work.]

Arny: The way that military leader modeled feeling the universe moving him as he dealt with the tensions within the military and battles in his country has changed my idea of the military. He demonstrated the courage of deepening himself while dealing with everyday reality. Those are the kinds of leaders we need. That military leader retaught us that we only learn what we already know. Being close to his deepest self makes him a true leader.

For example, I was really ready to play out a very strict opposing military system leader, an X, but our present military leader melted me by being so close to what he called that "god experience." His dance of the ancient one, his peaceful way of just being and brought me to home in the Universe. The X that I as trying to play stopped without conflict. His presence at the essence level created a noncognitive change in me. The world may pay you as a facilitator or military person to win or resolve a conflict, but that is not all that is needed. This military person encourages all of us to be closer to our deepest selves in public.

That reminds me to stress the human factor, the relationship issue that is in back of just about all organizational issues. We always need more organizational expertise and better CEOs. We need people who can make decisions quickly without contacting others. But the universal relationship factor is still central, though often hidden behind all other issues. For example, a group like GM produces cars. NASA was, at one point, mainly producing rocket ships. Whatever your organization produces, the problems often seem local, personal, or material. Yet there is always a nonlocal feeling problem in the background.

For example, NASA created a rocket ship a number of years ago that failed just after takeoff and killed a number of people. NASA then invited all sorts of scientists to investigate what went wrong, and they found that an o-ring had failed, a ring that should not have failed.[79] Just repairing the o-ring, however, was not sufficient to resolve the problem that led to the destruction of Challenger. There had been messages from one department to another about that o-ring prior to lift-off, and the bosses thought, "Oh, the chances are 85:15 that it won't happen, so I will go with the 85 part." But the 15% chance that it would not work is what happened. The problem was not just a bad decision. The deeper problem was that there was not enough discussion about the decision. Remember relationships!

Or think of the nuclear reactor breakdown that happened in Japan because of the tsunami that rolled in from the sea, breaking up entire cities, including nuclear reactors. The person who was at the head of the reactor in Japan said that 20 years earlier, in the 1990s, he had never thought his reactors would be disturbed by tsunamis. We can all think, "Well, that's a mistake in judgment." However, *Tsunami* is a Japanese word after all. He should have realized his error. You might think he is to blame, but the bigger problem in the background is that there was too little community or no organizational meeting about it that might have brought forward all sorts of possible problems. Why didn't the reactor builders, the scientists, meet with seismologists and oceanographers and elders from the villages? Some of these people might have predicted tsunamis? Such a meeting never happened. The moral of the story is, for every country, don't forget community. Bring all the parts and parties involved, into a community meeting. Bring in as many stakeholder parts as you can into your organization. Make every organization you are part of a place for community meetings to discuss things. It could be a matter of life and death. Have as many different parties as you can come together to an open forum, even people who do not like your organization. Don't side just with the *u*, but invite the X energies too.

Dictatorial X energies are most troublesome in all groups. You can hear these energies in some of the following comments:

- You are the problem!
- Cut the crap, just do it! Don't feel about it, just do it!
- My job is to tell you how it must go! I know the best!
- You were wrong! I was right! I know best!
- I envy you but won't admit it. I'll just criticize you behind your back.
- This organization is rubbish!
- I don't want to stay and hear that! I won't listen!
- That is not part of our department's responsibility.
- The regulations don't allow it.
- I quit! I am totally burned out!
- I am a new CEO in the organization and I wouldn't have hired half of the people in it!

A leader who is not at home in her processmind, relative to all the parts in the universe, will push some people out the door and create conflict even though those people are doing good things. Knowing and applying the sense of home and dancing with the X's in public forums helps organizations perform identified tasks and creates a place where people can interact and discuss issues, concerns, and shared accomplishments.

Σ   FOR REFLECTION ON CHAPTER 15

- All organizations go through (dancing) cycles.
- The processmind's dance of the ancient one in back of our world has been seen in dancing universe figures such as Nataraja and Shiva.
- Dance to be at home in the universe to bring your organization home.

CHAPTER 16

The Mediator as Meditator

World change happens when we remember some form of space–time dreaming movement meditation while working with others. We live in a relational world — that sounds like an obvious statement. But what do I mean by relational? For me, relational means that we live in a field of coupled, interacting processes. For example, you can kill the person — a dictator — but not the dictator ghost role. We need large-group awareness processes; not just hiring, firing, and war!

I would guess that many people will agree with me. Why then don't we do such group awareness processes more often? Most people avoid public processes in part because they fear that a divorced energy, X, that we have always disliked will grab us! Perhaps it is a divorced energy that we have been avoiding since the age of 3. Or we fear its appearance in public. Perhaps we fear that we will become possessed like the X. What's the solution? Bring X consciously with you into public life. For example, before doing a large-group process, try to play out in your imagination the worst X energy that might trouble you. Your facilitation work begins before you meet any real people.

Help others to realize that we live in a world filled with ghosts waiting to be related to! We live in a relational world. As I have said so often, we can kill, for example, Saddam Hussein — I think very few people who I knew liked him. You can kill the person, but you cannot kill the role. Hey, that is such a simple thought. Remember, someone else will fill that role right away. So all your energy is consciously or unconsciously focused on, "Get that person!" And we forget that the dictator role is actually needed. It has the power to get things done. Even the so-called *terrorist* is needed in a way: we may need the essence of the *terrorist*, that forceful commitment to stand for something. It is in the background of all of us. It does not just belong out there in the newspapers and the public situations. Be careful of going after the people only and forgetting the roles. If they scare you, bring them with you and play them out in public in some way.

Imagine a new world in which leaders make a home for their opponents and even model becoming them for short periods of time! Think of a country leader saying to one of her or his enemies, "You know, about once a month I feel a little bit like you!" People would laugh. Of course, it has to be done in a way that fits politically, but somehow saying that you are a little bit like the other models a new world politics. Elect leaders who can go deep inside to the system mind and explore the shared roles in the space between us. It is the Tao or, as I have said before, space–time dreaming. Let yourself be nonlinear. A linear speaker is usually a nervous speaker because there is always something trying to curve her or him. Call it an X, call it what you like. With space–time dreaming, you are a little bit looser in the middle of tension. Nature says, "You should be tense," but she also says, "Remember your dreaming and let your body be moved!"

Something in me says, "Arny, do you expect people to look relaxed while walking around like they are tipsy and drunk?" I laugh when we see the police stop people driving on the highway who look like they are weaving and doing space–time! The mark of the normal person is supposed to be that he or she walks straight! That is only a very small part of us.

Learning how to follow the universe and space–time curvature makes us creative. If you are sitting at a board meeting in a very straight situation that doesn't know you very well, just slightly swaying in your chair will help you move into your space-time dreaming. You look reasonable enough; you look like you are thinking, but you are not. You are swaying a little, feeling, *thinking*, then suddenly **aha**! It is just your creative mind, your dreaming mind. Getting to that dreaming while awake state is something that modern organizations around the world are beginning to realize is important to do. This is a very powerful way of doing it. You can do it sitting, you don't have to do it standing. We will be exploring that sitting version in a few minutes.

I always hear the voice, "What if I can't do it under difficult circumstances?" What is the answer? What if you can't do it under difficult circumstances? My answer is, "That is right, you can't do it, but *it* can!" You cannot do it with your everyday mind. It is something that happens to you through space–time stochastic dreaming. I can prove it. How? Every night when you go to bed you relax and all sorts of weird stuff comes up. You are so relaxed in bed that sometimes you blow a fart. Now, that is not necessarily a creative act ☺ but it shows that you are freer to dream!

In this part, Part 4 of the book, we have been focusing on a feeling skill, that of the mediator as a meditator. *Mediator* means being in between two or more parties. But meditate is connected to *medi* or healing as in medicine. Process oriented meditation heals the split between your everyday mind and your deeper self, your dreaming. And mediation occurs in between people. Meditation involves healing the split in relationships. Being closer to your basic self will help you enjoy whatever you are doing. Stop, if you are too uptight, and go deeper.

Meditating as a mediator will help you with what I call the A-B-Cs of world conflict.

- Your problems are not just yours. They belong to the environment. Anybody who knows you, anybody who bumps into you, might share the same problem. There is no such thing as a problem that is only yours. Now that sounds pretty strange because psychology works on your problems as personal problems. But *your* problems are often conflicts between your images of what is in the field. If I start meditating on myself, I can just about read into the field of people or organizations I work for.

- Even if you claim you have no problems, the earth around you will give you some. Some people say they have no problems. I respect that, but the world gives you problems even if you have none. Because of nonlocality, the world out there is your problem.

- Everybody is forced to become part of a conflict, but you can choose to become the whole, the home, for the rest of your earth family. It is being a bodhisattva, someone who returns to help everybody including her or himself. Either you are part of the situation or you are the whole. If you are the whole, you feel a little better, at least temporarily. It is quite natural to be a part, and it is important that you feel the whole at the same time.

Metaskills of Home

The process oriented mediator makes a *home* for all the parts. If you can help all the parties to feel more or less at home, without any further skills, many of the difficulties are already resolved. "Come home, have a cup of tea, do this or that." If you feel a shared sense of connection with others, that all parts and people are aspects of your universe family, then a kind of community atmosphere helps to resolves problems. Can you make a home when you are in a muddle with somebody, with others who you don't like very much?

I am going to show you the biggest muddle that I know [Arny enacts a fight with Amy]:

Arny: You did it!

Amy: Are you crazy? You did it!

Arny: No! Days ago, when I was feeling so quiet, you did it!

Amy: That's not true!. You started it before then!!

Arny: What are you talking about? I am just a quiet, peaceful person!

Amy: That's not true! I am the one who is always peaceful in this relationship!

What is the structure of that muddle?

There is a u and an X. The u is the part with which we identify ("I am a quiet person!"), and the secondary process is X ("Grr! The other made trouble for me!").

In the front there are Amy and Arny so to speak, and underneath is a u and an X for each, which are entangled; a quiet energy and a louder, noisier, aggressive energy. Who plays the roles of u or X switches back and forth. We unconsciously role switch. People fight and, without realizing it, rotate between the u + X without awareness. There are two people and one process. Therefore, you need a system mind, a process-mind, or your dreaming mind in order to be able to process those role switches. Can you get deep enough when you are in the middle of a muddle? How can you make a home for both the u and the X? How can you make a home for both the quiet one and the noisy one? Imagine being able to be both a part and the home for all parts at the same time. Doing both makes you an enlightened mediator!

The world needs a whole lot of social changes, ecological insights, and environmental fixes. We want to solve these things but rank differences abound. Some groups have more money and more power, some have less, and many have been abused. Can we solve things with simply a few changes? Not easily. But more than anything, we all need to go deeper for ongoing community and world teamwork.

Audience: When you are in a complex, it is impossible to get to this place.

Arny: It is impossible! On the other hand, you go to sleep at least once every couple of nights. You do go to sleep once every couple of nights!

Audience: True, I must remember sleep!

Arny: I want you to look forward to a bad conflict and think "Yes! This is my chance to develop!" I am exaggerating, but I am excited and it is a big thing. Thank you for asking that. It is a meditation practice and it takes time, so be kind to yourself while learning to mediate.

WHAT IS A COMMUNITY?

We live in a world that is relational and often adversarial. That adversarial quality is one aspect of the world, and another aspect to the world is the entanglement underneath, which humans have perceived in varying ways for millennia (think, Tao, *unus mundus*, Shiva, Tilopa, Nataraja, to mention just a few). Most of the time we marginalize these entanglement experiences and deal only with parts at the surface of reality. But the sense of *home* and of community is not complete without these deeper levels as well. The elder in you knows that. If you have been through enough trouble or have been pushed around, you survive in part by becoming a bit of an elder. That helps you create a home and sense of community for others around you.

Let's practice meditating while mediating. I suggest you do this exercise with three people. If you work together with others as a mediator, you should do this exercise with your colleagues before any outer work you do. In any case, one of you will describe a problem, and, after working on herself, facilitate that problem while the other two act it out. Choose a family, team, or organizational relationship issue that you would like to be able to facilitate better. It is possible that you are one of the members of the relationship trouble on which you want to work. If you are in an organization and have trouble with a person, you can work on that connection, or you can work on a relationship between two other people. The goal is to create a home in which conflicts can get resolved. Here, let's think about a fight or argument between two parties or people who are on a team or in a family.

When your partners act out the two parts of the relationship conflict, first try facilitating them by using any relationship skills you have. Then we are going to ask you to stop, and the two helpers will support you to get back into your universe dance. Let that dance guide you to facilitate further, until things flow. Maybe your *ancient one* will read deeply into one side and maybe it will read deeply into the other. The idea is that from its perspective, it will know even more how to facilitate the situation.

Please note, the facilitator is beginning to succeed if one of the role players changes sides while playing a role. As a player, don't push yourself to keep going in that role if you feel the facilitation beginning to change you.

Exercise: The Meditator as Mediator in Family or Organizational Relationship Problems

In triads, you will need paper and pen.

1. Meditator-facilitator: Choose and discuss a troublesome family, team, or organizational relationship problem. (You can be one of the sides of the problem.) One of the helpers should guide the facilitator in the following inner work:

    What energy, X, bothers you most in this family, team, or organizational relationship problem? Act out this X energy. What does it feel like? Where do you feel it most in your body? Feel it there, make a posture that goes with it and a movement with your hands or whole body to express it. Then make a quick sketch and name this X on paper.

    What part of you, *u*, is most disturbed by that X energy? Act out this *u*. What does it feel like? Where do you feel it most in your body? Feel it there, make a posture that goes with it and a movement with your hands or whole body to express it. Then name and sketch this energy on your paper.

    Now choose a special earth spot that you love. If there are many, spontaneously choose one on which to focus in the moment. Imagine that you go there and look around and notice where you see the X + *u* energies represented by some aspects of that earth spot. Now, feel yourself on that earth spot and let it breathe you and begin to move you about. As it dances you, let it express the X + u energies as it moves back and forth between them.

Now, as you are moving, sense how this earth spot is also part of the universe all around it. And let the universe's atmosphere begin to move you spontaneously about. Feel the sense of being moved and continue until you feel yourself moving unpredictably. Notice and let spontaneous motions happen. (Be careful not to hurt yourself.) When you sense the universe moving you freely, bring this movement experience back to the earth spot and let this dance help you explore and swing between the u + X energies there until some insight occurs. Write your insight down.

2. Helpers: Please now act out the people or u + X sides of the facilitator's problem.

    a. Facilitator: Now, enter that dyad problem: For 5 minutes use any first training methods you know (e.g., double signals, edges) to work with the problem. After 5 minutes or so, facilitator, STOP and remember to re-feel your universe dance and *meditate to mediate*: that is, stay deep inside while outside shamanizing, reading into the u + X energies. Write down any insights.

    b. All together: Discuss insights and the effect of the facilitator's processmind dreaming.

       There is a deep intelligence in everyone that can bring up all sorts of understanding of the different sides that the ordinary mind probably won't understand.

Audience 1: This worked for me. I found out that I could sit more quietly in the midst of an intense family battle. Being so detached enabled me to understand and support the other people without actually being interested any longer in the battle. Things relaxed by themselves in part because of this surprising detachment.

Audience 2: What is the theory behind always being able to find the X and the u energies in any earth spot? What is the thinking behind that idea?

Arny: Aboriginal thinking and the scientist in me think that certain earth spots are similar to energies that we have. You love certain spots, you feel certain spots. First it is just a feeling thing. You can feel very connected to earth spots. They are healing spots. In my *Shaman's Body*, I bring out Carlos Castaneda stories where his Yaqui Indian shaman, don Juan, says that the mark of somebody who is going to become a shaman is the ability to find a healing spot any place on a porch, on any porch or in any room anywhere. One spot will feel a little bit better to you. It is just a feeling thing, but it is really an ancient ability that people have reported since the beginning of time.

There will be a part of the room that makes you feel less well, that you stay away from. Anywhere, anytime, nature's diversity is always abundant if we perceive it. This is the basic idea here, diversity is always present on this planet. But she, the planet, and the universe are also the earth beneath our feet and the *home* space between us and behind all diversity issues.

Audience 2: In the exercise the X energy was a stinging knife pointed at me, and in nature it turned into a seagull, moving down with its beak pointed toward its prey. And what I realized is when I go to nature, it relieves my everyday mind, my judgments. It is neutral. In nature it is something that just *is*, and it opens my heart to the energy and the people in my life personifying that energy. The seagull had an overview and was able to fly. This was an aspect that the stinging knife did not have in consensus reality.

I learned a lot about detachment from the near-death experience of C.G. Jung, that I described in chapter 8. Remember that in his heart-attack vision he went into the universe. I thought about that for years and realized that he was actually trying to get more distance from everyday life. Something in all of us says, "Let me get away a little bit and look at the whole mess from a distance." It is a psychological move. My direction is to help you see that the world is your ashram, the street fight is the place for your development. Facilitation is both a mechanical meditation method and also an unpredictable art.

Learning this space–time dreaming facilitation skill depends upon your movement meditation practice whereby you physically anchor the feeling sense of space–time dreaming. I remember that sense and I look for it again when I am in a tense spot. Remember to stay open to the X energy and seek what it could be giving you because it is an energy you need. Some people are helped by the teachings of Buddhism. It reminds us that everything only looks fixed or stable or solid, but that really it is *maya* or illusion. Some people may be helped by thinking that every tense situation is a chance for nature to reveal her wisdom. Some are helped by remembering dreaming and altered states. Being grounded and tipsy at the same time really is the whole point, the practice, of bringing those worlds together.

Seeking detachment is what I call the fourth great drive. Sex, hunger, and thirst are the first big three. I call *the fourth drive*, the great drive to transcend the present moment and the need for ecstasy of some sort, for finding community as a living fluid, conscious experience. Not valuing this drive, drives people to various edges: to high-speed cars, to drugs and addictions, or to depression. Remember that creating a sense of home means that you are making a home for the way people are, as well as for what has not yet been expressed. Some of you have been doing it all your lives. You do it automatically, which is why you are interested in facilitating. Otherwise, you would not be here. You already know how to do this. Remember that meditating and mediating are similar. They only have one "t" difference.

....

Σ   FOR REFLECTION ON CHAPTER 16

- Meditate while mediating organizational processes.

- The world is filled with ghosts (roles) waiting for relationship!

- A next step in politics is for everyone to make a home for opponents by modeling becoming them for short periods of time.

- Seeking detachment is the fourth great drive.

CHAPTER 17

Race, Religion, and LGBTQ Conflicts

Serious ongoing conflicts worldwide often center around themes so-cially identified as *race*, religion, and tribal associations. Since everyone belongs to one or more races or religions (including agnostics and athe-ists) and sexual orientations, international facilitators need to be aware of their own issues in these areas. We all need training in detachment and fluidity and to more deeply understand each of these categories. We need to realize that some of these categories (such as *race*) are so-cial constructs that are defined by momentary human thinking, not by natural or biological law.

Working with highly emotional issues pressed me to find a way to deal with charged scenes. I have learned a lot from Patanjali, the mythic parent of yoga. Remember him from chapter 6. He implies in his *Yoga Sutras* that enlightenment is a matter of "becoming a dead man in life" or, I would say, a "dead person in life."[80] This statement refers to the process of letting your little *u* die and being reborn with more connec-tion to your deepest meditative nature. I also want to speak in favor of remembering your personal history and using it to help people today, not just dropping it but gaining a little detachment from it and remem-bering it from a distance. This *remembering* is a form of what I believe Patanjali meant by twice born.[81] Once is enough for some of us! *Twice born* means you renew your experience of life through connection with deep meditative states.

If you do inner work with the periods in which you are tired and depressed, you can *die* in a metaphorical sense, and if you can consciously let go while connecting to the processmind, a second birth, so to speak, occurs. If you don't do it consciously, your body will just sink you down sometimes: "I have had enough!" This could be an important moment to go down inside yourself. Normally, most people look down on times when they get tired or depressed, but it is not necessarily a bad thing. It is perhaps the beginning of the twice born experience.

I speak of enlightenment experiences in the midst of conflict work because facilitation is both a real and a spiritual task. An enlightened person, in my mind at least, is someone who is sometimes in touch with the whole universe and can help others feel that as well. I don't like seeing great leaders being shot, Martin Luther King, Gandhi, John Kennedy... these incredible people. I don't like it when I see teachers of mine who were fantastic people die on a stage because they were trying to stand for something new and unknown. I have worked with world leaders who were afraid of being killed, and actors and actresses who were afraid they would be shot on stage. Learning how to drop down, go down underneath, is not only an aspect of everyone's natural process, it may also be protective.

Please try to *die* before you are killed. There has never been a mediator who is not nervous, at one moment or another, that he or she is going to be shot down. It is the same thing. There is going to be someone who says, "You stupid idiot! You are the wrong age, race, color, gender, religion, or sexual orientation or you are too big, too small, fat, thin, et cetera!" Boom! Your abuse issues in the background are always waiting to get reconstellated.

If you are nervous about something, that could be your lucky moment! You might think, "Someone does not like me, someone is after me, someone is going to hurt me. I will repress that, just take it, breathe deeply." But don't repress it, for this feeling could be the beginning of enlightenment. Perfect! Instead, take the next step and bring your human family, the *u*'s + X's, *home*. This is the best approach for you both outside and inside.

Now, before dealing with large group conflicts around race and religion, let's think about *tokenism*. Everyone has had the experience of being lower in rank at one moment or another. Everyone has at least a tiny experience of being a minority person, even if it was just being a child in your family system. Some people always have more rank.

But everyone has some experience of rank and some have lifelong experience, whether it is around racism or sexism, homophobia, age-ism, healthisms, et cetera. Everywhere on earth you must be careful about Islamophobia (fear of Muslims), anti-Semitism, ageism, sexism, healthism, homophobia, economic differences. All of these things give you a sense of rank or lack of rank. At some point or another, every-body knows what it is like to have less rank.

I have spoken of rank before in my book, *Sitting in the Fire*. Now I want to explore tokenism, which is a most subtle abuse of someone with less rank than you. Tokenism occurs when a person with more privilege acts inclusively toward a person of lesser privilege or less rank without there being a true interest in the person. Tokenism can be unintentional. For example, if a newspaper hires someone with a Jew-ish name to write against Israel and then fires the person shortly after the article came out on the grounds that the paper "no longer needs" that person, tokenism may have been involved. A US example would be hiring an African American person to write against affirmative ac-tion and then later dismissing her or him. This may be conscious or unconscious tokenism.

Tokenism can be expressed as a double signal that is due, in part, to national or global systemic unconsciousness. One signal says, "I like you," and the other says the opposite. Tokenism is often ingrained in the whole system. Some modern democracies insist upon being nice to groups of people who have been hurt by the system. This stance is good but can also be hurtful. I am stressing the tokenism concept be-cause when it is unconscious, it is most often hurtful. As the minority person, it can leave you with a sense, afterwards, of, "Hmm, they don't really like me for me!"

For example, rewarding a gay person, or more generally an LG-BTQ (lesbian, gay, bisexual, transsexual, queer) person, to take a stand against gay marriage can be a double signal. The primary signal is, "I want to model being a good system, I want to be a good heterosexual person and hire minorities. I want to be nice, even though I don't re-ally care about them and am not conscious of my invisible privilege or of how I am using others without really caring about them as people." Behind tokenism, on the part of the tokenizer and also of the token per-son, is often ambition, wanting to get ahead, and the subtle belief that, "Your worth depends upon public opinion."

Another example: Worldwide, I have a great deal of privilege just because I am a man, speak English, am American, and because of my light skin color. But in some places, at some times, I may have less privilege. Some years ago a large organization in Germany hired us. At first I was quite enthusiastic about the prospect. I thought, "That is a great idea! Why not?" and in the process I marginalized aspects of myself that were suspicious and doubtful even while saying yes. The experience with that organization did not work out very well because I did not really feel liked by these people. They were not really interested in me and in what Amy and I were doing. They wanted to use us, in part, because, "We need Jewish people. They will help us on our path." And so we separated from that organization after a while. I said yes to them originally because I thought the association would help us "get ahead" and I marginalized my other feelings: "Who cares about you as a person, Arny, and your feelings? Maybe what they are doing, they are doing because of tokenistic reasons?"

My point is that the tokenizer is not just outside, it is inside us as well! We all need awareness and the courage to discuss our awareness of personal and social issues.

Amy: I was not conscious of it at all, of being identified as Jew-
         ish or any of that. I was just happy to be able to be with the
         big group. We shared ideas, and I thought that was really
         great. Then afterwards, realizing that they were not really
         interested in us, I felt used in a way because of our back-
         ground in that particular place and, for various reasons,
         we decided to separate in a decent way.

Arny: Remember, most of the time people don't realize they are
         being tokenistic. It is often unintentional. It is a systemic
         problem, and most individuals are not conscious of it. That
         is why I say it can be a subtle thing that looks partly well
         meant. The main point: Tokenism is often a double signal.
         One signal says, "Let's both get ahead in the world and
         appear open-minded," and the other says, "We don't care
         about you as a person."

In consensus reality, you have more power or less power depend-ing upon the situation. But from the dreamland viewpoint, everyone, even the so-called *minority* person, can have a lot of power. As a mat-ter of fact, feeling like the victim of a situation can give you what I call *victim rank*, which means a sense of spiritual outrage. This too can be as harmful as it can be good. But my bigger point is that you can be the victim of a consensus reality situation and, at the same time, the facilitator of the mess in spite of its complexity. From the deepest level of understanding, there is no clear fault (though fault or blame surely is assigned in consensus reality). From the deepest viewpoint, it is not just this side or that at fault, everybody needs to know their greatest powers and use those powers consciously when possible.

9/11: Race and Religion Diversity Issues

Before doing large-group work around the US issue of 9/11, let's work on the sense of marginalization because it brings up uncomfortable feelings in everyone. Knowing how to work with those feelings inside yourself requires an open-heartedness with yourself. The following exercise is an opportunity to work on a sense of being marginalized in your life. Marginalization may be something you feel all the time—it may be based on your race or gender, sexual orientation, financial situation, or health. You may have areas of more social rank, for example, for how you look, for your intelligence. There are many different factors. The point of this exercise to make it easier to work as an individual or team to prepare for an organizational or open forum on such issues.

Inner Work: Marginalization and Your Zen Mind

1. Think of some situation where you feel or felt socially marginalized or hurt. It may be something you feel all the time; based on race or gender, sexual orientation, age, health issues, et cetera. You may have been put down for how you looked, for your intelligence, or for your lack of intelligence. Everybody has had something or some combination of things. Who used rank against you in that situation? Make a note.

2. What is the X energy like of the person or people who used rank against you? Act out this X energy and sense where you feel X most strongly in your body. Now express this energy with a body motion and make a sketch and name it on your paper.

3. What part of you, u, is most disturbed by that X energy? Act it out and sense where you feel it most in your body and then express it with a body motion. And then, make a sketch and name this u energy on paper.

4. Now, choose a favorite earth spot. If there are many, spontaneously choose one on which to focus in the moment. Imagine that you go there and look around and notice where you see the u + X energies represented by some aspect of that earth spot. Now

feel yourself there, and let the earth spot breathe you and move you. Let it begin to express the $u + X$ energies as parts of itself as it moves you back and forth between them.

5. Now, as you are moving, sense how this earth spot is in the universe all around it. Feel how the universe's spaces move you spontaneously about. Feel the sense of "being moved" and continue until you feel yourself moving unpredictably. (Be careful of things and of others around you.) When you sense the universe moving you freely, bring this movement experience back to the earth spot and let the dance, with its universe perspective, help you explore and swing more deeply between the $u + X$ energies there until some insight occurs. Make a note.

6. Move back and forth until some sort of little tiny insight occurs; you must write it down because such insights are noncognitive and easy to forget. Those insights might be useful; they may give you lessons about how to use your various energies, how to deal with them, how to deal with outer circumstances. Then we will go on to our group process.

GROUP PROCESS

There are various ways of doing group process, as you know. The exact form of a group process depends upon the culture. If you do group process in Japan, it is often a little quieter. In South America, people often speak simultaneously with one another. If you do it in Russia, it can be quite dynamic. The specifics depend upon the culture. They are different in African cultures and in European cultures. There is no one way that is right.

I want to recommend to the person who is facilitating that you remember the various cultures and that some cultures may be shy and need to be invited to speak. It is important to remember that there are various peoples, cultures, countries, and nations here. So let's see who will facilitate the next group process.

[Arny spins the pen among the participants of one of his seminars and it *chooses* Mohammad as facilitator.]

Arny: Thank you for offering to be the facilitator! What sort of things happened when you work on yourself just now in the exercise? Being Palestinian in the United

	States, I can easily imagine that you have plenty of outer things that would disturb you.
Mohammad:	The name Mohammad itself is huge.
Amy:	When people hear your name?
Mohammad:	Yes, especially here in the US…
Arny:	Islamophobia is painful. What X's + *u*'s have been coming up for you?
Mohammad:	X attacks me for being a terrorist, and the *u* is pretty peaceful, happy, the opposite of what people would think. I am not going to bomb you right away!!
Arny:	That is well said, and such a hard thing! It is good to laugh about it. The *u* part is the opposite of X. Is there anything that can help you in your own learning?
Mohammad:	This is my first time here as facilitator! I am glad the pen, or the Tao or whatever, has chosen me. My inner work gave me some distance, let's see what happens.
Arny:	Yes, we can talk with you especially afterwards and go into things personally after we end.

After an hour long group process dealing with much pain and wonder …

Arny:	That was an amazing group process! To be more complete, we should now break up into small groups to discuss specific diversity issues that arose. After that, a next step would be to take all that we learned into the public, to TV, and the Internet. Take it out on the city streets. But since this is a training session, first, let me interview Mohammad.
	Dear Mohammad, let's talk about your experience of facilitating that complex situation! First, let me ask, do you have a sense of any deep reason for being on this planet? Just luck? I know that's practically impossible to answer, but still…
Mohammad:	Be yourself. Do not let someone else represent you, show who you are really, not those who say they are representing you. And live your own sense of democracy again.

Arny:	To hear that statement just once is enough to make me forget everything else. Live your democracy!
Mohammad:	It is hard. I think I hope to make change in a way. I know everything on the side of the victim, and now I am trying to learn things over here.
Arny:	Thanks for saying that. Sometimes you are a little shy, sometimes not. May I experiment bringing out your strength more? Let's grasp each other's hands and push. [Arny and Mohammad grasp hands and press gently and then more strongly against one another.] Don't hesitate, keep going… I love that strength about you. You are smiling, how come?
Mohammad:	I like it, too! I am surprised.
Arny:	I am trying to show you that you are a person with a lot of inner and outer power. It is like this [pushing against Mohammad's hands] and you handle it really well. Your specific style of mediating is generous. You say you are on the side of the victims, but you were anything but one-sided. You have a lot of power. I could never teach you that. It is in you as a person, and your quiet strength and inner composure are facilitative. These are qualities from your processmind and you use them very well.
	Now, I have one question. As our arms meet, feel your strength, and imagine using your full strength also to lead everyone. How can you use that power to speak the truth of what you feel? How can you use that power even more to go deep in yourself and help others? How can you use it to flow a little bit more? There is no one answer to these questions. The answers will change every week, but how can you feel those things now? You are looking at me, and we are smiling at one another.
Mohammad:	I see my strength there, it is obvious. I am trying to bring it here, but I need the support to bring it here. This Western world, this is my problem and my playground! I know what is going on here. And I have been living for a year here but don't understand it well. So I cannot advise Americans and Europeans.

DANCE OF THE ANCIENT ONE

Arny:	But you might advise us, a little.
Mohammad:	OK… be aware, educate, bring awareness! I want all of you to open your minds for the others!
Arny:	Very good! We should open our minds to other people, and we have not yet. Telling us to do it is a really good thing. Can you support us in how to do this?
Mohammad:	I am here in this country for a year. Could you open up for me, too? I am pretty safe, so if you are not open for me, then you will not be open for the people there. Try to be open with me first.
Arny:	We need encouragement too. We are troublesome but also we are babies about opening up, as you say we must. We are babies and we are adults. That is, a new identity is growing; becoming the adult, the parent, the one who is the *home*. To facilitate the very thing that is driving you insane you are called upon to facilitate a situation in which you are a minority. That is almost impossible. And there is some crazy, amazing power inside of you that is you. I don't know where that damn thing comes from, but it is the thing that makes you dream. No mind, empty mind, processmind, god mind, whatever you want to call it; you know the things that move you and that is the essence of the facilitator, that allowed you to move from one side to another, remembering that you are the parent and not the child only. Thank you.

[Now addressing everyone]

People, feel your power, your presence. It precedes us. Your own processmind, your special powers, your beauty precedes you. It was that presence to which I was referring with Mohammad; his presence is not something that someone else can develop. It is a kind of power each person possesses. Making it conscious and using that power is a big thing. It takes years and years, and at the same time, it takes not even one minute. Maybe you can see it in your baby picture. Ask your friends what it is they sense about you, even when you are not around!

Even if you are in a group that has a minority status in one culture, and you feel hurt and downed by that, your sense of power is still there. In fact, with some people (this is not true for everybody), a minority status may even bring that power out more; sometimes it comes out as an aggression, but whatever, it is still there. I want to stress this point. Having been marginalized is really hurtful and downing, and at the same time there is another rank that comes from living through it. It is a rank, too. I sometimes call it a spiritual rank.

Remember, we are in the universe's space even though we only identify with the spot on earth on which we are standing. We are not just parts in dialogue, but the dance between the parts. Your process-mind is a stochastic dance. The parts are connected with your identity, but the dance is your larger self.

Let's turn now to using meditation with conflicts around the LGBTQ scene. Before we do group processes around this area, let me ask a question: Do you know how many countries or sovereign states there are in the world today, in 2012? There are around 204. Do know how many allow same-sex marriages? There are 12. That means 1 in 17 allows such marriages. It is a massive issue and one that is, to some extent, invisible. As a result, people who have other than heterosexual orientations in relationship are frequently troubled by fear of others. So, it is a huge psychological problem as well as social issue. I have worked with family scenes where teenagers wanted to kill themselves because they could not come out to their family. But their story, the pain of these kids is not just awful and is not for nothing. It has helped me move major groups in the United States that are against gays. This social issue is a medical emergency. The government, the school systems need to change everywhere.

I am in pain about those near and actual suicides. Why do people have to kill themselves to bring about change? It has been many years since we did an open forum on sexual orientation issues in Portland, but the forum we did is still run on the public cable channel. Do a forum on social issues, call your local TV program, and have them come and video it. It cannot hurt and can do some good.

Let's go through a quick inner work first, one that we have been practicing. Everybody needs to find their center in this issue before we work on it publicly. I am going to be asking you about the worst and most difficult X energy in the whole issue around sexual orientation. It may be something you have experienced personally, it may be something you react to or hear about in the world or whatever. It will be your own experience.

Please note: If you can't get to your deepest self on this or any issue, there may be one of three things to consider:

- Your little *u* inside of you has not been expressed enough: For example, "I am scared. I want to do it but I don't know how." Give voice to whatever that little *u* inside of you is feeling. It needs to come out completely because if it has not been expressed enough, it will inhibit you.

- The second possible problem is the X: What exactly disturbs you about that X? What are you afraid of? That disturbance or fear needs full expression first, otherwise you cannot just drop out.

- The third possibility is that you are just at an edge to let go and relax, move around, and dream.

  OK, let's try to apply this *u* + X exercise to LGBTQ issues.

INNER WORK

1. Think to yourself: What is the worst role, person, or group in the whole issue around sexual orientation and LGBTQ issues? What is the worst and most difficult role for you? What is the most painful, difficult, disturbing area? It might be a particular kind of person or group that disturbs you, a particular energy, or a lot of them might disturb you. See if you can find one main focus to begin with.

2. Remember what that role or person or group is like. What is the X energy of that role or person or group? What is the energy like that is so disturbing for you? See if you can feel it and make a gesture that represents the energy that is so disturbing or difficult. Feel what that is like in your body. Get a good sense of that X energy.

3. Now ask yourself what part of you, *u*, is most disturbed by that X energy? What is that part of you like? Make a gesture and feel what that part of you is like in your body.

4. Now think about one of the earth spots that you love. Imagine that spot, imagine you are there, and look around that spot. See if you can identify those energies. Where is that X energy represented in that earth spot? Where do you see the quality of energy of the *u* in that earth spot?

5. When you feel those earth positions, sense yourself as if you are each of them, and let each one move you about. For a moment, express that X energy in motion and then let it express its *u* energy.

Go back and forth between the two energies for a few minutes. Experience both of those things. As you are doing that, moving back and forth, feel how those earth spots are connected to the larger universe, cosmos, or solar system.

6. Let that universe feeling move you a little bit. Relax a little bit into it and let it move you even in your chair, let it move you about, feel a little bit of looseness. Feel a little bit of that spaciousness and looseness the universe brings as it moves you. And then, when you are ready, let your experience of that space, that universe, that relaxation come back and explore a little more deeply the X energy and u energy of those earth spots. Perhaps those earth spots of the X + u energies will give you an insight you did not know or had not experienced before from this new perspective. Let that insight flow back and forth between those energies from the universe perspective and see what it adds or brings.

7. If you get some insight, go ahead and make a note about it.

After this inner work, people facilitated a large group process. Very rapidly, the large group entered into a vehement group process around LGBTQ issues that brought up fear and abuse for many. One group of lesbians at one spot in the world was irritating to some heterosexuals because those lesbians were so powerful. Others rallied against the heterosexuals in part because, without that powerfulness, those women would have no place to live and be.

The process ended with an uncanny moment of mainstream understanding of minority LGBTQ experience. But this moment also brought forward all sorts of other problems in the group, problems connected with feeling hurt and powerless against larger forces. This often happens. Working well with one group process encourages people to go further into new or as yet untouched subjects.

Under these circumstances, one woman was reminded of her experience of having been kidnapped in a South American country. It seems to me that her difficult story was characteristic not only of her own experience of being mishandled but of all LGBTQ people.

ABUSE AND RELIEF: WORKING WITH SOMEONE WHO WAS KIDNAPPED

Sonia: Thanks everyone for letting me go into my history around the topic of abuse, I must speak about the fact that my country, Colombia, terrifies me. The painful part about being in that horrible place is trying to find how to enter the social issues in that country and what to do about it in a way that really contributes to helping everyone, the abusers and the abused!

Arny: [Realizing that people do not know what she was speaking about] Sonia, when you say you are trying to find what to do about it, what is this *it*? Let's say I did not know the story of Colombia, what is this it?

Sonia: It is the hopelessness about violence. The numbness about what is going on. It is like we have erased what is really going on and have continued with our lives.

Arny: What is it that is going on? Rebel groups fighting one another, drug cartels, violence between ethnically diverse groups?

Sonia: War, death, killing, kidnappings.

Arny: You seem to know a lot about that, too much! I can guess what you have been through, so I want to be especially delicate.

Sonia: It is ok. I bring it up because I am really looking for the way to get into working with it. Should I just let it go? What should I do?

Arny: [Playing the suspected roles for Sonia] If you have been kidnapped and been badly dealt with, you know there is an aggressor out there who is violent and will do almost anything to get what they need. Since you are open to working on this, let's say that there is an X that needs to be expressed. There is also a *u*, which probably says something like, "I want to do something but am nervous about it... the people who are violent are..." How would you describe them?

Sonia: They are blind killers. They have blind revenge.

Arny:	Are you at the point where you can show some of the blind revenge energy of those people?
Sonia:	Right now? They are cold, like a stone. Nothing can penetrate that. They are like a bomb that will take out everything in its way, it does not matter... it just walks through everything. There is no heart there or feelings or anything there.
Arny:	[Checking to see if Sonia is well enough to go further] OK, are you ok?
Sonia:	Yes.
Arny:	I like your strength. And I also want to support the part that is most nervous about that, the part that hates the X aggressors and is the victim. Can we give that a place to speak?
Sonia:	I am afraid to die, I don't want to die, I am too young to die. I don't want to get killed. I am scared...
Arny:	[Speaking for the *u*] "Don't kill me! I am afraid to die!"
Sonia:	[Suddenly switching to X] "I don't care about anything or anybody!"
Arny:	What is happening now? You seem to be smiling. What is happening with your hand, what is it doing?
Sonia:	My hand is here, by my heart. It is like I am protecting myself.
Arny:	OK, bring that protection out more to the surface if you can.
Sonia:	As *u*, I am protecting myself... against anything!
Arny:	There you go! The *u* picked up the X's energy. So touching. When you are ready, go ahead and tell us how you might use these energies in every day reality.
Sonia:	I am going to talk to people about this... that is what I am going to do. Fearlessly almost... I will say, "I have been through hell! It is painful... it is a pain, not only my pain, but the pain of all the people of my country. I am not talking only of myself. And it seems that whatever is going on in Colombia goes unheard in the world. There is a great deal of pain from kidnappings, war around there from ex-

ternal forces because of the drugs down there, and money pouring in that continues funding that war.

Arny: [as the X] What are you going to do with us? We have guns and are poor, and we want that money! I want more money, more drugs, and will kill.

Sonia: [Going on with the u] We have forgotten you. [Almost apologetically to the X] We are like unconscious zombies, doing whatever we want to do, and outside everything seems ok. Everything is fine, people are happy.

Arny: I am moved by what you said. What should Colombia be doing?

Sonia: We need to really be aware of the deep pain of living in a country that is at war, a daily pain, day and night. We cannot forget about that. It is hard for those who do not live there. Try to imagine! It is really tough to go to bed at night and not know if somebody is going to break into your own house and take you.

Arny: In your own house? Someone might come and take you?

Sonia: Yes. They enter into your own house. It is so hard! We listen to the news about kidnappings but how to get in touch with the feeling of death that is around us everyday that we rationalize! It is hard to get in touch with the feeling of real annihilation.

Arny: [Playing an X role in Colombia] What will you do with this energy that says, I want anything! I will kill for a little money! What will you do with me? GRRRRrrrr!"

Sonia: I don't know what to do!

Arny: [To Sonia] Follow your hands. Your hands are out. What are you going to do?

Sonia: I am not afraid of you. I have to say that, I am sorry I am not afraid of you!! [Now playing the abuser] You don't have any idea who I am! You do not know what I am like! You don't understand what it is to be forgotten by God. You don't know what it really means to be forgotten by God. There is nothing in me, there is nothing for me to hold onto.

Arny:	What happened to you? How did that happen? We don't really know you? I want to know you! Before you kill me, at least tell me who you are!
Sonia:	[Still playing the abuser] Life has no value to me at all. There is no value, there is no future, I have nothing. I have nothing to lose. [Becomes quieter] I have nothing to lose.
Arny:	[To Sonia as herself] That statement is so touching, it almost makes me want to join you. I see you are beginning to relax so let me say, let's bring this dialogue out on TV in Colombia and everywhere. I will help you do it.
Sonia:	Thank you!
Amy:	Thank you so much for going through that with all of us
Arny:	[To everyone] With the processmind, both the *u* + X need to be recognized and brought *home* and can be heard. I am deeply moved by that Colombian scene. I am so touched by her courage. The biggest thing stopping her may have been not having access to her processmind and therefore not having been able to shamanize and read into the attackers, into the X. To work with such difficult national and international situations, we all need to work on our own abuse issues and social fears to find fluidity and understanding for everyone who is involved.

Σ   FOR REFLECTION ON CHAPTER 17

- Finding your deepest self is enlightenment, it is like being *twice born*.

- Creating a *home* for everyone is the essence of meditation and mediation.

- Our realistic, financial, power-driven democracies need a deeper democracy and facilitators who are in contact with the deepest part of everyone, with our *home* in the universe.

- It takes a lot of inner strength and wisdom to facilitate group processes in countries if you are in a minority role. Remember how Mohammad's power needed to work in the US in spite of Islamophobia.

- Some LGBTQ issues are connected to mainstream misunderstanding of the pain and power of marginalized people.

- Mainstream repression of diversity issues in South America and elsewhere exaggerates minority group reactions that endanger everyone. Remember Sonia's story.

PART FIVE

Process Oriented Ecology

The way we marginalize parts of ourselves is the same way we marginalize others that we don't know, don't like, or whom we fear. In almost the same manner, the way we marginalize parts of ourselves, we also marginalize and *trash* parts of the environment. While this dynamic is part of our nature, it is also part of our nature to go deeper, to find some form of space–time dreaming, and to help the environment and the world with which we are often in great conflict.

Process oriented ecology, or POE, integrates psychology with earth systems. POE is both a science and an art that not only supports understanding the individual nature of our earth's peoples and parts but that stresses relationship consciousness between us all as well. We need a global theory and eldership training. We need to learn about the details and the parts and to understand and feel how the universe can put them together.

CHAPTER 18

Ecology as Science and Art

In this chapter, I emphasize that the space between us is our home for everything that exists. Space is our habitat, the place we inhabit. It is our home. Not only the earth but the universe is home. Said differently, to help our earth, we need to think like the universe, just as to help any system we need to get into the system's way of thinking.

18.1 Earth is Our Home (NASA).

In Greek, the word for home or house is *ecos*. Ecology is the science that studies the distribution and abundance (or scarcity) of living organisms and their interactions with other living organisms and their environment. This environment usually includes climate, geology, as well as the other organisms that share the living area.

Process oriented ecology includes not only the distribution and abundance of living organisms and interactions with other living organisms and their environment but also the possible feelings, dreams, nonlocal interactions, and space–time dreaming of all concerned. In other words, ecology is the study of our home, which includes the interactional processes in and between us and the rest of our living and nonliving world and universe. Our roots in the space around us connect us to everything else in the universe, our home.

18.2 The Universe IS Our Home (NASA).

Shamans such as Carlos Castaneda's don Juan are *eco-shamans* in the sense of working with the feelings or dreams of the environment. My interest in shamanism was centered on the magical field that the *Yaqui* Indian Mexican shamans called the *nagual*, meaning the mysterious force of the earth that moves us. The *nagual* is a kind of space–time dreaming. In this book, space–time dreaming has appeared in connection with dreaming, the Tao, the quantum mind, and the processmind.

We all tend to be eco-deniers. Every time we focus only on ourselves as if we were independent of the world around us, we deny not only the local environment as a living entity but also the earth and universe. Since ecology means the relationship between the animals and all things and their natural environment, we deny this if we marginalize our sense of relationship to the living and nonliving world. In this way, we are eco-deniers and, even without noticing it, dump trash everywhere. Thus, ecology is not just a scientific domain, it is also a social and psychological issue. When ecology is intermixed with issues of money, privilege, and classism; when people dump and trash places where real estate is inexpensive and people are poor, we might have eco– or environmental racism.

Psychology needs to be more ecologically oriented to be complete. Eco-psychology tries to bring psychology together with ecology. The direction was summed up by Theodore Roszack in his 1992 book, *The Voice of the Earth.*[82] We are aware of people but we don't take our experiences of the waters, trees, rocks, and animals as seriously. Eco-psychology forwards our relationship to the woods and the oceans and all natural environments and promotes caring for the earth on which we stand. It is a crucial factor in creating a planet that is sustainable for all living creatures. Ecology typically deals with the biosphere, the surface of the earth that is characteristic of life. Ecologists more rarely deal with outer space or simply the spaces between and around the earth.

System Mind in Ecology

Imagine that I have a big table in front of me and there is a mess on the table. I pass by and see the mess on the table. I say, "OK, let's clean up that mess," and I knock the mess off the table, it falls on the floor, and I walk away. Do you think what I just did is a good idea? I cleaned the table, but I made more of a mess on the floor. This is not a sustainable solution. How come? It does not solve the psychological problem of *dumping*. I simply displaced the mess. I treated the symptom of the mess allopathically instead of dealing with the *trasher*. It would be more complete if I had a mess cleaning party and created a home for all involved, including the trash and the trasher.

What happens if the city officers notice that some section of town is a little run down for different reasons, and so they decide to let the city dump all of its stuff there? It stinks! In one spot in the Bronx, a section in New York City, a few years ago you could not see the river any more because there was so much junk there. Where my grandmother used to live there was a river, but I never saw it because there was so much junk between my grandmother's building and the river. I only discovered the river recently. To see the river from her building, you had to take some of the junk down.

What would we do if an earthquake struck and made the mess? What would we do then? Who could we blame? What shall we do? Of course, each of you has your suspicions about possible answers. But this is a big question. Ecology must deal with the movements of the deeper earth, otherwise earthquakes, like the terrible one that hit Haiti, appear to come as a complete shock to most of us. It is terrible what the folks are going through down there [this section of the book is from a class in 2010]. We just recently worked with a group that wanted us to go down to Haiti. I gave help to a rescue organization's helicopter crews who were dropping food to the starving people.

Ecology and Worldwork are intimately connected. People were hurting each other as everyone struggled to get the food being dropped from the helicopters. I did some space–time dreaming while witnessing those events and realized that the violence of the earth was nature, and that I should not just criticize those struggling against others for food. It's natural. So I suggested attaching loud speakers to the bottom of the helicopters that were carrying food to the people and speaking to the *bad* people down there taking food from the old and ill: "Everyone is hungry! You are hungry! You have not eaten for a while and we are going to bring you some food. It's natural for you to want to fight over it. We understand that." We spoke to the X: "Don't fight more than needed, though, because then you will get hungrier." And that worked. The strongest and most fit came first to catch the food but instead of eating it for themselves, they actually passed it back to those who were not as strong.

If people are in serious need of basic life-sustaining provisions and we just throw it to them, then we should expect the kind of desperate behavior typically labeled as *bad*. We need to learn how to dream into others' psychological states so that we can join them rather than throw more rocks (negative labels) at them. Becoming conscious of the whole field allows us to understand neediness and also remember everyone.

One aspect of ecology focuses on the atmosphere, on the climate and climate change. How do we deal with global warming? Is it happening? How do we deal with all the associated difficulties? Have you been following this issue in the news? What happened at the 2009 United Nations Climate Change Conference, the Copenhagen Summit? The rich nations said, "We expect the poor nations to join us. We will give them some money, if necessary." The poor nations did not jump at this chance and the rich nations, scratching their heads, wondered, "How come they don't want to go along with us?" My answer was, there was not enough interaction ahead of time. There was no group process! Our whole planet increases its suffering by trying to deal with people and the earth independently of one another, studying the earth without considering human relationships. In short, changing one part without reference to the whole makes solutions unsustainable.

Ecology is mainly seen in Newtonian terms: cause and effect. If there is an effect, something fell onto the floor, let's pick it up or let's stop the person from causing it to fall in the first place. We need an interaction that encompasses everybody and everything with dreams, space–time, and gravity included.

As an example, what would you do with the person who threw junk on the street corner? Should you just walk by it yourself? How many times do you walk by junk on the streets and think, "Somebody just threw that stuff there!" Did you ever pick it up? Sometimes. Depends on your mood. Did you ever process it? What could be good about the person who threw the junk on the floor?

Process oriented ecology says, interact with the trasher, don't just trash the trasher. Is there anything good about having some junk and throwing it away? Sometimes we need to just let go of things. There is a meditation procedure about precisely that: Let it go. A great deal of Buddhism is about that notion. Can you just drop something in the moment? I am not saying that is a good thing, but to really combat something you also need to know that bad thing and recycle it. Don't throw out anything.

Process oriented ecology is bringing everything and everyone home. In deep democracy, everyone has a right to be heard! We need a home with the right *climate* or *atmosphere* in which to gain more understanding and create more teamwork. Then we can actualize the field of ecology as relationships between organisms and their environments. Ecology is about home and relationships. The bad guy may also possibly have something to offer. Those *bad guys* are more likely to join you if you think that way. Meditators who drop their inner junk and people who drop Coca Cola bottles are *bad* only from the perspective of *good people* who say recycle everything but who don't recycle the bad guys. Recycling is the metaskill. We need to recycle the bad guy. Don't throw her or him out. For example, in the past some South Pacific Island people would normally throw out things onto the street because that trash, in those past days, turned into fertilizer. Now, however, we have new products that don't biodegrade and instead accumulate. Dropping things used to be good. Now it is part of the disaster.

Doing good things without a system mind is not sustainable. Think of the island of Nantucket off of the US eastern coast. The idea arose there of installing wind turbines to create energy on this huge piece of land that is empty and goes right up to the ocean. Most think that is a great idea because it will save money and energy, but some native tribes there don't like the idea one bit. Those people need a clear view of the sky to watch the sun rise everyday, and those turbines present a huge conflict for them in terms of their beliefs and their religion. So they are taking the island government to court. To take one action is to affect the whole planet. Nantucket is its own ecosystem, definable as an island, the atmosphere above it, the water around it, and all its peoples.

ECOLOGY AS TAOISM?

Let me give you another example of amazing problems with an eco-system. Think of an island, a little island, on which you raise sheep who eat grass. Everything has been going really well until suddenly a lightning storm strikes and all your grass burns. Your sheep soon starve and you are now in bad shape. Oh my God, what next? Should you buy more sheep? How do you get that grass to grow back quickly? You don't know what to do. You are about ready to go to an ecologist in town on the mainland but instead of going to an ecologist, you decide to invite the neighboring Taoist. (Let's pretend there is a Taoist there.)

The distraught sheep rancher tells the Taoist, "My grass has burnt and my sheep are dying. What should I do?" And the Taoist says, "Oooh, hmmm. What to do?" This divination-oriented Taoist now does something that I hope everybody eventually learns how to do: She goes into the Tao and does some form of space–time dreaming. Maybe she just did it by meditating on the Tao. In any case, she says, "Ohh, Tao," and gives the answer; "Do nothing."

> "Oh, but I am starving!" protests the sheep rancher.
> "Do nothing! There is nothing to do," responds the Taoist.

Let's say the sheep rancher believes her at last and relaxes. What do you think happens? The rancher could die, that is a possibility, but in this scenario some seeds drift across to our island from the mainland, and they take hold on the outskirts of the island, escaping the fish, and before you know it in a week or two, there is grass growing there again. Isn't that wonderful? How could the Taoist have known that?

The Tao of space–time dreaming is a system mind. Taoism has not played a large enough role in modern ecology till now. I just want to say, it is needed! We need someone to go into the processmind of the area and see what is happening. The Taoist felt that no action was needed because although there was no grass then, soon there would be, perhaps. But how this might come about is a mystery, and we want to know more about that kind of mystery. Of course, she could also have said, "Move to the mainland!"

Ecology as a science should focus on essence-level experiences as well as on chemistry and biology, physics, climate change, erosion, and evolution. In this picture, let's envision an MIT ecological model. I have been corresponding with scientists there, looking at their global system model and discussing how this MIT group understands the world. They have advisors to government on questions of ecology. I want to look at one of their models of the world very briefly.

In Figure 18.3, there is a square area in the middle labeled Earth System. And that earth system has four parts to it: Atmosphere, Urban or city processes, the Land itself, and the Ocean. In the center of the diagram, you see the term Coupled Ocean, Atmosphere, and Land processes. The ocean interacts with the atmosphere and, as a result, things change on the land even though the ocean may not have had direct contact with a given piece of land. That's coupling. Two things interact on the other side of the world and I feel it here even though I am not aware of the connection with the other side of the world. Another example of a coupled process is doing something now, like throwing out junk. Then, eventually the fish might eat it but we then eat the fish and get sick. These are causally connected coupled processes.

All our lives interact. They are coupled together. What one person does is coupled to another. In the earth system all the processes of the atmosphere and what happens on the land influence each other directly and possibly indirectly or nonlocally. Ecologists need to think about local but also about nonlocal or dreamlike feelings and interactions.

What happens on the earth is influenced by volcanoes. When Mt. St. Helens blew her top recently (relatively speaking), one of the MIT people (possibly over-) calculated that enough CO_2 went into the air to balance the whole Industrial Revolution since its beginning in the 1700s. Hello? We are working on recycling plastic, but if Mt. St. Helens burps, she won't help our eco-situation. Remember our relationship to the sun, how the sun spews forth all sorts of stuff and influences us and our planet. How much CO_2 gets into the atmosphere is a complicated business. Should we shoot up reflectors into the air to block the sun's radiation and heat? Yes and no. Mono-causal solutions generate problems too.

All of us diagram makers want the best for the future of the planet, but we sometimes forget to include the specific factor that I call awareness of our deepest selves. Science often treats people as one part among many in a causally interacting system. We need to bring in dream-like factors as well. What psychological change do we need? One is already beginning and many people are beginning to say, "Don't throw out your junk, try to recycle it." Business is beginning to realize that there is money to be made by developing machines that don't use as much fossil fuel and by creating energy without ruining the environment. (Fossil fuels are sources of energy like coal, oil, and gas that contain a lot of carbon and are formed from the decomposition of compressed, dead organisms.)

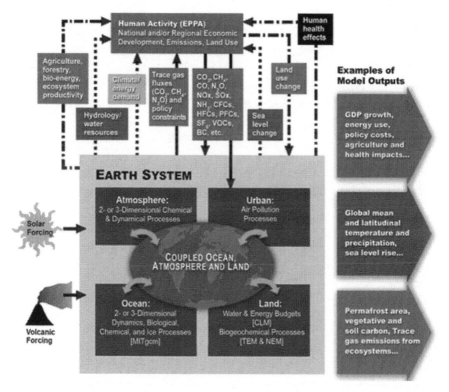

18.3 Earth System.

(MIT Integrated Global System Model 2011
mit.edu/images/diagram-igsm-)

Our sciences need to work with psychology and with government. Sustainable solutions require getting along with people who are too afraid to think of the future of the planet. We need to learn to get along with our neighbors—less war, please. We are trying to use normal allo-pathic medicine with our planet, which means if something makes the biosphere unwell for people or other animals, stop doing it. That is al-lopathic, and it is a very important and a very good idea. For example, take the air we breathe. When I take a big breath and then exhale, some CO2 comes out. We burn coal. Where do you think the coal's carbon atoms go in the smoke? Those atoms become CO2, carbon dioxide, and float in the air around the world. Will I ever see that molecule or those atoms again?

Tyler Volk, professor of biology at New York University, reports carbon specialists told him that the carbon atom we exhale goes into the atmosphere, and chances are that it takes only one year before it ends up in the leaf near to us.[83] So whatever we do will be back in our faces quickly. Oh! That is something to tell the person who threw the junk out! "Be careful, that is going to come right back at you one of these days!" So, the wonder of eco-theory is that it is trying to put all these things together but it needs a truly global, holistic theory encom-passing people, conflict, and teamwork.

HOLISM

Holism (from ὄλος holos, a Greek word meaning all, whole, entire, or total) is the idea that all the properties of a given physical, biological, chemical, social, economic, or mental system are not determined by studying its component parts alone. Instead, the system as a whole determines how the parts behave. In other words, changing *this* part because of *that* part—*me* changing *you*, *you* changing *them*—are all im-portant, but such an approach is not the full story. All parts interact together, so what we really need is a more holistic systems-theory.

WHAT IS HOME?

As I said in the beginning of this chapter, *Ecos* in ecology comes from the Greek word for house or home . What does our house, our home, really mean? It is at first a feeling about an area or space. Listen once to a song about a city you love. Think of the singer Norah Jones and imag-ine her singing about Manhattan. She reminded me of Manhattan, of good experiences I'd had there, of work I found in Harlem and nearby. Music describes a feeling of home:

I go back to Manhattan

As if nothing ever happened
When I cross that bridge
It will be as it always is
As if nothing else existed.

OK, now you may not feel the way she does, or like I do, about Manhattan, but it almost brings tears to my eyes because it reminds me of all the people and of really deep and important things. As artists and singers know, these indescribable feelings are also part of home. This music is part of home. It is part of the home field.

I want to bring another little piece of home here. People living in the little coastal town of Yachats say that Amy's song *Coastal Town* reminds them of their home on the Oregon coast. You should hear her song:[84]

Evening in this coastal town
People watch as the sun goes down
Fisher people drift out to sea
Their lights glow on the dark blue sea.

It is not just me, other people in Yachats say, "That reminds us of Yachats! That is home." And they put up her song on the internet as part of Yachats' description. Think about your country. You may not like your country very much, but think of city songs and national anthems. Many people start to cry when they sing their country's national anthem. Why is that? Why are they crying? What do those tears say about home, like it or not? What am I saying here?

We are often not conscious of the essence experience of our world, our home... and so we are often not at home. The parts of home are both real and dreamlike, inner, shared, musical-poetic experiences. Home is composed of animals with furry noses and birds, stones and air, trash, monsters and people, but home is also a musical feeling beyond any single part. My main point is that just working with the reality of things does not deal with the entire home situation. We need the dreamland experience of home that you can feel and hear to work with its system mind. Use the whole to work on its parts.

Holistic means that we cannot break something down into parts; we will ruin it if we break it all into parts. Atomism and Newtonian physics are real, change this, change that, but without a deeper feeling of the field in which we live they provide only one aspect of home. Ecology needs *ecos*; home, deep democracy: that is, the real stuff and dream-feeling stuff, values, fantasies and essence level processmind dances.

The Inuits, the Alaskan native peoples, and the Himalayan people think that we need to breathe into the earth to keep it alive and the earth's breath keeps us alive. All of that is holistic thinking. Holism also exists in quantum physics. In quantum holism parts operate together in some inexplicable, quantum entanglement-like manner.

Quantum holism is an aspect of home. If you look inside a quantum system box, some of the particles are entangled. How come once you look at a particle and see that one is up, you know the other one turns down? There is something connecting those two particles, something earlier physicists (e.g., Niels Bohr) called quantum holism. Some physicists say, "If you can't measure it, don't talk about it." You cannot measure that quantum wave function that says entanglement is possible, so we don't know what it is. "It's just math!" Other physicists say, "But the math is there, so quantum holism exists." We can't (yet) measure holistic fields like space-time dreaming, but I believe such fields lie behind Einstein's ether concept (mentioned in chapter 7).

Process oriented ecology is the deep democracy of ecology. Home has many levels: Home is real, home is dreaming, home is the essence level. And the essence level is the holistic background that will help us work with all the different conflicts. I remember when one of my clients was dying, the thing he said was, "We are entering home." I said, "What is home?" and he said, "It is the house of Christ." I said, "Tell me what it is like in there," and he said, "It just feels real good." I am talking about the practice of sensing things at the essence level.

Audience: In Buddhism they might call this essence level *kensho*—no separation.

Arny: *Kensho* is becoming aware of no separation, another holistic concept. *Nonlocality* is another term for a holistic situation. There is no space between us.

Recall that in chapter 4, I spoke about the holistic nature of atmosphere in terms of the Greek word *kairos*, meaning the weather and the right moment.[85] There, I spoke also of the term *Ma*, which in Japanese means roughly, "the space between two structural parts." Artists understand the power of space. In art, a picture has parts but they interact because of the space between them. In Picasso's Guernica, for example, you don't just understand one part but the whole of World War II is there. That's holism in art.

Holism is the middle ground between science and religion and the border between everything. Process oriented ecology is about being real, being atomistic, and getting the different little pieces together and it is about feeling deeper and working from the deepest feeling in yourself with the various parts of things. What does all that mean in political thinking?

Let's say a green group says, "We want to stop those guys who have been logging too much! We are going to get them and we are going to stop them!" At one point you have to say that is a good thing, to stop the deforestation process. But this is political, so what else can you say? What about the people whose lives depend upon the logging? They are going to starve. What about the farmers who live from the rainforest? It is not so simple. So the process oriented ecology viewpoint is that it is not this or that. It's about relationship, so let's sit down and talk and use our processmind.

18.4 Nonlocality in Picasso's Guernica (Wikipedia).

I want each of you to think of an environmental problem on which you would like to work. Which of the many environmental problems would most interest you? Choose one of them. For example, I would chose the earthquake that just happened in Haiti. Think of the energy of it. I am going to take the X energy of the earthquake, act it out a little bit, and then make an energy sketch of that; a crashing energy sketch. And then there is the little u part of me that is so upset about that earthquake and the horrible things it has done—that part of me is quieter and centered. The energy of this u part, I would draw as an infinity symbol. Then I will find the processmind as a body experience.

The idea is that you will find the deepest part of yourself as a body experience, feel it, and then I want you to associate this experience with a piece of the earth. I won't go through the whole meditation, but the idea is that when you get into your processmind and you are moving with it, there is a noncognitive moment that occurs that I cannot predict ahead of time. There you will find space–time dreaming and solutions.

DENIERS

Audience: Before we do this exercise, let me say that the environment for me is mainly a material problem. Basically we consume resources faster than they are replenished, and we create pollution faster than it is absorbed. We make our homes increasingly unlivable. I struggle with how consensus reality does not accept that simple fact, even though from the point of view of science and everyday reasoning, it is as simple as that. I don't know a single person who, in the way they live their lives, is not doing more damage with how they live. All of us are accelerating the problem, and we are not even close to starting to slow it down.

Arny: Yes, everything we do accelerates the problem; just being alive accelerates the problem. Having so many of us on this planet is a problem.

Audience: When I get that, it feels incredibly painful and most of the time I have to blank that out. It's just too painful to feel it. How do we help deniers, help the people face that fact and accept those feelings and the message those feelings give us about how desperate the situation is? Most people do not seem prepared to feel that bad.

Arny: I am on your side. One of the things that people need to hear is that the human race may possibly not be here for long if it does not awaken to its nature and the nature of the earth and universe.

Audience: I don't see us using the energy we have responsibly.

Arny: You are right. There is a huge X factor around, a denier! It's a ghost role.

Audience: Right, 90% of the species that have ever existed have become extinct. It is our more likely destination.

Arny: Yes, that is one of the reasons I am studying these concerns. How can we create a more sustainable future for all? There is a great great tension in the room to further with our eco-work.

EXERCISE: PROCESS ORIENTED ECOLOGY WITH EARTH PROBLEMS

Consensus Reality, Dreaming, and HOLISTIC Space–Time Dreaming

1. Choose an environmental problem of interest. What is one potential consensus reality solution? See, feel, and act out the energy of the environmental problem. Then sketch and call it X. Think of people that remind you of this X?

2. Who in you is most disturbed by X? Feel and act out this energy, u, and then sketch it.

3. Scan, find, and feel the deepest part of yourself in your body. Then breathe into that body area, and, when you are ready, associate this body area with some place on earth. Try to find the X + u energies at this place. Breathe into and be the earth spot until the resulting experience dances you.

4. Now totally relax to find your space–time dreaming experience again, and when you have found this dance, use this body experience to explore the X and the u on earth. Explore and make notes about what the space–time dreaming dance suggests about how to best deal with the X + u problem. How does this compare with the consensus reality solution you had at the beginning?

AFTERWARDS

Arny: This exercise brings forth a noncognitive solution. It is difficult to show nonverbal or noncognitive things, but you will know it yourself when you feel it. The idea is that just making people drive less or take buses, all of these solutions are important. But especially in the United States, the media says about 50% of the public and a small percentage of scientists do not want to make any social or economic changes and even that doubt climate change exists. There is a radical conflict in the background. Inspired by climate physicist Prof. Catherine Gautier-Downes, Amy and I conducted an open forum with scientists and people from different sides.[86] A conservative think tank that hires people and sends them to disrupt such forums did so at ours as well. There were lots of people sounding off about this and that! Surprisingly the forum went well in the sense of people on both sides of the climate change debate eventually began to switch sides, understanding and even befriending one another. There was obviously more work to be done, but this was a beginning.

Inner work such as we did in the last exercise helped find process oriented solutions, which for me meant opening up and supporting all sides one at a time. So my point with this preceding exercise is to stay in the processmind dance state until *it* informs you of something. Let *it* surprise you. I would like to hear what you are learning and any questions you might have.

Audience 1: My initial solution was to have a radical population control; the young, the old, the infirm, not so many kids in lots of different ways. And as I worked with $X + u$, what really came out was one part that wanted to grab control of everything, and the other side was frozen and terrified. Then the space–time dreaming became a Tai Chi style flowing with what was there in both of those parts, and neither of those were permanent states. I felt how both parts would exhaust themselves and would both evolve if I helped each of them. The point was to trust in those parts evolving and changing and not being so attached to what was happening in the here and now.

Arny: Thank you for saying that. Tai Chi, originally an earth dance, developed from the earth, the animals, the clouds, and the sun. The whole thing is in there, in Tai Chi, and it taught you that there was a dance going on between the energies that creates a *home* for things to work better together.

Audience 2: My experience was very similar. The issue was the vast farms that take over the little tiny farms. The energies were also hands moving slowly, one pushing up and one pushing down. The feeling was that we cannot solve the conflict, that we are not the creators, and that something else was trying to happen. I never had that insight before. I have always been a strong environmentalist, into action, but this is a new feeling. It makes me feel like relating and making more community. And from that I could imagine then going back into political scenes and having a sweeter attitude, a nicer way, an easier way of saying difficult things.

Arny: Right, neither the conventional activist nor the skeptic are the final point. It's all about relationship. I am really happy to hear the two of you.

Audience 3: I just wanted to notice the atmosphere in here after we all gathered back to talk. It was tense before the exercise, now I feel so much calmer and I felt so much lighter sitting here. After tapping into processmind and our earth spots, it just feels like such an important way of achieving the connection we need to bring this approach out into worldwork and open forums.

....

Σ   FOR REFLECTION ON CHAPTER 18

- Process oriented ecology deals with the reality, the dreaming, and the essence levels of all stakeholders of a given conflict or environmental situation.

- "Bring your family home" means, see even the disturbing factors as part of your family and bring all parties to space–time dreaming.

- We need contact with the universe in order to help the earth.

CHAPTER 19

Quantum Coherence in Personal Life and Ecology

In the last chapter, I related how I was asked about how to deliver food in Haiti. The helping organization that had originally asked for help revealed itself as a part of the Southern Command of the US Army. Originally, the person on the phone sounded like an ordinary executive trying to do something helpful, but, since the method worked, I learned who this person was really affiliated with and that shocked me. It turned out to be what they call SouthCom, that is, the Southern Command of the US Army based in Miami. So it seems that they have now encoded that method into their rescue missions in the future because it worked so well. Space–time dreaming made its way into the Army!

In the last chapter I spoke about how process oriented eco-created solutions are, in principle, holistic—they work with relationships between all parts. Before I worked on the Haiti problem, I used my own earth-based processmind to facilitate the power of X, the earthquake I felt in the crashing of the sea against the rocks and then the quietness of the distant sea. And then somehow the earthquake energy became OK, like a storm followed by quiet weather. I realized that the tendency to want to kill for food is, like an earthquake, somehow natural, and it was that attitude that inspired me to tell the *managers* of the situation to speak through their loudspeakers to the people on the ground and say, "It's OK, it's natural to want to fight for food, but it is not the whole story. Don't fight too much because it will make you hungrier."

It worked! The people actually stopped fighting. I was told what happened. The people on the ground heard that message from the helicopter loudspeakers, and the strongest and the fittest who were in the center to get their food first caught the boxes, formed a circle, and many of them passed the food to those who were frail, to the old timers, and to the little ones at the very edge of the circle who might otherwise not get any food.

Process oriented ecology is created around the sense of home. Home is a multidimensional concept. Home is not just the furniture in your house, it is a feeling. Before you work with somebody or with an organization as a client, notice and create *home* for all of the energies. Frequently people who are ill (or whatever) come to you as an individual therapist or as a business helper or coach because they need the concept of home, even though this feeling need is rarely conscious. People, perhaps many beings, don't feel at home with themselves or at home with their communities.

Help works best with a sense of home. What is stopping us from feeling at home? Sometimes people are hungry, afraid, or panicked, or just angry. Explore the X energies that disturb you and bring them into their larger field so that they are not just irritants but creative factors.

TOEs

In a way, ecology is, or rather needs to be, a Theory Of Everything. We need something that pulls all the parts together, something you can work with when you are working with helicopters, when you are working with climate change, or when you are working with an organization, the environment, or with yourself. Is there something that pulls it together? A theory of everything!

For ecology to be holistic, it must deal with parts when separated as well as when not separated. Three examples of holistic tendencies come to mind that I have already mentioned. Your first dream in childhood has a tendency to organize most of the events of your life. Aboriginal and spiritual belief systems believe in field spirits, gods that interconnect everything. Quantum physics and the quantum wave function and entanglement are holistic in the sense that parts of a system at different locations are connected without anything known about what is connecting them.

This is interesting theory, but can you use it at home? I had problem with my computer! How many people have problems with their computer now and then? It is like the common cold now. This week the wireless would not pick up the Internet signals! For me, when my computer does not work, like perhaps for some of you, it is a very big deal because a lot of my national and international connections happen there. So, I started to sweat. I don't know about you, but when I get nervous I sweat. I started to try to fix it! *Fix it*! It was not working!! Earlier the same day, somebody stole our bank numbers, and this made everything worse! Some weeks are a little more complicated than others. So, anyway, I was doing what I could, and I started to sweat. I said to myself, "Arny, something is not right with you!"

"But it's not me, it's the wireless!" said my *u*. So I asked Amy for help, and Amy called friends (Joe, thank you for your help!), she called upstairs, downstairs, wherever anyone had a computer in our building. I realized something was not right here. So, I went back to my own theory, of course! I worked on myself, and it was very practical. I had to say, "OK" to my nervousness. Then I went back in my half dreamy space–time dreaming state, and from that state my body went click, click and the computer worked! But I could not track what I did. I could not say exactly what I did. There was a logical thing that I did, but I didn't know what it was. I will have to study and learn more about wireless and the interconnection between technology corporations such as Intel and Windows and space–time dreaming. I love space-time dreaming because it is noncognitive, but it is also frustrating to the everyday mind, the little *u* in consensus reality that wants to know the details of everything!

Audience: Will you do a conference on computers and Processwork?

Arny: I will try! I am learning. So, what I want to say is that what was wrong—well, my wireless was not working—but what was really wrong was that I was not affirming my nervousness, which I was seeing only as a symptom. The pathologizer and the symptom were in conflict. As long as X said *u* should not be nervous, as long as it said, "Take it easy, what are you so nervous about?" instead of having an eco-mind, a processmind, that said yes to the pathologizer and yes to the nervousness and let's go deeper, I had a problem.

Now I must ask. If being in your processmind and having all the parts, at least temporarily, is so valuable, why don't we do it more often? Why aren't we biologically or psychologically or spiritually (call it what you like) tuned in all the time? Why don't we do it more often? And how do we get separated from something so deep and so useful? If it is so great, why do we come apart?

The processmind's holism is that the universe includes that earthquake, that starvation, and that murderous panic. It needs them, as I have been saying, to awaken to itself. Still, once we discover this, why don't we remember it? And why do we lose our sense of the whole again and again?

DECOHERENCE

There is no one answer to that question, or perhaps there are as many answers as there are people. To answer this, let's think more about what it means to be at one with your deepest self? Think of sleeping as one possible example of that: You are one while you are dreaming. In your dreaming mind, this side and that side are both part of the dreaming. You can be "good little me over here" and "roar over here" too. The dreaming mind has room for both. And when you wake up, you usually choose the one with which you identify. Before you woke up, there were all sorts of possibilities. After, there is one.

Being centered only in the world of parts, in consensus reality, is like being a fish out of water. When we are only in consensus reality, we look like a fish out of water, out of our sense of dreaming, of the earth, the universe, the field in which we swim. We need the field, that part of us that says yes to this and yes to its opposite. The field itself is not in conflict. Part of you may be in conflict, but the field has room and compassion for all of your parts. I am going to call the tendency to get out of our basic oneness *decoherence.*

COHERENCE

Coherence means being in tune, as I have said before. Thus, *decohering* means getting out of tune with your basic stochastic dancing self. It's easy to get out of tune because we are all partly determined and partly totally random. Your everyday mind has to be very flexible and ready for spontaneous changes to stay in tune. Where does the problem of coherence come up in spiritual or religious traditions? What do religious or spiritual traditions say about coherence? What do they say to you?

Their deepest message… though not always the dogma… is something like, "Get in touch with your basic self," regardless of its name:

- A oneness with everything.
- A oneness with God.

The Nez Perce in Joseph, Oregon said that when the Europeans came and said, "You have got to work and be on time," Chief Joseph responded, "My people will never work, they dream." I remember hearing this when we were in Joseph, the town in Oregon named after the chief. Now, do you think that he did not want to work? No. It had nothing to do with never working. What was he saying? He was saying, we are taking our wholeness with us. We must dream regardless of what we do. So, if you have to work nine to five like most of us do, don't forget you're dreaming while you are getting there.

Aboriginal Australians speak about the dreaming earth. Buddhist meditators speak of Buddha mind, and the Rinzai sect in Zen Buddhism speaks of *mu-shin*, being at one with all things. Are there other meditation procedures or inner experiences that you use to be your whole self? There are as many as there are people. I have been saying, "Be half in and half out." Be asleep and dreamy, and be awake in consensus reality, be in this level and in that level. Incorporating process-mind into consensus reality is a matter of personal development, we cannot press people to do that. There is also something also important about, "Woof! Alarm clock! Get up and get dressed!" Decohere!

Is There Something Good About Decohering?

Diversity! Decohering creates clarity, separate worlds, and diversity. In states of decoherence there is always someone who says, "Hey! You forgot me! You forgot me and my people!" There is a lot of good diversity and reflection and pieces and aspects of consciousness that are created, in part, from decohering. From the deepest viewpoint, catastrophes and one-sided diversity issues are a potential for more consciousness. Inside your psychology problems seem to reoccur: "Oh! This old problem again. What a good-for-nothing I am! Not that again! I have been working on this for 30 years. Why did I not get over that?" Asking instead, "How can I open up to this problem now?" is a very different psychology.

CONGRUENCE AND COHERENCE

I have to argue with myself for a minute: "Arny, why do you have to speak about coherence? Isn't that a new term for psychology?" Why not leave it in physics? Another part of me says, "No, it's not a new term, we see it in other places. And yes, it is a new term. I am using it because I want to update our idea of congruence and understand space-time dreaming better!"

Congruence in Processwork refers to signal congruence. *Congruence* is a measure of how together you are with your signals. For example, if my arm goes to the right here, all by itself, it means I may be incongruent if my body or arm did something without the whole of me. I am incongruent. If I go with it, that would make me more congruent with all my signals.

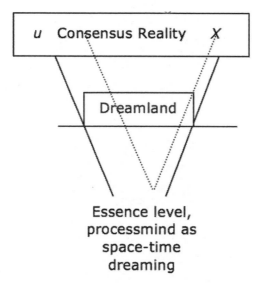

19.1 Processmind in Reality or Dreaming While Awake.

In Processwork, coherence means being at one with your processmind, with space–time dreaming. In this state you will feel your arm rising before it even rises and you will move with it so that the transitions are less abrupt. All your signals; your body, mind and spirit or whatever; all act as a unity.

Congruence refers to being together with the signals and the events happening in dreamland or in consensus reality or in both. *Coherence* is from bottom up, from the essence and dreamland levels into consensus reality. With coherence, you are in a half dreamy state and signals all emit the same message, so to speak, they all sing the same song.

Incongruence appears when you or others are double signaling or doing something they are not aware of. Then you can say, "Let me help them become more congruent by noticing the double signals and making them part of your conscious actions." It's like integrating a dream. That is why congruence belongs to dreamland and consensus reality levels.

Coherence is an essence level sense, the sense of being so close to your basic nature that you don't get incongruent. There is nothing wrong with double signals, it's just that coherence comes from the essence level and is more sustainable! Coherence is a processmind feeling that makes you completely congruent without working on your signals.

What I call the essence or processmind level, some quantum physicists would refer to as the *psi* function, that is, the quantum wave function. What is the quantum wave function? Let's say, it is an imaginary buzz, the basic pattern behind things. People who thought of it the first time thought it was real, but actually it is a dream-like imaginary buzz. No one has ever seen it. It is a mathematical pattern that works to explain things, but no one knows exactly what it is.

19.2 Tai Chi.

In chapter 2, I tell how Schrödinger first thought that his discovery of the quantum wave function was wrong because it implies that two things can be simultaneously true. It implies that two things, such as life and death, can both be present at the same time. His cat could be both dead and alive at the same time! Or we can be both good and bad at the same time!

This overlapping of opposites was a really big problem for early 20th century scientists. Until that time there had been only objects. Now, there were overlapping quantum states! How can two things be true simultaneously? Can you be good and bad? Can you be both horrible and fantastic? We all have processminds that embrace all parts of ourselves at the same time! Your processmind's space–time dreaming, the dance of the ancient one in you embraces everything. It is a home in the sense of a dance embracing all energies as parts of, or moments in, itself, the dance.

In *Quantum Mind*, I tell how Niels Bohr, one of my great heroes, was given a Tai Chi medal in his old age because of his Copenhagen interpretation of quantum theory. They gave him this Tai Chi symbol, a circle with a yin–yang symbol, because the Tai Chi, or *great ultimate*, implies that yin (feminine energy) and yang (masculine energy) are intertwined. According to Taoism, before there was anything, there was the Tai Chi, the yin–yang symbol, implying that before there was one thing, there were two rotating (wave-like!) things at the same time. I can flow between and be both an earthquake and a very quiet person at the same time, rotating one after the other, especially when I am coherent!

As I said, quantum physics embraces opposite energies. For example, in my diagram below, you see on each side there are two cats. One cat is standing with her tail up in the air. She is a live cat. The other cat is lying down with her feet in the air and a long flat tail. She is a dead cat. One is living and one is dead.

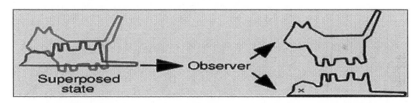

19.3 Schrödinger's Cat: Both Dead and Alive (Wikipedia).

The basic pattern of quantum physics, the quantum wave function, describes the cat as both dead and alive simultaneously (as on the left hand side). Schrödinger felt that this anomaly proved that quantum physics must be wrong.[87] But actually he was wrong about his work, as his work is very right. Though he did not believe it himself, indeed his cat could be both dead and alive. Inhabiting two or even three states simultaneously. Being a nice person, being a horrible person, and being something that says, "I am both those things" is absolutely possible in psychological processes, in meditative states, and in spiritual experiences.

We know from psychology—physics is still wondering about this—that you can be alive and dead at the same time in a dream. You can both be here and there at the same time. How, then, does reality arise where you are either one or the other?

When you wake up in the morning, wide awake, often you forget the dreaming, so you are like the cat with your tail in the air on the right side. Yet, though you don't usually notice, you are still dreaming, though now this dreaming becomes a double signal. Then you look like the cats on the right, which have decohered. You are split and live in parallel worlds.

Today's physics says that upon observation the wave function collapses. No one knows exactly what that means. But still, we may wonder, did the quantum wave function actually collapse? Yes, in consensus reality. But no, it did not collapse. Scientists simply marginalized the multiple realities of dreaming, quantum math, and parallel worlds, which we see on the left hand side of the picture. Processwork says that when we awaken we all develop our primary, consensus reality process and a secondary process that appears a bit split off in the dreaming. The dreaming did not go away. The dreaming is right there in your double signals and symptoms and in your relationship problems.

When you are awake, you are also dreaming at the same time, you simply decohere! That is, you marginalize that and call it reality! However, being coherent means carrying this dreaming attitude, the larger feeling attitude, into everyday life.

Audience: What do physicists mean when they say that the wave function collapses?

Arny: They mean that it disappears. Its imaginary qualities disappear and the result is just one, measurable consensus reality. Either the cat's tail is up or the cat's tail is straight out dead as on the right hand side of the picture. There cannot be two realities in our present consensus reality. But in psychology, the answer is that both realities are still there, you just don't see one of them. That is a most exciting point.

Parallel worlds exist, we just marginalize the dreaming world. Physics has been stuck with this dilemma since the 1920s. Psychology has an insight into this, but psychology has to ask the question, what wakes us up? The cats are a metaphor from physics. They give us some grasp of this slippery thing we are dealing with called consciousness.

Schrödinger used the cat to make things simple. He was trying to say that, according to the physics principle, the math implies that something can be dead and alive at the same time.

Chuang Tzu (also Zhuangzi) (Fig. 19.4), the ancient Taoist, must have understood all this because he awoke one morning from a dream and asked, "Am I a butterfly dreaming of being a man or a man dreaming of being a butterfly?" We are both the dream figure and the real person in a dream, and we are a process, moving between them. We are both people and dreams. The following exercise about quantum vibes may help you better understand and feel coherence.

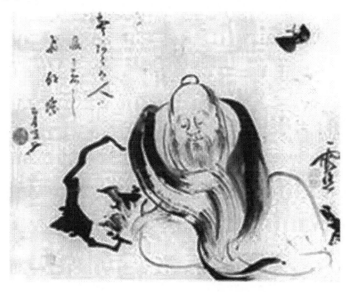

19.4 Zhuangzi dreaming of a butterfly

(or a butterfly dreaming of Zhuangzi). (Wikipedia)

EXERCISE: PROCESSMIND COHERENCE AND DECOHERENCE

1. What is your greatest energy conflict today (e.g., sweet and tough, wild and quiet, etc.)? Feel, name, and sketch the energy closest to you now as u and call X the one most troublesome to you.

2. Now, find your processmind's vibe. First, scan your body to find the deepest place in your body. Then, breathe into it and associate

the body experience you have with a piece of earth. Are the $u + X$ energies around that piece of earth somewhere? Breathe into the earth let it move and *sing* you until a rhythm, a dance, or a song emerges. Notice when you become coherent, that is, when you become one with your dance or song. Make an energy sketch of the processmind dance. How does your dance, that is, coherence, embrace or understand the $u + X$ energies? How are they both present in your processmind's earth dance or song experience?

3. Now remember your everyday self again and the world of parts. When you lose your processmind and decohere, do you notice these states in conflict within yourself and in your relationships or in the news? Now finally, let the space above that earth spot, the air and the sky, move you spontaneously. And when you are moving freely, bring this universe experience back to the earth energies. Do you feel the stochastic, random element in your dance? Notice your sense of coherence now. What would it be like to make yourself choose one instead of the other of your earth energies?

You may have discovered that you neither have a problem nor are you free of that problem. Instead, when you are coherent with your deepest experiences, you are a dance that can put together or resolve what seemed like a problem. When we as individuals and as groups decohere from our basic system mind, we split off parts and energies that seem like irresolvable problems. In this chapter we studied how to be at home, coherent with all that we are.

....

Σ   FOR REFLECTION ON CHAPTER 19

- Congruence is about being at one with signals.

- Coherence describes being close to your deepest self, the universe's dance of the ancient one

- Coherence lets two apparently opposing energies or facts in consensus reality both be true at the same time because they both belong to the same dance, to the same community.

CHAPTER 20

How to Avoid the Deluge: Coherence in Creation Myths

How can coherence help us with our ecological difficulties? Is there a big picture behind the evolution of our planet? What is going to happen to us? Where are we headed? Is there one answer? Remember, we have been talking about ecology from the viewpoint of consensus reality, dreaming, and the universe-mind levels. Environmentalism is a bit different than ecology; it tries to awaken those who deny that our earth is sensitive and changing, in part, due to the mess we make.

Remember that the essence of ecology comes from the Greek word *ecos*: home. Home is not only a dreamlike feeling, it is also real: Let's solve the CO2 problems. Let's get your house or apartment greener. Let's care for the seas. Home is real.

Our apartment had a big problem! The vent came out of our clothes drier where it fits into the ceiling. Oh! Just before we were going to bed, the drier went chug-chug-chug and then whoosh! It was blowing into the apartment! Has that ever happened to you? That is part of home.

The ventilation duct to the drier in our apartment pulled out of the wall, and Amy and I had to fix it. How do you deal with that? There are various levels. You have got to have duct tape to put it back in. If you don't have duct tape, prayer can help but usually it is not as important as duct tape to make things stick. And then equally important is the way how you put the hose up there into the hole in the ceiling that it came out of while your girlfriend or boyfriend is holding you around your feet so that you don't fall backwards. This requires the next level of dreaming! Are you pushing it or are you asking the vent to help you? Yes and yes. Perhaps you can remember your universe dance as you are putting the duct tape on. If you are going to be in a totally real home, you need everything.

Home is a very multidimensional and complex idea, and it is also a meditation. Holism lies deep in the background of your house. This holistic metaphor of the quantum wave function that I have been using, from quantum physics, is an aspect of the great pattern behind a closed system and may be a pattern behind our apartment and the whole universe. If I just look at that vent instead of feeling it, I marginalize the dreaming, the humming, and the coherence that organizes life.

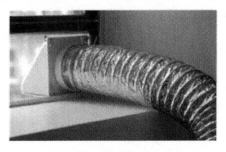

20.1 Ventilation Duct.

We are usually taught to forget the dreaming. But in the dreaming, all parts are superposed. My vent may be broken in consensus reality, yet it is also still perfect. People who work with others on deep levels know that even though their clients choose to be one of the dream figures inside their dreams, there are other figures around in their dreams and in their body and movements. I have been talking about those secondary processes. When I say, "I am Arny and I am not the other figures in my dream," or "I am not you," I become not only incongruent, I decohere. I identify with only me, and, as a result, the other figures bug me.

In any case, to fix that vent, I could just push at it and view it as a problem. Believe me, I tried that and got really tired! Amy reminded me to use my processmind to fix the vent. So I got deeper into myself and began dancing. Suddenly all the parts of the duct that did not fit together with the wall worked. And, to my surprise, the whole thing was fixed in about 10 minutes even though I had tried and failed for

45 minutes before that! I won't go into the details—you can imagine what I am talking about. Try your cognitive intelligence and strength to do things, and don't forget your noncognitive, system mind when you work on problems that seem difficult to solve in your ordinary state of consciousness.

OUR BIG PICTURE

People have always sought the big picture: a system mind, process-mind view of life. Most spiritual traditions and religions are based upon mythic stories whose meaning people try to stay close to but often fail to. Let's study these stories and see what we can learn about the earth or universe's process or system mind. This is like focusing on the big dream behind the universe. It's something like the physicist's search for a unified field theory or like the Tao, Shiva, or Pachamama.

First of all, let's ask ourselves again, is there a big picture? What is the story of our planet? Is there one? Is it connected to the whole universe? Is it the quantum wave function, space–time, dark energy, or a combination that I have been speaking of, namely, the processmind space–time dreaming? Will the big picture help with the future? If we knew there was a big picture, it could help us in dealing with local problems.

FIVE BASIC PATTERNS OF CREATION MYTHS

One way of looking at a big picture is to look at the world's big dreams or creation myths. The earliest written myths that we know of date back to 3,500 years BCE. Others may go back further, but some of these have been nicely collected in *A Dictionary of Creation Myths*, where the editors say that there are five basic patterns of creation myths.[88] For example, in physics, we have the *myth* of the big bang. It's a myth because we believe it, in part, because of what we today call empirical evidence, yet no one knows exactly what happened in the beginning or how. In mythology, the first common creation myth people believed was:

One: **Creation began from chaos or nothingness.**

Arny: How did creation start with chaos or nothingness? You know the answer from your own life.

Audience: From my own life I know the nothingness as a performer. I tend to perform from nothingness because I improvise from nothingness, and when I draw, I start from chaos and it goes from there.

Arny: Thank you. And are there any spiritual traditions that are based on nothingness?

Taoism

Zen Buddhism's concept of *mu-shin*, the whole idea that you have to be in the state of empty, creative mind.

Fukushima Roshi used to tell us, go into empty mind, creative mind, open mind, which he called *mu-shin*. He would grab his calligraphy pen and make a fantastic drawing. One of your most creative states is just opening up and seeing what catches your attention. That's creation from nothingness.[89]

Two: **Creation began from a cosmic egg or maternal ground, such as the *Dreaming* spoken of by the Australian Aboriginal people.**

This belief is partly reflected in my suggestion, "Go back to your processmind, inside the earth, inside the universe." We project or experience or discover feelings in the earth and universe, that is, in the Dreaming that can give us brand new ideas.

Three: **The world was created when united, world parents separated.**

You find this theme in many early myths. The universe was two people who loved each other and were close together and when their oneness split up, the creation of the earth began.

What do you think about that one? Very few of us see people breaking up as a creative act. What could that mythic theme mean? When two things are really together, they don't make much of a *bang*. Everyday reality happens when this coherence or congruence goes to pieces. And then separation and decoherence occur and we awaken in consensus reality to the world of parts.

These types of creation myths stress that separation from the creator can be very creative. We are one, and then we come apart. What is good about coming apart? Coming apart is not all bad. Splitting off from the gods can be creative, just think of Eve and Adam. They disrespected God by disobeying his one command and then the world began! It's not a perfect world, but it's sure interesting. Or at least challenging!

Four: **God orders the Earth to emerge.**

For example, in Genesis 1:9 of the Bible, God commands the water below to be gathered together in one place and for dry earth to appear. God names Earth and sea and commands the earth to "bring forth grass, plants and fruit bearing trees." He said to the waters, "Separate and make earth come about."

What is that about? God was asking for separation! Sounds a bit like the big bang! Out of a wavy *nothingness* came something! Wake up, come out of the waters! Separate and let's make something concrete here! And then the world is born.

Five: **Dive deeply beneath the waters to find the earth.**

In the beginning there are waters and first beings dive down and find something interesting and bring the earth up to the surface.

This theme depicts an innate power that everybody possesses. Start in consensus reality, then dive deep into yourself, or get *depressed* or sad. But going down and in and deeper can bring up something new.

The word depression is overused. Frequently depressions precede creative periods. During depressions or pre-creative periods, don't just say, "I am depressed and need some more coffee" or "I need to go get drugs," or something like that. Sink down in meditation. It may not be just fatigue that is sinking down. Go down. It is OK to go down into the earth. Perhaps something new will be fished up or born. Sometimes you must go down to fish up new things while at other times things seem to just emerge by themselves.

DELUGE

In just about all creation myths, according to our authors, every mythic beginning involves a deluge, a great flood, or its opposite, a great drought.[90] In such stories the creator often feels a mistake has been made. "Whoops! What I made did not work very well!" The creator gets disgusted with his or her work and thinks, "These people just are not right! They are not coming out right! Let's clear the decks, clear the table top off, and bring out the soup again!" So the creator makes a big deluge and sends creation back to chaos again. This deluge is a huge, huge issue. Huge! What do you think it is about?

The great spirits create this incredible thing—let's say, the world, the earth, the planets, and what have you—and then say, "Well, I don't know about that," scratches their noses once or twice and then decide "Let's try again." What is your view of that? What is going on?

Audience 1: Why should anyone expect to get it right the first time anyhow?!

Audience 2: There are many creations; life and death, deaths and lives; that emerge from going back into the chaos.

Have you never felt, "Oh, my god, it is all going to pieces! What next? I fear death! I fear inundation, I fear illness! I fear depression. I fear it is just too much for me. The whole world is going to pieces?" This is fear of the deluge. You feel, "Oh! I cannot go on any further. I am done!" This is a very common and very important experience. Therapists, coaches, organizations, and spiritual advisors are always called in at this crucial point of the deluge. Fear of being inundated, fear of failing or dying is part of the human legacy.

However, in this deluge there is always something like an ark, a large boat with some people on it and some seeds of new creation. What is it that floats on the water? Hope! Our hopeful dreams keep us afloat when everything in consensus reality seems doomed. The ark is a system that was built to flow so that its *cargo* could survive. The ark is a system built for going into altered states: systems that say, "You are going on a journey into the dark night of the soul," use the awareness within you to track and flow with these states. These essence awareness systems are *arks* that keep things afloat. Our basic essence level awareness and systems that work with altered states of consciousness can be extremely helpful.

Here again, Haiti comes to mind. The Haitian people are in the middle of a deluge. I was asked, "What would you suggest to the people who are waiting to get their friends pulled out from underneath the rubble?" What system would work there, in those particular conditions? I told them to sing their spiritual songs, their Voodoo songs about God. I guessed that those songs were close to many of their spiritual beliefs. Those processmind songs that people carry with them are also *arks*. Music can help people move through and with difficult times. The *ark* is a feeling, a theory, or a spiritual experience that people sense can carry them through impossible periods.

The *ark* is something you are commanded from inside to build, something that was only a potential and that you made conscious and built before the problem happened. That is the reason for developing your awareness, so that it can carry you through even difficult times. That is the meaning also of training yourself, to help you detach and float when your everyday reality seems threatened.

Can someone explain to me what happened up there in the Garden of Eden when God said, "Don't play around with that snake" and Eve said (or was it Adam?), "Well, let's try it anyway?"

God said, "Hey, you guys, that was not the right thing to do! You have got to go down to earth now as your punishment for disobeying me and there you will now experience life and death." Disrespecting God created a sense of time! The snake was slinking around, and Adam and Eve were gazing at the great tree of knowledge of good and evil and the apple and all these things. But what happened there? I understand that God here is an image, not the large power that is creating the story. God is just one image within a larger story, but, still, what is going on there?

By saying NO to our deepest and most coherent self, by identifying with consensus reality and marginalizing the dreaming, we get into trouble, create a world, and go through a whole bunch of things. And then through decohering we create time and wake up, creating the world. The deluge comes later and then a re-beginning happens all over again. What I am suggesting is that saying no to God is part of a process, part of a very big process: to say no and to lose contact with your deepest self. Saying "No!" to God creates a big problem, and many will tell you to say "Yes!" to God and to pray to God. But sometimes saying NO is good because although it leads us into trouble, it also creates new things.

In all stories creation happens from nothing, one way or another. The creation story I suggested in chapter 2 has aspects of all these myths. The story suggests that in the beginning there was *wonder*. That is, a wondering process that asked about itself and broke into parts, resulting in diversity, reflection, and consensus reality. Cohering and decohering are in all stories. Then there is often the deluge but also the process of the ark, that is, of the new beginning.

COHERENCE–DECOHERENCE CYCLE

Creation myths show coherence–decoherence–coherence cycles, which we go through. I think of the Tibetan Wheel of Life, which shows these cyclical processes and the potential of liberation, symbolized by a Buddha figure who is "off the wheel," pointing to a moon that is detached from the earth. I want to propose a process oriented ecology cycle that has the chance for detachment built into the cycle on earth. This cycle is part of the big picture, or the big picture itself. Decoherence ensures diversity and it is needed for consciousness. If I say no to my process-mind, I begin to do a lot of realistic things, but I also eventually suffer. And through that suffering I become more conscious of an earlier immense state, which I did not realize before. So one aspect of decoherence is saying NO and then having to rediscover what it was that felt so good originally. Create a mess on earth, and then remember one of your deepest drives: "Let me consciously seek the universe's wisdom that moves me and bring it back to the earth."

When you forget your deepest self, instead of saying, "You are foolish for doing that!" you might think, "Well, maybe now I can consciously rediscover that deep state." My point is that decoherence ensures diversity and inspires consciousness. The wave function collapse is built into us. Creation, agony, decoherence, and finally going back toward the oneness again with its many parallel worlds. The world is in a PROCESS, one where there is no one solution, only re-solutions and resolving and recognizing the flow of things and denying that flow and then attempting to organize what happens here when we deny the big picture.

At the very base of my next diagram, you will see a moment of coherence where we are in a coherent state of holistic oneness; for the moment. This picture works for individuals, couples, and all groups. Couples and friendships also have decoherence patterns; the partners love each other, they are friends, and they come apart. Most friends go through a little something or a big something again and again. The same applies to organizations. Perhaps the whole world is in the midst of such a pattern, and that is the larger picture behind the environmental problems that threaten the earth.

After the initial phase of coherence comes Phase 1 which I am calling creation. In this phase we are still more or less coherent. The group is dreaming up new ideas. We are dreaming, "Hmm, what could I do today?" And then in Phase 2 (upper left), we wake up. Each person thinks, "I have been dreaming. Now let me go into consensus reality." We are still fairly coherent in Phase 2 but the parts and conflicts are becoming clear, though there is no war as yet.

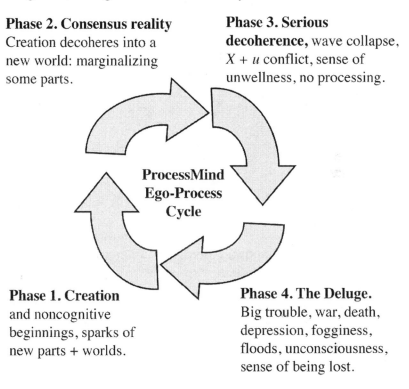

Phase 2. Consensus reality
Creation decoheres into a
new world: marginalizing
some parts.

**Phase 3. Serious
decoherence,** wave collapse,
$X + u$ conflict, sense of
unwellness, no processing.

**ProcessMind
Ego-Process
Cycle**

Phase 1. Creation
and noncognitive
beginnings, sparks of
new parts + worlds.

Phase 4. The Deluge.
Big trouble, war, death,
depression, fogginess,
floods, unconsciousness,
sense of being lost.

COHERENCE

20.2 Universal Process Pattern: life and ecology as a process.

Phase 2 is the world of consensus reality or a new world that everyone hopes to sustain. Things are booming, moving ahead. There are many names for this phase, depending on the person and depending upon the organization. Consensus reality means that we are trying something new: we want to begin again, we are beginning to realize our dreams and ideas. Although our wave function is collapsing, we are still fairly coherent, but we are soon going to decohere more seriously.

Phase 3, after the midpoint in the *afternoon* of the epoch period (be it a millennium or a day), brings big problems that can no longer be avoided. We turn against the other. X + u are now in severe tension. The X energy begins to get more and more problematical as u marginalizes it more and more, and we (or an organization) begin to seriously decohere. Like in the Industrial Revolution, things start well, but then they go too far. X (the dirt, the carbon, and pollution) becomes too much for the u in us and begins to decohere from u. We are still in the world of reality, but conflicts grow worse.

During Phase 3 we severely decohere and X + u now clearly separate. Relationship problems appear in the organization and in our personal lives, inside and outside we are in conflict. It is quite an extreme period here. This is the time when therapists, coaches, and rescue missions are called in to help. In Phase 3, there is support for one part against the other. Symptoms that bother us get worse, we get nervous, and things begin to threaten us; and suddenly we feel that our world is falling apart. In short, the deluge threatens us.

Phase 4 brings the full-fledged deluge. We have had enough! We begin to get more depressed or sleep all day or scream and shout or curl up in a ball of twitching anxiety. We want to die or we fear we are going nuts. We fear our world will go to pieces. We forgot that the world goes round and round. Tibetans make meticulous sand mandalas and then, poof, they sweep them away! The Navajos, the Tibetan Buddhists, many have realized that our original structure was OK, but they didn't hold on to it. Blow it away! Begin again! And so we go into deep dreaming states and the world begins all over again.

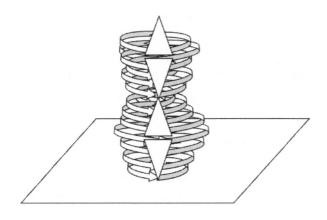

20.3 Eco cycles around our center.

Our world is a process. We cycle, we revisit problems we had long ago at least a dozen times. It is not because we are bad people or because we are stupid and unconscious (as many of us reprimand ourselves). It is not. It is natural and, in fact, it is needed. The point is, if we go around enough times, if we have the same problem again and again and again, maybe this problem gets a little bit better slowly, over time. We start to co-create together with the universe. That means, we start to know, "Aha! Now I am in reality. Now I am decohering." The whole cycle is easier if we are aware of it. When we reach the stasis point again at the base of the diagram, we begin again to co-create and thus can take a more conscious part in this grand scene. Taking part in the co-creation of our world, having some hand in it, makes it easier.

Initially, it takes us many years to go through the cycle. Next time it might take less time, and so forth. As far as most people are concerned, after we go around and around and around that cycle enough times, it gets a little bit smaller. The parts come closer together and it does not take so long. But then, once again, it takes longer, and then shorter. Over time, the cycle may be more like a spiral with an ever-changing diameter. We get closer to the essence and then further from it again as we go round and round.

We are all cycle dancers, like the dance of the ancient one, the universe. That is, we cycle through levels of consciousness (essence, dreamland, and consensus reality) and through the various phases of coherence and decoherence. In fact, it appears that our whole planet has cycled through four or five periods of mass extinctions.[91]

What makes us go through one period to another? What pushes us? What moves us from one of these periods to the other? Some call it god. I call it the space–time dreaming of the processmind. Call it whatever you like; we dream and sleep, then with a big bang we wake up and marginalize things. It's a basic process. I cannot tell you why it is there or where it came from. Nobody has that answer yet. The sun rises and sets.

When we are close to the center, close to our processmind's space–time dreaming, we begin to co-create. We begin to get the sense, now this and now that, and now I am breathing with myself, I can go with my life process, and I am *with it*. That *with-ness* is a kind of co-creation. Co-creation means moving with our process, with the world's process, as it goes from inside to outside to inside again, from life to death, and so forth.

Global warming: Is it possible that our world is in Phase 3, at the point of sensing an extinction of human life though the planet will continue on again? In the past, there have been several proposed reasons for extinctions: for example, flood, basalt eruptions (volcanic rock), falling sea levels, and asteroid impacts.[92]

- Volcanic eruptions: Eleven occurrences, all of which were associated with significant extinctions.

- Sea-level falls: Twelve occurrences, seven of which were associated with significant extinctions.

- Asteroid impacts: Enumerable occurrences, giant ones.

Today, it sometimes seems as if we, as a world population, are in Phase 3 heading towards 4. Many people are speaking about a coming environmental doom. Skeptics call them *alarmists*. Is the end of our present idea of our world and planet immanent? I don't know, but that fear is surely beginning to make a lot of creativity happen. According to this big world picture, we will get depressed, fear a deluge, and then get more deeply in contact with nature again. My hope is that our demise as groups and individuals can happen in the sense of relativizing our little *u*'s to go and get in touch with space–time dreaming, which would help bring our polarizations and differences into a creative process. I doubt that we can stop the cycle, but we surely can make it easier, more creative and productive for all!

As I mentioned, if we are close to the space–time dreaming of the processmind, we go through this cycle more quickly. And we have more sense of community. For example, my processmind was decohering the other day as I was walking with Amy down the street. All I could see and stare at was the man ahead of us. This man was eating an energy bar. He took off the energy bar wrapper and threw it on the ground. Eating healthy and throwing the wrapper on the ground! Being in a decoherent phase, cut off from my processmind, I ran and grabbed his energy wrapper from the ground and was going to bring it to him. I wanted to say, "Hey! Look, here is your energy wrapper!" But I could not catch him! Thank god! You know why? I felt I was better than him! I was inflated out of my mind and in Phase 2 or 3. I was going to show him he should be recycling, that poor unconscious man!

But I did some of these exercises and I realized that I could do all this better. I look forward to meeting him again. Then, when he throws the wrapper down the next time, I will be in Phase 4—I hope—and closer to coherence. I have now meditated on what I would do. I would pick up that energy bar wrapper and then go over to him and say, "Oh, Master, thank you for showing me how to let go, throw it away, take it easy, because I am in a phase of life right now where letting go is important to me. I want to thank you for showing me how to let things go. Now if it is OK with you, either you throw this wrapper in a garbage can, or I will take it home and put it in my window to remind me to let go." See the difference?

I can move toward coherence and see both him and myself (in my little *u* form) as a needed diversity in the big picture. Otherwise I am not recycling, I am creating more conflict. Now, that is not bad, that is not wrong, but I want more than that Phase 4. We need to see the whole cycle. The more conscious we are, the more we might be able to short-cut that cycle in some way and avoid the disasters we fear so much.

Audience: The man who dropped the wrapper became your teacher. You were marginalizing him when you were going to pick up that wrapper and go after him. But were you marginalizing something in yourself at that point? What is that?

Arny: Definitely. You bet! My own *trasher*. I needed to recycle him! Then after meditating I could see him not just as the bad person out there or in me who disregards the environment but also as person from whom I can learn. I might teach something too, but the realization that he is a teacher was a co-creating experience for me.

Audience: So is that decoherence when you separated yourself from him?

Arny: You bet! In consensus reality, I am not him! I decohered, became split and incongruent, un-integrated, and close to a deluge point! Then by working on myself and entering space–time dreaming, I could see, yep, we belong together in the same dance!

....

EXERCISE: YOUR CREATION AND POLLUTION STORY

Let's now explore our deepest self and how can we use it in the world.

1. Find your processmind in the deepest part of yourself in your body, breathe into it, and relate the experience to an earth spot. Be that spot and let it dance you.

2. Now relax some more and let the whole universe dance you. Is there a universal experience in this space–time dreaming dance, a sense of being at one with the universe?

3. Notice your tendency to decohere. What's positive and negative about decohering? Let a brief story come to mind about this loss and gain. What do you look like when you have decohered and cohered again?

4. Consider a messy spot in your apartment or house that catches your attention or your memory just now. What is the energy, X, of that mess? What part of you (*u*) is disturbed by X? Now, be a process oriented ecologist and dance your space–time dreaming again. Let it dance you back and forth between the mess of energy, X, and *u*, the one who is disturbed by this mess, to value both X + *u*.

5. What is good about the mess? How does your dance advise you to deal with the mess? Note insights: please write them down and keep them. (At your leisure do the same exercise with other messes around the world.)

AFTERWARDS

Audience: My mess was, is, a big pile in my file cabinets. All the papers and bills and magazines are piled up. It gets so high and then that one last piece of paper can make that whole pile crash.

Arny: Everybody is laughing as if they understand that! Look at the guilty-looking faces around the room. It's the funniest thing.

Audience: So I tried to hide from the mess by huddling under the coffee table. I tried to hide from the mess.

Arny: You hide from your mess? That is so creative! Imagine talking to your mess, "You scare me, I want to hide!"

Audience: So from underneath the coffee table I started to rearrange the papers and bills and magazines and to dance with each one. I really got to appreciate each one: "Well, what is beautiful about the electric bill?" And it was like, "Oh, well, with that electric bill, if I go right over to my computer and pay it, bing! I can go over to the recycling bin and bing! Put that in there, it's done!" And it is a dance. If I pay that bill then there is light and my electricity won't be cut off. And I can dance it to and from the mailbox. I can pay it right away rather than hide it in the pile, and then I only have so much time, so I could get rid of a lot of that shit. I don't need all that. I can distill and decide how much I can dance with things.

Arny: Oh! You are hypnotizing me as you are speaking, which is really important. That altered state is so important. You are doing a little dance over there and there is a very different attitude toward those things than your everyday mind had before the exercise.

Audience: I decided not to have anything against the paper, whereas before I hated the pile.

When I was beginning to study ecology, I would walk down the street and sometimes open up garbage cans. Amy filmed me doing this. And I looked in—you must once try that, or maybe not. Open the garbage and look in to see if there is something that you could use. Become a kind of garbage person. Talk to the garbage. Make a dance out of it. There are lots of creative ways to deal with reality besides avoiding it.

....

Σ   FOR REFLECTION ON CHAPTER 20

- There are a number of typical motifs in creation myths around the world, each describing how the earth comes into being.

- All creation stories have some sort of creation and near annihilation or deluge later on.

- Perhaps the history of our earth, perhaps ecology itself, has cycles in which we cohere, decohere, become incongruent, fight, and experience a deluge that eventually brings us *home* again.

- Awareness of the dance of the ancient one might shorten Phase 4, making personal and global deluges a little easier.

- Recycle the *trasher*.

CHAPTER 21

The Gold Diggers:
Pollution, Ecology, You and Me

Remember Phase 3 of Figure 20.2, that is the conflict and decohering period I discussed in the last chapter. That phase is followed by Phase 4, the deluge. Our experience of the *uni-verse* (which means one turn) is cyclical. After the deluge, world myths show that creation re-begins (in part, because of arks) and just after that, we get to the bottom point, which I call the coherent point, the essence of things. That is where an experience of the processmind occurs.

Individuals, groups, organizations, and perhaps the whole world probably cycles through similar phases. You are coherent, beginning something new; you run into conflict with yourself and eventually you get disoriented, tired, or even a bit depressed. Your process goes into the depths, and then your dreams begin to create new worlds all over again. As relationships and groups, we start out very close to one another. Then we do new things together and troubles arise, and then it seems as if we go down and around, recreating organizations. We all sense these things, but we tend to locate ourselves only in the moment, forgetting the larger view, the universe dance.

Audience: I was wondering if this concept could be in conflict with the concept of balance? Because if you are in balance, then you cannot go through that cycle?

Arny: Jung suggested that an individuated person became herself by balancing the opposites. Today I think he would agree with me that that balance is actually a cyclical process. Being in balance means fighting then accepting all these various phases at different times, including being totally out of balance yourself.

The universe is a process. Follow your process. If you are close to the dance of the ancient one, you go through these phases a bit easier. We need such mythic overviews to work together as a planet. I have been stressing the idea of *ecos*, of home. We need to feel at home in the universe to work with all our earth-based problems on this earth. Recycle uncomfortable feelings, don't just throw them out.

Let's consider home, not-doing, and working with pollution. Besides the CO2 from fossil fuels, our second worst pollutant is said to be mercury. Most of the global mercury pollution comes from the small-scale gold mining sector, from our desire for gold.[93] Most of the mercury ends up in the water, which we drink; and in the fish and trees and the plants, which we eat; or in the air, which we breathe. Mercury in the body is not very good for us. It makes lesions in brain tissue, it wrecks the heart, it is toxic. Eat too much fish with too much mercury in it and you are not going to be feeling very well.

GOLD MINING

Focusing on this one pollutant, mercury, can teach us about working with global problems. First, we must ask, why and how is pure gold made? Why make it? Imagine I am an economically disadvantaged person. I am a child living along a small river north of Shanghai, or I am a man near the Amazon in Brazil, or I am a big industrialist who likes gold because it makes me a lot of money. You basically get your pan, get some gravel from a stream that is supposed to have gold in it, and you put the gravel in a pan. Then you mix mercury you brought with you into the gravel and mix it with your hands. The mercury amalgamates with the gold and gold-mercury combination sinks to the bottom while the other stuff stays at the top.[94] You tip your pan a little bit to get rid of the stuff you don't like, and you have got your silvery (mercury) gold metal underneath. Next, take a blowtorch and heat up the remaining gold–mercury combination to drive off the mercury into the air and into the ground. Heating the mixture releases the mercury into the air, or you may dump some mercury into the water. And that's where a lot of our mercury pollution comes from! Now gather up the gold and get a lot of money for it!

If you tell somebody who is doing that with his bare hands that, in time, it will make him sick, he might say, "Yeah, but it will make me a lot of money in a short time. It will feed my family and get me ahead in life. My life is shorter but so what?"

Gold making, mercury, economics, psychology, and the environment are coupled ecological processes. People want gold for jewelry and because it's fast money. Gold prices go up especially as currencies go up and down. In the diagram, you see a couple of people talking together. Let's say their relationships are stressed because they don't have much money. "What are we going to do? We need some money!" Or maybe they just became greedy for other reasons. Their relationship stress may be connected to the push: "Let's get some gold." Relationship and individual processes are linked to releasing the mercury poison into the fish environment. Their human relationship process is coupled with the processes in the atmosphere, the trees, the soil, the sediment, and the whole earth.

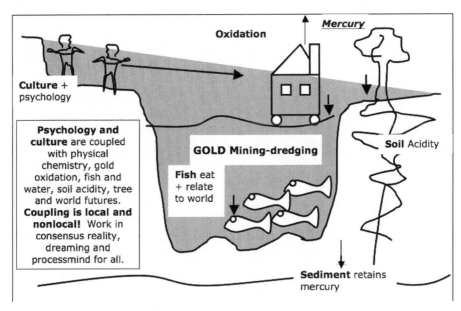

21.1 Coupled Ecological Processes.

In psychology, coupled processes mean, for example, that if people in one city have trouble, other people feel it, even without TV or the Internet. They can also hear about the trouble through gossip. There are local causal coupling connections and also nonlocal couplings going far beyond any given locality. Whatever you do is linked directly or indirectly to everything else. It is like *Indra's* net, her universal great net. If something on one side of the net is pulled, then something on the other side is moved, even if it is not directly on the same line. You could say a net gives you the sense of coupling. Things are not only directly connected, they are also coupled indirectly through space–time dreaming.

Complex couplings are characteristic of physics, chemistry, and ecology. I just wanted to give you a feel for coupled processes, the amazing interlinking between many separable processes. For example, if a 2-year-old baby sitting on the beach decides to play with the sand pile, water will come in and go out. "Let me make my sand castle," thinks the child, and that castle influences every nation in the world. Everything is intimately connected directly through the water, the disturbances of the water, and the whole atmosphere. Everything we do is interconnected.

So how can understanding these complex coupled processes help us with the world? For example, when I say, "Mercury is one of the worst pollutants in the world," what is missing in my description of this pollution problem? The whole complexity is missing. To begin with, the observer's psychology is missing and clarity about the u is missing. We see the X but we don't know what the u is. The u could be someone who says, "You should not be doing that! It is bad!" Or it the u might be someone who is financially well off and who says, "You should not be stressed out over money. Let the gold go."

Our first thesis is that this u (say, a conventional environmentalist) and this X (call that greed for gold) are both aspects of nature and are both needed. The u who is saying, "Stop being greedy" is ok, but I do not think that statement really works because I have never met anyone who is not at least a little bit greedy at some point. Our second thesis is that we need an elder who is there to recycle BOTH the u and the X. The facilitator, your processmind space–time dreaming dance, is like music. If one step in the dance is you, wishing for better health conditions, and the other step is an X, pushing for its own gain, for example; then you will need space–time dreaming to bring these two rhythms into one coherent dance where they work together.

Not-Doing

All of us have this *pollution* problem inside and around our bodies. The so-called *greedy* part of us pushes in a manner that is split off from body feelings and may contaminate us. If you start working too much with just pushing yourself, that contaminates your body. It is not only bad, but it stresses your body. In relationships, one person ends up pushing him or herself and the other. It stresses relationships to the maximum, this particular problem of, "I must push, things must be done!"

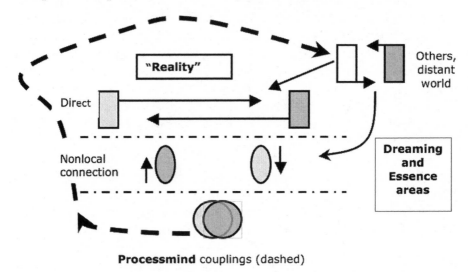

Processmind couplings (dashed)

21.2 Processmind helps with nonlocal couplings.

**Real people (as squares) connect in reality and dreaming
(as ovals) with the processmind (shown as circles).**

It must have been fifty years ago that I first read the *Tao Te Ching*. It speaks about *wu-wei*, not-doing. The sage *does* everything, and yet she does not *do* anything. Fifty years ago I said, "Good luck, buddy! How do you do things without doing them?" It is our big project! Today, this seems to be our central planetary project! Remember the deepest thing you want in your life, staying close to that as you move forward or meditate on some supreme being or experience can help make you feel rich as if you had some special kind of *gold*.

As we saw in chapter 14, the alchemists believed in an experience of a unified world, which they called the *unus mundus*. The alchemists were after gold! The best known goals of the alchemists were the transmutation of common metals such as lead into gold or silver and the creation of a panacea, a remedy that supposedly would cure all diseases and prolong life indefinitely.[95]

What is it in that panacea that makes you feel well and rich and can dissolve all things into the highest ideal? It's not just money. For the richest can still feel poor as well! A couple of years ago Amy and I worked with fifteen of the richest people in the United States. We had a group process with them, which we did for nothing because we suspected that they might be poor. We did not charge them. And the reason that I say that is because the rich can also be poor... well, you know, all of us are frail human beings, we are all going to die. Panic or fear of deprivation or poor health makes everybody a *poor* person. We were shocked that they were poor people in the sense that their health anxieties terrified them. They were greedy, but not just for money. They were looking for the gold of healing and the gold of timelessness and health; that is, detachment, whatever that meant for each of them.

GREED, PANIC, ANXIETY, AND DOING

Your own inner critic can wake you up to get your life together. But more often this critic just impoverishes you. That inner critic will tell you, "You are not perfect in consensus reality. Push yourself to be better than others!" The basic critic for just about everybody always says, "Something is wrong with you!" This is a universal message: "Something is wrong with you! You have no *gold*!" Measuring yourself against others can be positive or negative. Get some medicine if your blood readings suggest that, make money if you can, but be careful. The most common critic says you should ignore dreaming and push to *do* things. "You good for nothing! You will never be good enough! You are a loser! You must PUSH!" That critic is coming about from consensus reality and also from biological drives that translate as, "You have got to succeed! You won't make it!" or "You are sick and dying!"

Doing freezes the everyday person and makes us more rigid as we seek security in our fear and panic! As a result, most of us are inadvertent *gold diggers*, killing ourselves to *make it* in life. The gold-digger behavior is due in part to anxiety, biology, psychology, and global economics. However, there may also be great wealth in dreaming, that is, there is a precious *golden* inner experience, your processmind. Collapsing the worlds or bringing them closer to one another is very valuable. In chapter 19, I spoke of Chief Joseph who said, "My people will never work. They are dreamers." He did not mean that they would lie around doing nothing. He meant that they would not come out of contact with their dreaming. Also I mentioned the *Tao Te Ching* and *wu-wei* or not-doing. In *wu-wei* you do things, but it is not just *you*, for you are being moved in the doing. Your processmind moves you. Carlos Castaneda's don Juan said that the shaman should "stop the world." For the Thai people, this shaman is the Golden Buddha, the world's biggest solid gold statue. It is located in the temple of Wat Traimit, in Bangkok (district of Samphanthawong, in Chinatown), Thailand.

21.3 Golden Thai Buddha (Wikipedia).

Meditation, stillness, and getting out of our sense of ordinary time not only quiets down our nervous system, our parietal lobe (that has to do with our sense of space and time), it relaxes our sense of self in relation to consensus reality. That sense of inner quiet while moving is part of the inner gold-making task. It is the essence of gold everyone is looking for on the outside. Without this gold-essence, we tend to abuse ourselves, push ourselves around, decohere, and move out of the essence area, thus locating ourselves solely in consensus reality.

TRUE GOLD IS TIMELESS

Remember, particles can go forward as well as backward in time, at least in theoretical quantum mechanics. Learning to do that psychologically is a medical issue: Stepping out of time may be good for your health and it may allow you to do more as well. Physicists have never seen this in reality because photographing something that is moving backwards in time is an experimental problem. But psychologically, you can *step out of time*, out of the world of your *u* and your X. Try this next exercise for some alchemical *gold*.

Exercise: Gold Diggers at Home with True Gold

1. How are you a *gold digger*? How and when do you push too much, and how does this pushing contaminate you? Act out your inner pusher and sketch its energy, X.

2. Who in you is most upset by that energy? Act out and sketch this *u*'s energy.

3. Find your space–time dreaming. Feel a favorite earth spot and breathe into it and let it dance you. Do you see the X + *u* energies there? Let the earth dance you, and relax even more. Now let the space–time universe dance you. Dance until your dance shows how to deal with pusher. Can you feel this solution in your body?

4. How does pushing contaminate or influence your body, your bedroom, your relationships? Now return to your space–time dreaming dance and let it transform *pushing* so that it is even more useful for all. Feel your space–time dreaming. In what sense is it *golden*? Make notes.

Try this noncognitive approach if you start to push too much. Try it as you are going to sleep at night and watch your dreams. Try it to learn more about sexuality. When you are getting up in the morning and you have gone to the bathroom the first time and you are about ready to wipe your rear end, remember space–time dreaming. This book is about having awareness of your dance 24/7.

To help ecology, begin with trying to save energy and recycle moods and plastics, and then when you push too much, find the *gold* you are looking for. Let your dance of the ancient one do things locally. Then stay in your processmind when doing things, when working on environmental problems. This will help resolve issues and perhaps may even work nonlocally.

Bring yourself back home to your *ecos*. Pushing is ok, but then really get what you need. Make a home for all people and energies.

Remember, when you are on the toilet, *push*, but don't push too hard! And carry that insight around the rest of the day into the world.

Σ   *For Reflection on Chapter 21*

- Ecology is composed of multiple coupled processes that are in need of a holistic system mind.

- Gold is a symbol of security, but the essence of gold is access to the fabric of the universe that does things with the least pollution.

PART SIX

Earth, Money, and the Big Picture

CHAPTER 22

Your Body, Our Earth

I want to clearly show that the better you get along with your body, the better off our whole planet will be. Body awareness, contact with space–time dreaming, knowing yourself as the *dance of the ancient one* is central to meditation and to your inner and our outer worldwork. In chapter 9, we dealt with body symptoms in depth. Now in this chapter, I want to focus again on symptoms but this time emphasize how working on body problems can be used for our little planet's ecological well-being. In the next chapter, I'll show how your body experiences can help you with your financial situation.

As you may have already experienced, space–time dreaming, which is the basis of process oriented ecology, can help you facilitate group processes as a new kind of *leader* who taps into the relationship field that is between us to find concrete personal and political answers for many issues. A main thesis of *Dance of the Ancient One* is that all the parts of tensions and conflicts are *family members* and that to solve these tensions we have to bring our families *home* to the universe. To some people this idea may be obvious. After all, the universe is where we live. The earth and all the people, animals, plants, chemicals, and everything else are aspects of our family. So let's bring our families home. Families have problems, that is almost the definition of a family or any group. Families have differences of opinions; let's bring those differences home, back to the basic part of ourselves, the most detached part of ourselves.

The problem is that, most of the time, you think of your body experiences as *your* body experiences. Most people don't think of their body experiences in connection with the environment unless they have an allergy. But it is very unusual to think that the thing that is bothering me, that headache, is possibly connected to the world around me. What is the relationship between your symptom, your relationships, and our ecology?

There are few single causes to most problems, whether in relation to people or to our planet. As I said in chapter 1, the perspective of mono-causality says that one thing causes another. Mono-causality, looking for one solution to a problem, can be good if you can find that solution. For example, you have a headache, so you take an aspirin. That is good as long as it works and you don't have to repeat it frequently. But often, the single so-called *solution* is not enough. Mono-causality is reasonable, but it separates disciplines: medicine is here, the environment is there, physics is over there, and psychology is in the background.

Remember parallel worlds? Physics says, "We don't want to bring psychology into physics." As I mentioned in chapter 3, a book reviewer from the American Psychological Association liked one of my books but said, "What is physics doing in psychology?" In consensus reality, we live in parallel worlds, parallel universes: physics, the environment, psychology, spirituality. Even spiritual teachers split up the world and may say, "Don't get too materialistic!" We need our system mind, the processmind, to work with the biggest problems that involve overlapping coupled processes.

In a way, even if you don't have any body problems, because of strong couplings between various inner and outer processes, if something is bothering somebody out there, you can sometimes feel ill here. You think, "this ill feeling is me," and of course it is you but maybe not only you. The sciences of consensus reality have mainly adhered to the notions of mono-causal connections and parallel universes. Develop a detached system mind. If you were a Buddhist, you might say, "Oh! Everything comes and everything goes." We can broaden that idea a bit by saying that sometimes holding on to things can be useful, as long as we don't make a program out of holding on! Our greatest conflicts are not between countries or between people. The biggest problems are between parallel universes that all say, "We are not the other!"

Stressing the importance of consensus reality makes all of us sometimes marginalize shamanism. Shamans know how to touch upon the essence of community and individual system minds. Civilizations grew into modern times and people started to use the internet and most forgot the ancient dance of the shaman. The definition of shamanism depends upon the group that you ask. Shamanism is the belief system of a given culture, usually aboriginal cultures, that suggests that to resolve certain problems, we need to go into an altered state of consciousness and connect with some unifying principle (the name depends upon the group). In my book *Shaman's Body* I discuss how Castaneda's shaman figure, don Juan Matus connects to the *nagual*.[96] There are all sorts of names for that sacred, relaxed space. The *nagual* is, however, not just a space but the shaman or sorcerer herself who shape-shifts, who leaves consensus reality and can experience herself in another form. I am using the term *shaman* here to indicate our ability to connect to space–time dreaming and to bring information from that space back to everyday life. That's a very shorthand description of shamanism. Our shaman healers from Africa called themselves medicine doctors.[97] Today, therapists should remember this part of their work.

In any case, shamanism goes back to the time before we awakened with a big or little bang, before this basic dichotomy of "I am this and not that." Finding your way back to that original shamanistic experience in psychology, going back to, "who was I originally?" is a major spiritual and shamanistic task.

The universe and our own mind create a big bang when our unity breaks into parts and we begin to think, "I am this, I am not that." We then need to bridge parallel worlds. We need a large perspective so that all the diversity in our world is not just a bundle of problems but somehow can be useful and needed as reflection.

Audience 1: The way you talk about things reminds me of Thomas Aquinas who said that the goodness of the creator is reflected in the goodness of each creature, and the more creatures you have together, the more love there is. And on the other side you said that bad things have happened like genocide and ecocide. I cannot fathom that this is just part of diversity, that there is something else that we are doing.

Arny: I am shy about words like goodness and love because they are a little overused in some areas. So, I just suggest there is a need for reflection or consciousness. That's why we have dramatic pushy energies and also quieter energies. We have dictators, now we have the 1% and 99% in the Occupy Movement. Diversity is always there.

Audience 1: But that we can destroy the whole biosphere, calling it just diversity is bland.

Arny: I see what you are saying. I am too bland! You want me to say the world is stupid!

Audience 1: It is not stupid but it is not enough to name the enormity of what we are able to do and what we are on the way to doing. It bothers me. It worries me!

Arny: Good for you. You should use more violent terms than I do. I love that. You help to balance me. I am like you, I do want people to wake up quickly! And there is another viewpoint too, that only when human beings disturb themselves enough do they reawaken. It is awful, it is stupid, and calling it stupid helps awaken us. So I am with you there... in part.

Audience 1: Thanks.

Audience 2: An old saying by Heraclitus states that "strife is the parent of all things."

Audience 3: I noticed that as you were talking about that, I was getting tired. Then I became interested in what you were saying. I was sleepy until there was some intensity in the room. That woke me up and got me interested in diversity!

Arny: Woof!

THE BODY AND THE ENVIRONMENT

Our body is frequently giving us "wake-up calls," that is, something frequently bothers us. All the people you dislike who appear most frequently in your thoughts, also frequently appear as energies in your body that bother you as symptoms. So, you may not be open to those people but your body sure is. Think of a really nasty creature. Think of the worst dictator that you can imagine either in your family or in your country. And there she or he is, someplace in your dreams and your body. If an X really disturbs you, it is natural to say no to it, but, at the same time, you need to use that energy somehow. I use the letter X to represent this energy because it reminds us of something we have divorced like an ex-partner or an energy that you have divorced inside of yourself. Energies that we divorce appear in our body as symptoms and dreams that disturb *u*, the dreamer. It's important to remember that you have a $u + X$ *inside* of you as an individual and because $u + X$ are also in dreamland, they are nonlocal.

Thus, you find $u + X$ inside yourself, outside yourself as another, as well as in the world! You get into conflict not just with yourself but also with close friends and partners. So the $u + X$ in your body also appear in partnerships, and the same energies that bug you in your partnerships and your body also bug you in the world as a whole and in the environment as a whole.

Now, you may be bugged by a million things in the environment, but I want to focus especially on how you can deal with the eco-problems on our planet by first dealing with your own body. Then we will take those insights into environmental work. I want to study how you can work with energies that are troubling you in your body and with that body experience learn how to deal with environmental issues.

The simplest example of how body awareness is connected to the environment involves our discussion of doing and pushing as we saw in the last chapter on gold diggers. As the *doer* you think, "I have to get something done and I have to do it quickly!" In a way, you become a gold digger and get stressed out from that, and after a while you get really tired. That is an X that is a problem for you personally in your body. If you push too much and you neglect your other body signals that are saying take it easy, then your body feels unwell or worse than that.

A similar psychology is also characteristic of our environment. I have to get someplace fast so I will drive 10 miles an hour faster than needed, thereby using more gas and creating more pollution. Who cares? I will get there faster! Or, I don't have time to think about the environment. So what? So, if you have the money, you think, "I will just purchase something I don't actually need! Forget the world! Just get something quickly!"

That same pushing, doing, rushing psychology stresses your body and can bother the environment. Pushing and doing are psychological and material issues that are in the body and in the environment. Some physicists at MIT are saying that, as a result of what we are doing, we are using the planet as if it were a planet and a half or even two planets. Some people speak of using the planet as if it were three planets! If you think about that, doubling or tripling what is expected of a planet is not a sustainable activity. That is a big problem. We are over-using (abusing?) the planet. As a result, warming increases, pollution increases, species are dying, and some people are saying, "Either we change in a hundred years or else! Stop the bad people! Stop these things from happening! Cut down that greenhouse effect!"

22.1 *The same u + X.*

The same u + X appear within yourself and in your relationships, communities, and planet.

My question to you is, why is bringing climate change to consciousness so difficult at this point in the US?

- Greed
- Diversity of opinion
- Fear
- Laziness
- Stupidity
- Economics

There are many reasons. One of them is apathy ("Who cares?") and another is panic. Panic is something that is rarely addressed. Panic means, "I cannot afford to stop what I am doing, I am panicked! If I stop or if we stop what we are doing, our economy will fail, and I won't be able to make enough money!" and so on. Panic is one of many difficulties that is split-off and in the background.

Another reason the US public does not seem to realize that the environmental problem is serious, is due, in part, to scientists who don't communicate as well as they could with others. In any case, there is a diversity of positions around climate change. There are people on two opposing sides and they don't like one another and so there is very little coming together. Those who want to do something about the environment, about the climate warming up and all of that, and those who don't care about it and who refuse to be pressured by scientific opinion. We are just now in the process of trying to bring them together in an open forum. We need more appreciation of diversity and also more teamwork. For that, we need more distance, more space, and detachment to work together.

Remember Einstein's universe's space-time. Relativistic thinking says that the space between us is not straight. Instead of saying to people, "I want to get something straight between us," what you want to say is, "I want to get something curved between us!" Don't forget curvature. If I send a light beam to Amy, she will see it because she is not far from me. But if there was a big planet between the two of us and if I were to send my light beam straight over to her, it would go towards her but would bend away because of the other planet. Being direct and straight in relationships is not enough!

To communicate with her in a powerful field, I will have to aim my light differently if I want her to "see the light." Remember, our universe is not straight and square. It is curved. If you really want to get something straight between you and somebody else, you need to be a little curved. And that means you need to be a little bit altered also. You can "say it straight," but it may not reach them. If you aim straight, you may miss. You need an altered state to communicate. Don't forget the *nagual* and space–time dreaming! That is the altered state. That is relativity.

Space–time dreaming is the basic common background process. That altered state is a common ground. How do I know it is a common ground? Because I can sit in a restaurant and if there are ten people in a group in a restaurant they all seem frequently to drink a lot. I have been studying that. You must study that! That is nature right in front of your nose. What are they drinking for? People miss each other, with just *straight* talk. They are seeking a common, *curved* ground.

Audience: I don't understand your concept of the common ground.

Arny: The *common ground* is the experience that we are all together as a unit on the same earth location. Imagine a group of people who work in an office. Then imagine them out drinking. There is an atmosphere they share, a kind of common ground. People who are a little drunk may experience more connection to one another. The equations of Einstein describing the universe's spaces are a kind of a common ground. Using his space-time, observers from anywhere in the universe will be able to understand or *tune in* to one another as far as their observations or measurements are concerned. Using space-time makes it possible for our different observations to be expressed in a way that makes sense to everyone everywhere. So space–time is a common ground. Likewise, if you, as a facilitator, use your own relaxed space–time dreaming to communicate between cultures, people will understand you because of the atmosphere of *home* that you create.

When you work with yourself on space–time dreaming, remember to notice the tiny stochastic motions. They are like myoclonic spasms (brief, involuntary twitching of a muscle). You know these sensations perhaps from falling asleep. Did your body ever wake you up by dreaming that you walked downstairs and then your legs moved and you awoke? You are falling asleep, you are taking a step in your dream, you spasm, and you wake up on the steps? That is myoclonic. That is one description of a dreaming state. Your movements are stochastic.

As I explained in chapter 2, our psychology is partly deterministic and can be guessed from your childhood dream and partly random. I cannot tell you when you will do something, the given moment, or where. As I said in chapter 2, the mathematical term for this combination of being deterministic and random is *stochastic*.

The theory of relativity has a lot of deterministic qualities in it, but the quantum world implies that there are jitters in there too. Thus, when you follow your experience of space, your movement is stochastic. I have movements that you can predict (demonstrates movements) that are very characteristic of me and yet this wiggle (demonstrates a sudden shaking motion) is random. This random moment that comes up is very important because it shows that you are close to dreaming, you are really close to the dreammaker.

Audience: How do random and secondary processes relate to each other?

Arny: Great question, thank you. Remember, secondary processes occur when you are identified with the little u, your primary process in consensus reality. Then, dream like processes appear in your body in terms of symptoms and double signals. However, when you experience space-time dreaming, you are the ancient one dancing, so to speak. You are at the essence level and processes flow from one signal to the other without any one of them being either primary or secondary. There is hardly a primary process. At the essence level, energies flow into one another without conflicting. They are no longer really separable. So the essence-level experiences like space-time dreaming are outside the control of your normal cognitive mind, your normal identity. At the essence of who we are there is something that is partly predictable, yet there is also an occasional hop! Don't forget the hop! A person who has forgotten the hop, has forgotten herself.

Let's work on a symptom with your global system mind, your deepest self, to work with body energies that pop up. Later we will look at the planet as an aspect of your body. I will be asking you to choose a most difficult body symptom that you have now, or that you had in the past, that you can feel now or that you remember feeling in the past or a symptom that you imagine you could have. Then we shall go further as in previous classes and chapters.

Audience: I am wondering if you have any advice or guidance for beginners. I am a beginner, and I get the impression that some of us have been doing this for quite a while and may have an easier access to this universe-dance state of being moved.

Arny: Great question. Let's be simple about it. What do you feel right now?

Audience: I have a headache! Ouch!

Arny: Show me how to make a headache. Sometimes beginners understand the $u + X$ best by thinking about how to create a headache, for example, pretending to create the headache in another person. Anything puppet-like will do. Every kid I ever met can do this. Show me playfully how to make your headache pretending that you have a ball in your hands. Ah ha! I see you squeezing the imaginary ball with your hands! OK, now we see the X, that squeezing energy. Now what part of you doesn't like that motion? Imagine being the puppet or ball, and imagine its reaction.

Audience: It hates that fierce pressure and squeezing. The ball wants just peace and quiet!

Arny: Great! Next, start to experience space–time dreaming. Some beginners can imagine being a little tipsy from alcohol. Just be plain tipsy (but no alcohol please!). Imagine being tipsy, and that will give you some distance from those consensus reality energies.

Audience: Uuuu, Aha! Got it! Got the feeling. From here, I will now be able to make recommendations to the u and the X!

Arny: OK, let's everyone try this.

Exercise: Body Symptoms and Space–Time Dreaming

1. Choose a worst real or imagined body symptom that you feel now or felt in the past. Remember it, re-feel it, and ask yourself what is the worst energy like of that symptom (e.g., poking, stabbing, fatigue, pressure, heat)? Feel this energy and make a motion to act out this worst energy (e.g., a fist) and say some words that go along with that. Take some time to really express it, to get a sense of what it's saying and what it wants. We'll call this worst energy X. Make a sketch of this X energy on a paper and give it a name.

2. Who in you (u) is most upset by that X energy? What is that part of you like (e.g., peaceful, wild)? What kind of energy does it have? Feel this energy and make a motion to act out this u energy and say some words that go with it. Take some time to really express it, to get a sense of what it's saying and what it wants. Now make a sketch on your paper and give it a name.

3. Now recall a spot on the earth that you love. There may be many. Let one come to mind just now to focus on and imagine that you are there. Look around and notice where you find the X + u energies represented somehow by various parts of that earth spot. If it helps you to draw the earth spot and its energies, do so. If possible, stand and feel yourself on that earth spot. Imagine the earth breathing you somehow back and forth between the X + u as you express one energy and then the other in movement and in words, if they come to you.

4. Now take a moment to relax. Relax your mind and eyes and sense the space around that earth spot (whatever that means to you) and between the X + u energies. Now imagine that you begin to move up into the air above that earth spot and the X + u. (Put your paper on the ground if that helps.) Continue to move even further up into the universe as you gain even more distance. Sense, feel, and relax into the universe's space all around you, and sense them beginning to move and curve you about (like a leaf on the wind). And as you continue to be moved about, notice smooth motions and random, spontaneous, unpredictable little jittery wiggles and movement flirts, and just go with them. Let them be part of your *dance*. Let the universe continue to move you freely and unpredictably. (Be careful not to hurt yourself or others.) And as you are moving, imagine that you are some human or spirit or nature-like

figure that is moving in this way and ask, "What is the name of this dancer spirit?"

5. When you know this figure and feel yourself moving spontaneously, bring this experience back to your $X + u$ family on earth. That is, as this universe dancer, look back at the $X + u$ on the earth, and notice if the $X + u$ energies are somehow parts of your dance. Continue dancing until the universe dance spirit gives you a tip about the $X + u$ and the body problem. It could be surprising and noncognitive. Please make notes about your $X + u$ resolution and the name of your dancer spirit. In what way has this dancer-spirit somehow always been true of you?

Now, after this exercise, I want to ask you a question, "Who are you?" The answer changes, of course. You will have different experiences. But who were you as the dancer? I would just like to hear a couple of them. If you got a hunch or a hint, who is that dancer in you? Did it name itself?

Someone said, "Great spirit." Someone else said "Bravo." Other people said, the Rising Sun, the Wounded God, Jiggly Puff Smile Monster, Pranja, the wisdom of Emptiness in Buddhism, The Wolf, Spirit Bird, Even Flow, Thunder and Lightning, Dragon Wings, Josephine Baker (an African American dancer who broke all the rules and was way ahead of her time!), The Diamond Mind, Doggie after his bath!

Woof! Please wear these "experiences." We should see them more often. Thank you!

Audience 1:   I was working on my knees. I noticed that there is something so poignant and dear about the fragility of the body from that cosmic distance that really touched me. I was surprised by the sweetness of it. My two energies were the crashing waves and the lava rock. Over time they wear down, the bank crumbles and changes with erosion. I was working on my knees and there is some erosion in there over time. It made it feel like... like there is something that made me feel my humanness or that fragile quality of that moment of life, which really touched me.

Audience 2:   I was surprised by what came out for me. It was coming out of my most pressed-down state, a pain in my back, scar tissue from carrying too much weight, and it makes me and my *u* very depleted. And out of the depletion, from space-time dreaming, I learned, "punch back!" That surprised me!

Arny: The good thing about a symptom is that the symptom forces us to eventually become conscious of the diversity of forces within us and of our tendency to side with just one of our energies, one part of our infinite dance.

The Environment

Remember as I said earlier in this chapter, that the u + X that bother you in your body are, in a way, aspects of troubling energies in relationships and also in the environment. Many, many things, thousands of things, can disturb you about the planet. Now, we want to work with the difficult energies for you, finding the X again, this time relative to the environment.

Your body experience is a reflection of the environment. Or is the environment or the world a reflection of your body? We are going to focus on an environmental X that reminds you of your body symptom X. Choose an environmental problem that reminds you of the X that you were working on in your body. The X energy you were just working on may be in the environment. When I say the *environment*, what I mean is, it may be inorganic thing or a human being, for example, an environmentalist, or it could be an opponent of climate change who bothers you. Years ago the environmentalist Al Gore bothered me with his one-sided vehemence. Thus, the X may be a person or group in environmental movements who bothers you; or it could be physical materials like chemicals in the atmosphere that create global warming or kill different species, and so on. There are millions of things associated with the environment. Your own nature will choose which to work on today. Find the energy X that bothers you in your body, and find the energy X that bothers you in the environment, whether it's as a material thing or a person or a group. What pops up in your mind just now?

- Burning plastic
- Hospital waste—incineration and the waste itself
- Urban development
- Cigarette smoking
- Wasting paper
- Destruction of native, wild ecosystems
- Owning land. Dividing, owning, exclusive land owning

- Over-consumption
- War

War is the one big environmental issue we always say that people don't calculate, the carbon produced by war itself. It is a major one. The expense and the carbon produced by war itself are rarely entered into the calculations that I see. Let's keep going.

- Acidification of water
- Whale and dolphin slaughter
- Fracking for oil
- Deforestation
- Garbage in the Pacific that is the size of Texas
- Clear cutting
- Genetic modification of crops, foods, agriculture
- Canadian tar sands as a symbol of the oil industry
- Electronic, cellular, microwave pollution
- Wild fires
- Junk in space!
- Slaughtering the wolves
- Business and the constant pressure to profit from production and increased consumption
- Medications polluting our waters
- Oil spills
- Dam building, destroying the land of indigenous people
- Carbon emissions, large and small scale
- Non sustainable lifestyles
- Manipulation of data for political agendas
- Designing for obsolescence, so we buy new things all the time
- Large-scale open-pit mining projects

In Basel some years back, the city government thought they had solved the problem of heating by utilizing the thermal heat under the earth. They meant well, but tapping into the earth layer created an earthquake in the city. So, environmental solutions are not always sustainable.

Amy: I heard a story about herders of goats who make cashmere in Mongolia. During the global recession, people were not buying cashmere, and that hurt the goat herders. On top of this, the goats live on this arid, dry land, which they dig up to get to their food. But the cloud of dust from the dirt on their mountain drifted into China from Mongolia and added to the pollution already there. The dust created so much pollution that the Chinese tried to forbid the herders from keeping goats on that land, which they have always had. Poor goats! Poor herders! But at the same there was a huge snowfall in Mongolia that caused the goats to starve! Truly, the life of the goats is not mono-causal but an entangled, coupled web of problems. The life of the goat herders is influenced by the Chinese, and the goats are influenced by the weather and by the desire for cashmere in the West!

Remember I discussed the Greek word *kairos* in chapter 4? It refers to the times, the world atmosphere, the Tao feeling! A system mind approach is needed here for our local and global atmosphere. We need to improve the *kairos*, the feeling atmosphere, literally, the weather between us. Recall that *chronos* refers to the actual, that is consensus reality time: 3 o'clock, 4 o'clock, 5 o'clock, 6 o'clock. And *kairos* is the feeling time, the weather, between us. To work with the environment, we need to improve the weather, the climate between us: *kairos*.

One of the biggest global challenges for human beings today may be the climate situation. Maybe climate change is the first truly global problem, because, although there are wars, not everyone is as directly involved as we all are in the climate. The climate, our global warming, needs everyone to be involved; there is no one who is not involved in it. To work on a global issue we must work on our global *kairos* to get more community feeling between us. As I have said, we need to "recycle the bad guys." For example, we need to fight dictators, but we also need to remember that the dictator is a role, an energy. Amy speaks about recycling in chapter 6 of her book *Metaskills*.[98]

Recycle the dictator and use the power inherent in the role better. Recycle! We breathe the polluted air and we also breathe in the bad atmospheres that we create. If we can recycle that polluted air and those bad atmospheres, we might be able to work better on climate change not in our personal lives, but for whole planet as well.

Amy: Oh! You walk into a room with a family that is in conflict, and it takes a toll on your body. It physically makes a difference! Change that atmosphere and there is more community.

Arny: Let's start by working on the world as if it were a body symptom. Choose a body problem, a symptom. It can be the same one you worked on before or another one. We are going to find the energies in that symptom. Then ask, when you find the X energy, where do you see that X energy reflected in some environmental issue? It might be an event on the earth or a characteristic of a person that really bugs you. We are going to ask what part of you is upset by that X, and then we are going to go to an earth spot. If there is a specific spot where your environmental issue is taking place, you can choose that or you can go to any earth spot that you love; you can do the exercise using either place. We are going to find those energies there, then go above to our universe dance with its stochastic nature, and see what advice it gives us.

When doing an exercise, if you are working with a partner in dyads, sometimes it is helpful for your partner to act out the u + X for you and then see how you would actually facilitate that issue if you were there working with people. Don't forget to write down your results.

EXERCISE: BODY AND ECO-WORK

1. Choose the worst real or imagined body symptom that you feel now or felt in the past. Remember it, re-feel it, and ask yourself what is the worst energy of that symptom like (e.g., poking, stabbing, fatigue, pressure, heat)? Feel that energy and make a motion to act out this *worst* energy (e.g., a fist) and say some words that go with it. Take some time to really express it, to get a sense of what it's saying and what it wants. We'll call this worst energy X. Make a sketch of this X energy on your paper and give it a name.

2. Who in you (u) is most upset by that X energy? What is that part of you like (e.g., striving to be peaceful, wild)? What kind of energy does it have? Feel this energy and make a motion to act out this u energy and say some words that go with it. Take some time to really express it, to get a sense of what it's saying and what it wants. Now make a sketch on your paper and give it a name.

3. The helper should use her or his processmind to act out the partner's X + u at some point if needed.

4. What environmental problem or people connected with an environmental issue remind you of that X energy? What u is most upset by that X? (This may be a little different u than the original u of your body symptom.) Now, imagine that you go to the earth spot

of that environmental issue or to one of your favorite earth spots and find the environmental X + u in some aspects of the earth there. Draw this spot and the X + u energies if you want. Now feel yourself on that earth spot and imagine the earth breathing you somehow back and forth between the X + u as you express one energy and then the other in movement and possibly in words, if they come to you.

5.   Then take a moment to relax your eyes and mind. Sense the space around that earth spot in any way that feels right for you and between the X + u energies. Imagine that you begin to move away and rise up into the air above that earth spot and the X + u. (Put your paper on the ground if that helps.) Continue to move even further up into the universe as you gain more distance. Sense and feel the universe's spaces all around you. Relax into those spaces; and sense the spaces beginning to move, curve, and pull you about. As you are being moved, notice and follow possible little weird movement wiggles and begin to dance freely and unpredictably. [Helper: Say this last sentence again and stress little weird wiggles.] Just go with those little weird wiggles. Let them be part of your "dance." Let the universe continue to move you freely and unpredictably. (Be careful not to hurt yourself or others.)

6.   When you feel spontaneous movements happening in your dance, bring this deep experience back to your *family* on earth. That is, look back at the earth spot as this universe dancer and notice if the X + u energies are part of your dance. Then while in your universe dance, look back at the X + u on the earth. Recall the problem related to the environment [Helper: Act out the X + u again, if needed] and continue dancing until the universe dance gives a tip to help the eco-environmental or human problem. Act out or imagine facilitating the X + u environmental issue. Make notes.

AFTERWARDS

Audience 1:   I worked on global oil problems. At first, I was a zombie, a combination of movements between this jerky movement and this flowing movement. My helper acted it out for me to see, which was really good, and he pointed out that the whole right side of my body was running the show and the other side was limp. During my life I have had an inguinal hernia and torn ligaments in my left leg and ankle. When the processmind *saw* me walking that way, I realized that there is a dominant and a submissive split in me between left and right, a split psychically and a split also in my experiences of the environmental issue: the oil industry; this harsh, propelling, driving energy polluting the earth and waters energy; vs the earth; submissive, poisoned, the vulnerable aspect.

I could see the correlation in the body on a continuum, and in my life as well, between polarities of more outward and aggressive vs more passive and open. So then I worked on pollutions of the waters, on plastic dumped that is so permanent, accumulating in the oceans and it is so disturbing that it is there forever. But then the universe dance reminded me of my eternal nature, which I forget—we all forget. That *eternal* plastic made me suddenly realize that I am eternal, and the permanency of that plastic is trying to awaken that dreaming! What a surprise! I needed this to continue on in my public work.

My inner work was about that, about remembering that Yes, I am finite and somehow that I am also going to be around forever so it matters to me that the plastic is going to stay around. Realizing this enables me to move forward to working on this in open forums.

Arny: Wow, what a paradox. By being the junk, you learned about how to deal with it!

Audience 2: My worst symptom is in my knee, between the bones. I had surgery there. What I imagined was the pulverization of the bones. The structure was disturbed. I imagined the same energies disturbing the world, deforestation, and the industry, the machines, the destruction. Then my space-time dreaming dance movement came, and it showed me how to "let go and give, then and take." Take what you need, give back whatever you can. The circulation: Give and take. Don't take more than you need or more than you can give back.

Arny: Take and give back, equal measure, sustainable lifestyle. That would be your political message.

Audience 3:   I had a strong feeling come up for me around learning to value what has already happened on this earth in dealing with waste! My family of origin focused on waste management, so what came out of this for me was to say to everybody, when you see trash collectors, send them good energy. Say "Hi," say "Thank you for doing that." Appreciate those trash collecting people who have been really looked down upon and shunned. They have been and are doing the best they can.

Arny: Thanks for awakening all of us.

Audience 4:   I am in my forties now and was an activist for many years, in my late teens and early twenties, for the environment and the world. It was very painful work and I got burned out and disoriented. So instead, I chose to live a very simple life and live by example and stop trying to save things because it was just too much. I have not really been involved in activism since then. But this exercise was very touching because I realized how, in stepping back from that activism, what I had left behind was the polarization that I am good, but those people buying tons of things are only bad, only thoughtless, have no good qualities at all, are only destructive. This exercise gave me the opportunity to really have a conversation with them and appreciate their choices in a very personal way. You have taught before about the loggers, trying to make a living, put their kids through school, paying their bills, getting in touch with those very real life motivations. I recalled how back in my twenties we were all so fierce and fighting, chaining ourselves to things, demonstrating, and always forgetting that on the other side there was a person with a story, too. It was nice after twenty years to feel myself able to come back into that world again.

Arny: Yes, thanks for being an activist, and thanks for going even further. We need to improve climate change and the relationship climate between everyone .

Σ   *For Reflection on Chapter 22*

- Use your processmind dance with yourself to facilitate environmental problems.

- Your body belongs to you, and at the same time, its polarizations are a mirror of what's happening on earth.

- We might say, "your body, our earth." So work inside-out on the world.

CHAPTER 23

Process Oriented Economics: Contagion and Community

I introduced the idea that the space around us is stochastic, meaning that it is both predictable and deterministic and that it also has spontaneous random elements. In chapter 9, I said that *space*, in that sense, was like a child. I saw a great example of children in front of our apartment in Portland. There was a family, two parents and a few kids. They were all walking along in a sauntering sort of way; and one of the children, a tiny one, was distracted, looking up, looking down, wandering here and there. The parents were amazing. We learned later that they had home-schooled their children and had decided to let them do whatever they wanted! So the smallest and youngest child was just himself. He would look around for a while and then instead of going forward on the sidewalk he would suddenly toddle up the alley away from the sidewalk. The parents let him. He plopped down in the alley for a few minutes and then got up and walked back to his parents. But then he saw something on the ground and just sat down and looked at it. It took a long time for the parents, as you can imagine, to get anywhere!

The message for me from this story is that it's ok to be a predictable, basically deterministic adult. But at the same time, it's ok to be a random, child-like creative, nonlinear creature that must explore all paths while still going forward. The parents plus the kids together sum up to being a stochastic process.

Amy developed a simple, very short exercise to experience the stochastic nature of space. When you are going toward a particular task that you want to do in life, ask your open, creative processmind to show you how to do your task. This exercise goes quickly. The idea is that we have a more or less straight path in mind that we want to follow, but often your process is not simply linear.

EXERCISE

1. Think of a task you would like to do in your life. It could be anything from getting a degree in a university to going to the store. Write the task down and put a piece of paper on the floor about four or five feet in front of you.

2. Now relax, and sense the space between you and that task. Then I am going to ask you to move and notice how space starts to curve you about, causing you to make random movements, and see what happens when you go toward that task. Space may turn you around, it might send you in the opposite direction, you might just sit down or go straight forward. We don't know what you are going to do, but we are going to find out what that space says about that task toward which you are moving.

3. Have a little bit of a dreamy mind. Let your head and neck loosen and bobble a bit, your eyes get heavy... relaxed... dreamy... and as you are doing that just sense the space between you and that task—whatever that means to you—just feel the space between you and that task.

4. When you are ready, very slowly begin to walk toward the task and sense and let space begin to curve you and move you about. Let little random, spontaneous wiggles happen along the way. It may move you forward or backward or whatever.

5. Do be careful as you follow your little spontaneous experiences. Just trust those motions... and just unfold them a little bit. Ask, what are those motions trying to bring you? Follow the nature of space and its wiggles and curves and just ask, what are those spontaneous experiences trying to tell you about that task?

6. When you get an idea, if you get an idea, make sure you write down what it might be saying about that task. Make a note about what space-time dreaming is saying about that task that you want to do.

7. The basic idea is you can wait till you go to bed at night and have a dream about the task, or you can let your movement dream now.

Amy: Something very funny happened to me when I did this exercise. It is kind of embarrassing, but something funny happened when I tried this exercise at home. I was working on how to do the seminar and I was kind of uptight. I was trying to get my notes together, but I could not get my head together. I was trying to figure out how to do things, and I walked toward the task of preparing this seminar and did this exercise as part of my preparation.

As I was walking, feeling space moving me around, waiting for random things to happen, I started to curve around a bit and suddenly Arny came behind me and pulled my pants down! That was so funny! [Both laugh.] And then I thought, "Oh god, now wait a minute, I am waiting for my random thing to happen! I have got to concentrate or something!" We both started laughing, and I realized, oh that was the random thing! Sometimes it takes a while to understand! Things happen all the time in the day, and you think, "Oh, that is just stupid, let me do the real thing!" And you miss the real thing! I realized that I needed to be more playful, more relaxed, have more fun, and actually be more naked in a sense of, "This is who I am. This is all I am!" not try and be something else. It was really fun!

Arny: She is fun to play with! I want to remind you all again, let space time dreaming into your life. Connecting to space is as I have said earlier, in a way, a matter of life and death. Often our process seems to seek space-time in near-death experiences. People near death sometimes have experiences of leaving their ordinary consensus reality body, rising up and moving out, and then often come back to earth, sometimes to their frequent disappointment. They are unhappy about the fact that they have to return again, but something says go back. That crucial space-time experience that happens near death is something we are trying to integrate. Kids understand space-time and really everyone does in their deepest self.

Audience: When you are doing the dance, *what* part in you notices the random movements? Also when you do it in a dyad, to the other person observing the movement might seem unusual but to you does it seem perfect?

Arny: In space-time dreaming, depending upon the depth of your inner work, your deepest self, your processmind is looking at itself. It is on the verge of waking up while being in touch with dreaming. As I said in chapter 2, Wheeler and others would have said that it is the universe looking at itself. And yes, our *natural self*, the universe dance, does look unusual to someone else looking at you because they may not be used to seeing people dancing freely!

Now I want to focus on deep democracy and global skills, and then I'll turn to process oriented economics. I have not talked about that topic before. I am doing so now, thanks to philosophical leaders of the Occupy Movement. Some of them from New York City, Portland, Chicago, London, Cairo, and other places connected with me this winter with emails called, "Movement Looking for a Mentor." I don't consider myself a mentor, but they felt that Processwork might help their movement, their worldwide process that much of the planet is involved in right now. What is the economic change that is trying to happen?

23.1 Occupy Movement.
**Occupy US, Canada, Europe, North
Africa, Australia (Wikipedia)**

In the previous chapters, I spoke about your relationship to your X, to that part of you that you inadvertently divorced. Inadvertent means, you did not consciously intend that divorce, you did not even know that you had divorced anything. Nature did it to you in a way. Nature insists on parallel, divided worlds that don't always connect. That is why we all need to go deeper in ourselves to reconnect them.

The basic idea is "bring your family home!" That means, bring the *u* part of yourself, the part closer to your primary process, and the divorced X home. Bring their relationship home to a deep inner sense, to a simple *universal* viewpoint. Many problems are exaggerated due to not being at home. We need to go back to shamanism and to *ecos*, which, to repeat, means literally house or home and is a root for economy.

It is normal to split things off, but we human beings have split things off to such a degree that we need a shift, a global shift. Our old leaders energized and reinforced the polarizations. Now we need a new kind of leaders that pick up the polarizations with awareness and unpack them, which also depolarizes them!

THE NEW KIND OF LEADER USES AWARENESS

This new leader picks up ghost roles, enacts them, and brings in all levels of awareness. She knows that awareness is not hers alone and that power and awareness belong to everyone. Everyone is responsible. That is a new political and psychological direction for our future world. Of course, there are challenges to realizing this new form of leadership. It may seem so simple to just let ourselves be moved and dream. Really, there is nothing to it, and yet... we rarely do it. Why? There is no one answer, but there is one solution: Relax a little bit and just do space-time dreaming!

Nature herself seems to want diversity to be present; the parts, therefore, are important. It is counter-cultural to stand up in a meeting and say, "Today, I want to talk about a and b and also dream with you about those issues." Yet, there is nothing to it. Nothing! But most adults are shy about dreaming together with others, without the help of drugs.

There are various awareness edges to noticing fields around you. The consensus reality field is an atmosphere that appears, for example, during conversation. We may be sitting over dinner as a little group, talking together about other people, and a *field* or *atmosphere* arises. What kind of field is that? One aspect of the field appears when parts or people are mentioned but not represented or processed. That is a consensus reality field that leaves tension in the air. The conversational field is laden with a kind of *pollen*, so to speak; but if we remember the parts and act them out, the field becomes more interesting, more dynamic. Tension occurs when things are mentioned but not explored. When those things are processed, the field relaxes.

Another more dreamlike field is a mood between you and your friends. Here, there is a hidden, dreamlike, not-yet mentioned person or issue, an unspoken $X + u$ in the background of that mood that is not processed. For example, friends or housemates meet you for breakfast. They appear in the morning, and are perhaps grumpy, and you think, "Oh, no. Not that mood again! I cannot stand that. Let's talk about something fun!" That attempt on your part occasionally cheers the others up. But there is an X and a u in the field, possibly shared or even nonlocal, that is not processed in that level of interaction. Not processing that grumpy mood leaves information in the air that is an aspect of discomfort.

Organizations, too, have moods before there are descriptions of who is against whom and what is happening. If there is a mood in the air between you and somebody else, just ask, "What is behind this mood?" Is somebody down? Is someone or something putting down that person? What parts are not voiced out loud?

In the consensus reality field, the awareness edge is that people and things are mentioned but are not explored. In the dreaming field, the second awareness edge is to notice a dreamlike mood in which there are parts that have not yet been explored.

A third edge is noticing essence aspects of fields, those large, city-wide or global dreamy spaces. You look at the sea, "Oh, isn't that nice, such a beautiful sea." Or you go to the movies, see something, and a dreamy feeling mood occurs. Sometimes when you go to a new city, it sometimes feels as if there is a mood around a whole city or country!

Don't marginalize global moods and fields around organizations of any kind. Some amazing things can happen in a group. We see amazing things in group process all the time. I am thinking of a particular diversity situation in a large organization with which we have been working. Whenever something strong or amazing happened, there would be a sudden sense of "Ahhh, wow!" that would mushroom through the room. Everyone would notice it, then quickly drop that sense and move on. Everyone tries to just go on, which is ok, but at some point, that subtle essence atmosphere needs more time, and more notice.

In the governing leadership paradigm, the facilitator is often imagined to help or be the identified leader, the one who must do everything. In the new paradigm, try to be aware of the atmosphere and ask others to do so as well. After all, awareness is shared with everybody, in the same way that awareness itself is part of the field. You, as a leader, facilitator, as coach, as the therapist, as a teacher in a class; whatever you are doing; you are central and also remember that what is central about you is also a shared role. The field, the universe that is space-time dreaming, is the leader!

PROCESS ORIENTED ECONOMICS: THE DEEP DEMOCRACY OF MONEY

Now let's apply what we know to working on economics. Who has ever had a problem with money? [Hands go up everywhere.] Economics is a central issue; it belongs in psychology, in Processwork, in politics and in ecology. Economic differences create rank problems in all organizations and need to be explored.

A process oriented view of economics is neither materialistic nor spiritual but some combination of both and neither. Economic issues are defined by whoever is describing or discussing them. Your personal economics are individual and depend upon your personal history. Your feelings about economics depend not only on your financial situation now but upon how you grew up, in part, and upon your social history, gender, and race. Economic issues are linked with social issues globally. Your personal economics are linked with what is happening in the environment and with how you feel about life.

I want to again thank the Occupy Movement for inspiring me to think more about economics. The Occupy Movement is an international protest movement against social and economic inequality. Its primary goal is to make the economic structure and power relations in society more favorable to the underclasses. It was inspired in part by the Arab spring, the fight for democracy against dictatorial rulers.

The consensus reality perspective of finances, whether personal or public, is a matter of (at least to begin with) how much money you have in your pocket, in the bank, under the bed, or wherever you keep it. What material things do you possess? You may have little or no money, but you may have material things that consensus reality deems valuable. Do you have jewels? Is or was your family poor or rich? Do you have connections with somebody who is going to die who can give you money? Do you have property? Or do you not have these things?

Your financial property also includes the specific abilities and talents that you have. Does your brain work in such a way that you are liable to make more money than somebody whose brain works differently? These thoughts just touch the surface of economics.

What do you have that can be exchanged for a debt? It may not be money. In certain parts of the world people still don't use only money. If you have something you can exchange, you are lucky. If you don't have such things, your economic feeling and rank may be low in this area. Health plays a huge role in your economics; as does your age, race, gender, sexual orientation, religion, and so on.

What year and what country are you living in? You might be poor in a so-called *first-world* country and still be wealthy compared to people in other parts of the world. You may feel quite detached about money and think, "Finances? Who cares about that? So what!" You are lucky to feel so detached, but just know that such financial detachment is usually made possible by a fair degree of financial rank, whether or not you are aware of this rank. People with rank rarely realize it regardless of what that rank is. For them, unrecognized rank becomes the same as invisible privilege.

Audience 1:   Where would you put luck?

Arny: Luck is getting down to the essence level. Luck is a huge thing, both good luck and bad luck.

Audience 2:   Are you referring to one's personal psychology around the issue of deserving or not deserving good things?

Arny: You are speaking of dreamland where financial powers are related to feeling that we are good people and have value or we're not so great and have less valuable. The sense of being rich or poor is complex in its connection with personal history, age, health, and also race. In addition, gender plays a role. These are all huge factors. We cannot just talk about economics in the abstract; we have to talk about economics in relation to a given culture, group, and individual in order for the discussion to be meaningful.

There are various views around money. I am looking at money here as something that can be exchanged for something else, at a most basic, consensus reality level. Today's money has no value as a physical commodity, but gets its value because some government says it can be accepted as a form of payment, within the boundaries of the country, for "all debts, public and private."

The deep democracy of economics includes not just consensus reality facts and views but also dreamland and the essence or processmind level. As I already indicated, your sense of security is probably greater if you are at the top of the money ladder, but you are generally nervous if you are in the middle and lower part of the remaining 99%. Loss of money or fear of its loss creates panic states. When I say panic, I mean *pan*-ic. *Pan* is the mythical god that means all or all-embracing. Panic is therefore an experience of everything inside of you firing fear and terror. It is a very, very important and difficult issue for everybody who has that experience or who has had it in the past. Panic plays a big role in all money issues. Panic can make you push more, fear more. It can be depressing.

We can talk about being detached, and I will do that also, but first we need to recognize that if you are living in an area of the world such as today's (2012) Greece, or any place where you or your people live under financial stress; then you easily feel polarized and dislike your leaders and other parts of the world that have contributed to your area's difficulties. You feel that you can't afford to be detached; not to begin with, at least.

In dreamland, you may feel either rich or poor, depending upon the moment, to some extent. As I mentioned in chapter 21, Amy and I worked with a small group of the richest people in the country, and we were amazed to see how poor and afraid of life they felt.

Arny: We did not charge them because we felt that they were poor.

Amy: That was such a big thing to them, assuming that they should pay for everything.

Arny: These people have a lot of money, but they were panicked about this and that. The concept of the top 1% is right, but it is not enough. Within those who have apparent consensus reality rank, many of them are terrified, for example, about their health issues. They were rattled and terrified about the prospect of death. They could not stop talking about death, and no amount of money was going to help them with that. They were also troubled by the problems associated with having a lot of money: "What is the right thing to do with it?"

The 1% and the 99% are roles; that is, experiences unconsciously shared by everybody. We all have all roles in us. Rich, the 1%, as a role is usually projected on to that particular group and described as greedy and hyper-consuming: "I want to buy more and own more." The banks are often associated with this characterization, as are those aspects of governments that exhort: "Raise taxes but lower them for the rich! We don't care about the poor! Save more money by decreasing their benefits! We are not going to carry them anymore!"

Likewise, the 99%, that is, the middle class and the poor, are also roles involving fear for social and physical security, depression, hunger, and death. As I said before, panic is another aspect of fear in response to the reality or the perception of not having enough. Panic can lead to a violent reaction that imparts a dangerous power and a kind of *victim rank*. If you feel beaten down, you get upset and you feel like a victim and that gives you a kind of rank to go ahead and bash other people. Those are all aspects of the deep democracy of finances.

Now let's consider the essence level of finances: contagion, community, spirituality, and shamanism. *Contagion* refers to a particular process in which economic changes in one country will likely spread to other countries. Contagion is about experiences in one spot being *picked up* at a distance. What is happening in Athens is important today because of the contagion involved. We think the problem is situated in Athens, but what happens in Athens influences the markets in Cairo, London, Moscow, Tokyo, and New York.

Recall how the 2008 collapse on Wall Street reverberated, and still reverberates, around the globe . We live in a contagious world, not just with viruses but with feelings. A tragedy in one location *goes viral* and feelings, attitudes, and beliefs are picked up everywhere. So what is bothering you in your own personal finances may be part of a virus going around. Contagion is a causal and also, in part, a nonlocal aspect of economics. It is a field effect, now here and now there, like a disease at the essence level.

There is another aspect of the essence level of economics that I would like to call community. Why is it that when a handful of the 99% rise up and say, "Now we want," then increasing numbers of people on their street corner repeat that message: "Now we want!" That is fun! But then someone comes from the newspaper or TV or radio with a microphone and asks, "What exactly is it you want?" and some people respond with, "We don't want to say." What is right about their answer? They are implying that what they want can hardly be stated. What is it that they want? Listen, I will do it again:

"Now we want!"

[Group repeats] "Now we want!"

What is the message in that proclamation? It is community. Part of the essence level in the background of this message is the feeling of community, the security of "we the people," we the community, the atmosphere of togetherness. Together we are here and within this community. Of course, they are speaking in this way in part because they don't have a microphone and are showing they don't need one. But they are giving the world another message. Community implies that financial issues are not the main point. In essence: "Let's share." We don't need the money thing, you understand, we need the relationship thing, the community thing. That relationship component is a very deep aspect of finances that is usually overlooked. For example, do you need the radio or TV or whatever, or do you need the musical feeling you are looking for? Sharing! It is like this: "May I use your radio? I need the feeling, not just the radio." These are some essence aspects of finances. In this way, people can be *rich*, even if they have little as long as they have community. This is another view of finances that is very different from the view of consensus reality.

The last essence-level characteristic I want to mention is the spirituality of the middle way. I appreciate how the Dalai Lama stresses Buddhism's middle way.[99] The middle way means that things neither exist nor are they absent. What we call a *thing* in consensus reality has a paradoxical existence at the essence level. Something is not real and, at the same time, it is not unreal. I am a person with a body, and I am still a person without a body. Don't hold onto the state-oriented idea of *thingness*. This is one of the great gifts of Buddhism: Don't hold onto the thingness of something. The Dalai Lama calls this practice of not holding on the *in-between-ness* of the middle way.

Also remember Gandhi. His idea about ownership is that we don't own our shoes, we don't own apartments, houses, or cars. Gandhi said, we are the trustees of these things, holding those possessions for the future of the world. Whatever we are doing is considered in relation to future generations. I think that is a really deep, essence-level concept. We are trustees; we care for and will share whatever we own with everybody else. From this viewpoint, we should care for our bodies well, too, for they are ours, but in a way, our lives also belong to everyone. We are the trustees of everything we *own*, holding it all for the benefit of ourselves and others.

Gandhi said that the British in India were not solely responsible for India's problems. He writes that his own yoga practice taught him that it was not the British, per se, it was Indians' attachment at that time to the British way of life and to the materialism that the British introduced, which germinated India's problems. Getting the British out would not solve the problems of India. He recognized that the British were in a dreamland-like role, and it seems to me as if he was seeking detachment at the essence level for the Indian people.

Let's say that this patch [marking out a section on the floor] is my land. My people have lived here for a long time and now you come and move your chair here onto my property. The normal part of me says that I have to push you off with everyday battle tactics. But my essence-level economics says, the problem is not just with your chair but also with my attachment to what you stand for. When I remove my attachment, that shared dreamland possessiveness, you will be able to leave. You, alone, are not the problem. This does not mean that we should accept an intruder on our property. Fight that intruder in some way, but try to detach from what that intruder represents!

A final aspect of economics I want to talk about comes from the Arabic word *Inshallah*, which means god [Allah] willing. From this viewpoint, what is happening financially to us, whether it's "Oh, my god, a catastrophe!" or "Yippee! I got lucky!" is another aspect of this essence level. *Inshallah*, let the process decide, nature knows best, is a Taoistic perspective.

Audience: Does *Inshallah* involve luck?

Arny: Yes, *Inshallah*! Nature knows whatever god wants, and god willing, nature willing, what it wants will be part of the greater process. My point is that all levels of economics belong to the overall process of any individual or organization.

God willing, that is a deep notion. Use consensus reality first to try to resolve your financial problems, then use all the other levels. Maybe you can get down to, "OK, it is the Tao, my process." Reaching that level at some moment can be very helpful, too.

Audience: I want to tell about an experience I had 15 years ago. I was in graduate school and living in a car with my children, and I was panicked around money. How would I support my children?! One night I had a profound dream that I had won the lottery. Yet in the dream, I was still panicked. It took me time to understand that dream. The lesson that came really deeply and still informs me today is that it is not about the money. It is about this universal credit or abundance to which I have access, despite my external circumstances. It was profound. I was so poor but also so rich.

Arny: I understand... even if you say you are still panicked, you are *rich*.

Audience: Thank you.

Arny: Remember the Bushmen. Some have claimed that in their community there is no financial problem because everyone seems to share everything. The whole community cares for everybody. That may be an essence-level community method that has worked for the oldest aboriginal community on the planet.

Shamanism also belongs to the essence level of money. When we were in Africa years ago, Amy and I had only debts, no money. We did not have any money, and we needed money. We met a shaman who danced for us and went off into the woods and made a little something for us. She just followed her process and returned with a little tiny something that she gave us. We still have that amazing gift. We came back to Switzerland, to all sorts of financial trouble at the time. We focused on this little shaman's gift and suddenly our luck got better!

Amy: When I get into those shamanistic states, all kinds of things come that are very surprising for me. Isn't there an aboriginal community that believes that if you dream something negative about somebody else, then the dreamer has to give something to whomever he or she dreamed about?

Arny: Yes! That is dreamland economics and it is a great idea. If you have a bad dream about somebody, better give them something! That person is both inside and out. Finances in that aboriginal community are dream-oriented work on relationships and community.

Audience: Can you say something more about that feeling of people being your family... about how to have that feeling?

Arny: We usually feel a sense of family with those who look like us and speak like us and have the same culture and stuff like that. But if you are deep enough in yourself for a moment, you might somehow feel and understand the other person even if you have never talked to her or him before. It is an important, essence-level field experience, and when you act or say something from that level, you will see that people somehow smile, and when they smile, there is something wonderful that happens.

Even if you are the most introverted, quiet person, and you never say anything, try this: If you see someone walking on the road with her or his dog, try saying, "It's a great day for a walk," but without looking at the person in their face. Just, "It's a great day for a walk," and you might see them smile. I think those moments are important. Just speak about the space, the field between you.

How easily you can talk to strangers depends on where you grew up. The inclination to connect is in everybody at least a little bit. You might consider trying it, even if you are shy. Everybody has their process, so if it is not right for you, then of course don't try it. But even if you are shy and you see somebody gazing at the sea, you can say, "Boy that sea looks really nice," and a giggle may slip out. Something amazing happens by joining the field of other people. In a way, everybody is your family! Experiment with this experience of connecting with people you don't think of as family in your consensus reality world.

Let's now work on financial situations. In the next exercise, work on a difficult situation around your personal finances. What are some of the most difficult parts of your personal finances for you? There may be a lot of things, but if you can, choose just one for now. What is the most difficult aspect of your personal finances? Is anyone willing to share?

Audience 1: Ownership of property. Feeling guilty for being able to own something, feeling in conflict with the idea of ownership of land, considering history of place and displacement of indigenous people.

Audience 2: Whenever I have a job or work I don't like it. It is not that I don't like working, I just don't like what I am doing so I never really can stay in a job. I don't have a fixed income ever. For me, the most difficult thing is finding something I really like to do and that is meaningful for me.

Audience 3: I love the work I am in, and because I have chosen the field of education I am compensated with half of the value I would get if I worked in a different position. I love teaching but teaching is not very well-paid, and other people with the same education get a lot more in my field.

Audience 4: Today's difficult economy has separated us as a family. My husband is in another state now that there are no jobs here, where we live. So we are going in the direction of separate lives. What we need to do to make the living, to meet the requirements is not easy. How can you be together and work together?

Audience 5: I have a hard time charging people for working with them.

Audience 6: I would like to just give it all away but I cannot. I do acupuncture and homeopathy.

Audience 7: I work in business. It is edgy, and I feel like I have to take the role of the 1%. I cannot complain about my financial situation, but, at the same time, I feel really disconnected from my heart and the spiritual aspect, so in a sense I do feel poor.

Audience 8: Sometimes I make a lot of money, sometimes very little. Either way, everything I make disappears. I am not a big spender, I don't waste money, it just goes somewhere. My account is almost always at zero.

To work on your personal finances, first see if there is something you can do in consensus reality to help yourself or others financially. Please don't ignore that level, and then remember the dreamland levels. The sense of panic that is sometimes there, or perhaps an obliviousness, those also belong to the work on finances. And, of course, the essence level, the Buddha's middle way or some aspect of the essence level, is important too.

In the next exercise, work with the various polarities in your most difficult financial situation and see if you can get some advice from your processmind about that situation. We will ask you to choose one of your most difficult situations (it might be real or imagined) you have with money. You might be afraid you are going to lose it or that you will get robbed or attacked. Maybe you are unemployed and have social security issues. Maybe there are dependency issues: You are dependent or you have dependents that you have to support, big debts that are difficult to pay, or you do not have enough money for health care.

EXERCISE: PERSONAL FINANCES AND YOUR SPACE–TIME DREAMING DANCE

1. Describe and think about your own real or imagined financial situation (dependency, job insecurity, nervousness, unemployed, etc.). What is the most troublesome part of that financial situation for you?

2. Now feel the atmosphere of the most troublesome part of your financial situation and identify the most troublesome energy, X, for you in that scene. Feel the X energy, make a motion to describe it, and say a couple of words that go along with it. Take time to really explore this energy: What is it expressing and what does it want? Make a sketch of this X energy, a little figure to represent it on your paper, and name it.

3. What part of you, u, is most disturbed by that X energy? Feel this u energy, make a motion to describe it, and say a couple of words that go with that energy. Take time to explore it, find out what it's expressing and what it wants. Make a sketch on your exercise paper of this u energy, a little figure to represent it, and then name it. Take a moment to go back and forth between the X + u energies, expressing them in movement and words. Now, place the paper with your exercise results on the ground.

4. Stand, if you can, and look at the X + u on the ground to help gain more distance from them and then imagine moving further up into the air above them. And imagine that you go even further up and feel yourself in the universe. Relax and let go of your every-day mind temporarily as you flow into the universe's space and sense it beginning to move and dream you spontaneously (like a leaf on the wind or being moved about in the sea). Sense it curving and pulling you about. And as you move, notice little weird wiggles and movement flirts that happen. Follow them and let them dance you about freely and unpredictably. Be careful for yourself and those around you.

5. When you feel yourself dancing spontaneously and freely, let your dancing spirit name itself. Who is it that's dancing in this way? Still feeling the dance as this dancing spirit, look back at the X + u finance energies on the ground and catch quick fantasies, in-tuitions, or a tip that arises about how to deal with them. And let

this dancing spirit give the X + *u* some advice. Make a note about the advice and your dancing spirit's name.

The advice the universe dancer gives you may be very practical advice, it might be a feeling kind of advice or a dreaming kind of advice. We don't know exactly what it is going to be. What did you learn from processing your own personal finances? Anyone learn something they will remember tomorrow?

Audience 1: It's all noncognitive as you say. But the answer was clear: Charge more, work less!

Audience 2: Be practical about the dreaming and take little steps. Go forward with the dreaming.

Audience 3: More and more appreciation, gratitude for less and less.

Audience 4: Be creative with the tax department. I am a break dancer. My dance had too much rigidity in it, and I could let it go.

Audience 5: How long can you go on this process journey? I have a background in a Tibetan Buddhist practice in which you go into a *sadhana* and usually you work with a mantra that represents energy, body, and mind. Usually in practice you use all three. It resembles what we did in Processwork in this exercise, but when I do a practice, it varies for me. Sometimes I am more in touch, other times I float away and get lost in myself. How long do you let the process go on here?

Arny: Thank you for the question. I don't have a formula for that, only the suggestion to follow the individual. For some people, their process brings them into their processmind for one moment, and then they come back out again. And other people connect to their processmind, and it does not bring them back to everyday reality right away. Others can hold the essence level and consensus reality level together for longer.

Amy: Sometimes I go into that space and keep going and let it flow and all sorts of creative things start happening—writing, music, dance, all kinds of things—it takes me into creative stuff. Sometimes there is a real crunch when I am working with a difficult conflict or something and I need to try to access it quickly. Sometimes I can't access it at all, and sometimes I can. It can be a really fast connection to help me get through something or work with something or it can take more time, more waiting.

Small Group Process

Now let's apply this work to all your group economic and financial processes. Do this work in your family systems. Whenever money problems come up (and they do come up frequently), create little group processes with your families or with your friends. Or, if you are coach or a teacher and the issue of finances comes up, make people more conscious about what is happening, and do a small group process on it. Now, work together in small practice groups of about three to give you all an experience of small group organizational process.

In this small group work on economics, remember the idea of rank and of roles. Remember that *things* are roles in the sense that when we project or see them in another person, there is also a role in the background.

Remember the 99%—or name that role whatever you want. Recall the problem of being nervous about the future, about your social welfare. There may be some depression, so notice that if it comes up and get into that area also. Feeling frozen around the issue of money, feeling in shock or panic about money—work with whatever arises.

Remember the rank feelings that belong to the 1%: "Who needs it. Don't worry about it." In some areas, people with rank think that the others, those among the 99% who are protesting, should just shut up because, "They are all idiots." That is a rank problem. And don't forget all the ghost roles around immigration, race, and gender!

Above all, remember "we the people" at the essence level, and remember the community feeling. Bring forward and show your essence experiences, your processmind experiences, if you can and with your own limitations. Remember them and use your awareness to emphasize these states of mind and use them to flow with, to process, whatever comes up.

You can use the same $X + u$ you contacted in the previous exercise, or you can access any new states that come up around world issues and finances. Everybody together will find their universe dances and, while working in that shared field, we'll see what advice comes out of that field for these world financial issues.

In the following exercise you are going to get together in groups of three. One person will be the timer and the guide as well as being a participant. We want all three people to discuss world financial issues that are on your mind. You might all have different issues. You might discuss community problems, some large-scale issue, anything that is larger than your personal scene.

Then the chosen timekeeper will guide and lead all of you through some inner work where you will focus on an issue that is important to you. What happens will be a combination of inner and outer group work. Continue until you all come to some insight or a resolution.

....

EXERCISE: MONEY AND UNIVERSE MIND (IN SMALL GROUPS OF THREE)

1. (15 minutes) All Together: Choose one of you to be the exercise timekeeper and guide. This person will also be a participant. Discuss as a threesome:

    What is a worst national or world financial problem for you (e.g., home foreclosures) and the worst X in that problem? (e.g., depression, greed, deprivation, fear). It might be a community, city, or international issue. Use something that is larger than your personal scene. Just discuss together, no need to agree.

2. (10 minutes) Now stop talking and the guide will lead everyone through this inner work.

    Alone: Each participant does inner work on the following areas before getting together again as a group.

    a. Again, choose and describe to yourself a worst real or imagined national or world financial situation. Feel the atmosphere of that situation. What does it feel like? What is the most troublesome X energy in that situation for you? (i.e., greed, depression). Feel and then express that X energy with a motion and words. Explore it a bit further to find out what it's really expressing and wants. Make a sketch of this X energy on your paper and name it. Then ask yourself, what part of you (or what part of the world), u, is most disturbed by that X energy? Feel and then express that u energy with a motion and words and explore it to find out what it's really expressing and wants. Make a sketch of this u energy on your paper and name it.

b. Now, while still doing inner work, stand up, if you can, and recall a favorite earth spot and imagine that you are there. Look around and notice where you find these two energies in that earth spot. Now, feel that earth spot again and imagine that it begins to breathe and move you back and forth expressing the $X + u$ energies in movement and perhaps in words.

c. Relax and sense the space and field around that earth spot and between the $X + u$. Then, imagine that you rise above that earth spot and move even further up into the universe. Feel the universe space–time field around you and sense it beginning to dream and move you about. Relax a bit more and as you continue to move, notice and follow little movement flirts or wiggles that move and dance you spontaneously and unpredictably. Be careful of others as you move about.

d. When you feel yourself dancing freely and spontaneously, let your dancing spirit name itself. As that dancing spirit, look back at the $X + u$ energies of that financial issue and let the universe dance give you a tip about them. Make notes about the tip and the dancing spirit's name.

3. (35 minutes total) OK, now everyone, come together again.

4. (25 minutes) Do a group process bringing the $u + X$ family *home* by facilitating and speaking with space–time dreaming.

(Helper: Read all of this section before starting):

We shall spin the pen to find the person whose issue we shall all focus on. This person should tell us about the financial situation she or he had chosen and the $X + u$ worked on. Each of you should remember and re-feel your own universe dance with its unpredictable wiggles, sense the space between all of you, and when ready, any one of you can begin to spontaneously express the chosen person's X or u energies. Act it out! Then someone else should come forward to represent and act out one of the other energies. Everyone, follow your universe dreaming as it moves you spontaneously about the room while expressing various $X + u$ roles, switching, and playing out energies and adding ghost roles, (that is roles that have been mentioned but not yet represented). If you get lost or too "pulled in," re-feel the detachment and spontaneity of your dancing spirit and continue with the group process until some resolution or insight occurs or the time is up.

5. (10 minutes) Discuss what you learned.

AFTERWARDS

Arny: Did you notice that you cannot always track in a linear way how solutions came about? You cannot always say that A follows B. You don't know how A appeared. Did it follow B or was it before B?

Audience 1: I think that it was Bruce Lee who said, "Learn the form, master the form, and forget the form." That is what happened to us! At one point, we just had to forget the presenting issue and follow the energy. Before we did that, we did not feel the sense of a team, but when we let ourselves go into the energy of what was happening, it created something pretty interesting.

Audience 2: I want to share what went on in our group because I think it could be useful for a lot of people. I was talking about parental short-sightedness, that is, not worrying about the future of the children. When we were playing it out, one of us said that she only wanted to care about her family. I supported that, saying, "I want you to care about your children, your grandchildren, and your great-grandchildren, about multi-generations." That generalization of the meaning of family was a great insight for all. Then someone else picked up the role of a child that wanted to have a good life, which very quickly changed the short-sighted parent.

Audience 3: In my group, the issue was war, and how such obscene amounts of money flow to war, carbon junk into the air, massacres, destruction. And then the energy that was really disturbed, the *u*, was the love of the mothers. So in this process the goddess Athena appeared at first as a ghost role. We played her and she showed the bigger picture, and *she* said it is sometimes necessary to break the heart of humanity, to break it open. The place was Greece, and so the goddess Athena appeared and helped us come together by opening us up. It was awesome.

Arny: Thank you for telling us that. Here Athena is saying the problems are here to open our hearts. That is one viewpoint on the mess we create, surely not the only one, but an important one behind the re-creation of community.

[A prolonged group silence ensues]

Arny: What happened to you in that quiet moment just now?

I felt the heart open... broken open.

We all connected in that moment.

For a moment, one field.

Audience 4: In our group, we were dealing with the problem of the rich and poor in Iran. It was interesting because some awesome unnamed feeling, a ghost role, appeared that was interested in both the rich and poor, in people who have and people who don't have. When the rich and the poor started arguing, this ghost was not happy. We tried to label the ghost as some power, and later on we discovered that it was not a human structure, it was greater than that. So I became the opposite energy or entity that feeds on conflict and was interested in us not communicating. I reminded all of death, of all of us who die. I said, "I will feed off your children. I am powerful, bigger than you, endless, and I am happy to be your fear!" Then something really beautiful happened. Someone countered me, this nasty spirit, by wondering, "Well, what are you scared of?" I said, "I am not scared of anything." Suddenly I realized that I, as the monster, am afraid of shrinking! Love and light make the monster shrink. I, as the monster, I feed off fear. But those playing out the love roles said, "Great! As much as we care for each other, we can care for you, as something that we love." I started to feel that it was shrinking me and that I could relate to them, and I could feel their pain... it was so beautiful, I learned so much from this.

Arny: You were part of the family even though you were a monster! Yes, awesome!

THE POWER OF COMMUNITY

Audience 5: I wanted to share what happened in my group of three. One of us is from Thailand, one from Chile, and I have a Philippine background. We were working on the fragile economic situations in our different countries that are destabilized by others from outside sending money back. Overseas workers send money back, this is a huge common cultural process embedded in these cultures. But this *gift* destabilizes the self-sufficiency of the country itself.

So we worked on the one in need and the one giving and the one saying no to that and encouraging the indigenous people to manage on their own. This was really powerful because each of us was organically able to change positions, moving back and forth between all the sides. All the role changing with the processmind helped to readjust the roles and depolarize them. Then at one point, an awesome quietness, the silence moved in… and I could feel the connection among the three of us. This deep sense of connection made me feel how much all of our countries need this kind of Processwork to depolarize all these stuck places. Sometimes it is so hard to feel this way when you are in the middle of doing Worldwork in our countries.

Audience 6: In that group, I was playing the role of the X energy, "Give me, give me, give me. I have nothing. You have everything!" What I experienced for the first time is the people with money then saying, "We don't have everything!" That stopped me, because I realized that I was projecting this idea that the wealthy live in paradise and therefore they can give because they have *everything*. So to hear that they did not have everything reminded me of what you have said in the past, namely that the 1% and 99% are roles in each of us as well as outer realities.

I realized, too, how rich I felt to be part of the community, even though we were asking for help. I saw that the so-called *other* side, the rich people, don't have what we have: namely, that we are able to feel and speak as one voice as a community. Suddenly it dawned on me, this is where the shift happened for me, the realization that there is power in the community. There is power in having a community that is able to get together and, in this case, ask for help.

Arny: Yes, the so-called *poor* may ask and need help but they have a power and wealth themselves.

Audience 6:   I flowed with the processes and suddenly something just came out… "Everything is in the right place."

Arny: Everything is a mess but somehow, from the deepest viewpoint, everything is ok. It is good to hear these process descriptions. There is a nonlinear moment that happens in there that is hard to formulate exactly, the moment in which the elder who can hold the various sides appears. No one is only one thing only… for long.

Σ   *For Reflection on Chapter 23*

- You or someone else may be the identified leader but the real one is the space between us all.

- Economics is very real! It's about money, capital, and rank and consists of shared roles such as *rich* and *poor*. Economics is also dreamlike consisting of good *gods* and *monsters*.

- Economics also has a field-like essence level giving rise to feelings of detachment, contagion, community, and spirituality.

CHAPTER 24

The Big Picture:
Street and Worldwork Training

In schools, organizations, and governments, in conflict areas and in city squares; present situations in 2012 and onward indicate that the world is moving toward democracies in more and more countries. It seems almost obvious that the world is looking for a deeper democracy. To actualize a world that is more aware of itself, that values various positions in its social and ecological fields, we need elders, people who are in touch with a big picture. This big picture is one in which everyone and everything seeks and finds a home, where individuals and organizations learn to debate but also appreciate themselves deeply as individuals, roles, and as aspects of the universe.

Democracy needs more deep democracy. I would love to see more world theater. Please go to your favorite street corner or coffee house and do a 3-minute theater on that corner about an issue that is important to you. My point is to occupy all the roles: the 1% and the 99%! Occupy everything including the universe!

But once again, before going further, let's first meditate:

- Think of a question. It could be about your entire life, it could be about what you are going to have for lunch, it could be anything that is on your mind. Choose either a question or a problem. Make a note on a piece of paper, or use something else to represent this question.

- When you have that written down, associate it with something on the floor or around you.

- Relax a little bit; relax your mind and your shoulders, your neck. Let yourself have a foggy mind. Sense that space around you, and let it move you slowly toward that object representing your question. Let the space curve and move you with little wiggles as you go toward that question or problem. Space–time dreaming might take you forward, backward, around, down; we just don't know what. Just trust your experiences... they will bring you an insight.

- Catch an intuition and meditate on it. What is that intuition telling you about your question?

- When you catch something, make a note about it so you can remember it. Give thanks to your dreaming mind, the creator of dreams, the processmind. Don't ever forget your magical wiggle. We usually have a more linear mind but the wiggle just says, "Hey! There is something else happening." Opening up to opening up is the basic point of that exercise: remaining open to all the unpredictable things, not just to one process or the other, but to the consistent ongoing flow of processes. Otherwise, you procrastinate instead of wiggling.

CATCHING YOUR BIG PICTURE

What is your picture of what life is about? I ask that not just as a philosophical question but also as a psychological one. If you work with tense situations, you need a big picture. I am not thinking just about group work or organizations or even big forums. We all seek a big picture when life is stressful. We all feel more secure in ourselves when we have found a satisfactory answer to what life is about. Each of us has to formulate that answer for her or himself. What is it all about?

In this book, I have been trying to update the global village concept that we are all one village with the idea that we are all one family, which is in need of a home. We live on earth, but we don't often notice that earth is in the universe.

EDGES TO THE PROCESSMIND'S SPACE–TIME DREAMING

So many of our problems are due to our worldwide lack of openness to different sides. We are at war with conflict. We don't often see polarities as *family*. Everyone's little *u* is a firm, often rigid part of who we are. Most of us think that the X that bothers us is the problem. But one of the reasons that X is difficult is because our everyday minds, our *u*'s, are unconsciously unbending. The opponent often appears impossible, but remember, too, that opponents are roles. It is such a simple thought, but I have to repeat it again. Remember democracy, then remember deep democracy. The opponent is very real—take that X seriously— but it is also a dream-like role in the field, capable of changing, at least temporarily.

You cannot kill a role. You can remove a person from office but you cannot remove a role. Roles are there to be processed. Dictators removed by democratic revolutions don't disappear. They reappear again in the new regimes and in everyone! Then the *freed* people are troubled by their own dictatorial tendencies, like everybody everywhere.

Remember, your own space–time dreaming manifests often and is often pathologized. It manifests, for example, as a tendency to be depressed or moody. These tendencies are normal, to some extent, but I just want to say that in those heavy moods there might be a letting go, a going down deeper through which you can find your relationship to the earth and to the universe. Don't pathologize these tendencies. Mild chronic depressions may be connected with needing to go deeper or to finding your roots in the universe.

Another reason why we do not always follow our deepest self is that the little *u* thinks, "I must do it," "I don't believe in nature. I have to do it. If I don't do it, it won't happen." Your *I* can be important to get you off your rear end to do the things that you can do, but be careful. You can *do* those things, but other parts of yourself may get marginalized in the process.

Bring out polarizations before they burst out as symptoms or relationship problems! Notice the X + *u* and play with them. Then drop into your processmind. Expressing the X + *u* is important because nature loves diversity, and you may not be able to go deeper if you don't appreciate diversity.

Any big picture includes the many little ones. On the top left in Figure 24.1, there is a person in a room saying "It is all me." That is one of the little pictures: "It is all me. It is all in my head." This vantage point has made psychology popular, and it is so helpful: "It is my problem, it is in my head, I have to work my stuff out—help!" This picture is important, it is all about me, but notice that in this room the windows are basically closed to the outside.

In the second picture on the upper right-hand side, the window is more open and you can see a tree and other things. Now there is a second person inside that room. This second aspect of this big picture is, "It's all about us." You would think that the transition from the first to this second picture would be easy, but the idea of the *us* means that it is not *I*, and it is not *you*. Instead there is an *us-ness* on which we need to focus, a space between us, a field, which is still an unusual frame of reference for most people. Yes, it looks like you are the problem at one moment, and I am the problem at another moment, but, basically, there is a field between us. It is about us and our community.

1. It's all about me

2. It's all about us

3. It's about *u* + me + us + universe

The Universe is home, the relationship space behind the dance of the ancient one.

24.1 The Big Picture.

There is a still greater perspective, another aspect of the big picture, one that I have been stressing in this book: the space between and beyond us. This aspect of the big picture begins with the *us* in the relationship and then moves to the third picture. I think, "Oh, it is my friend. He is doing that again!" Then at some point there is a sense that it is a feeling that is not just about my friend or me. The feeling is something in-between. There is an *us* in that in-between space that needs to be processed. In short, the third aspect of the big picture is opening up to the universe and seeing the truth to the fact that, yes, "it is all me," and paradoxically, "Yes, it is between us" and at the same time because of the space between us, "it is the whole earth, it is the climate, it is the entire space." In a way, our individual situation is universal. Bringing that universe in is a matter of personal need, transformation, and community intelligence.

I dreamed about this last night. I dreamed that there was a stage. It was the stage of a Taoist nun or monk. The dream showed that the person who is connected to the Tao or to space–time dreaming is in the next stage of human development. This dream was about me, in that it was *my* dream, but maybe it's also about us and the whole universe. This dream message is shown in the fourth quadrant of Figure 24.1. There I am trying to make the point that the universe is a magical and Taoist space that is moving us all.

This reminds me of Figure 2.5 from chapter 2 on page 26 in which a woman is tossing a coin. There is nothing very miraculous about her. Sensing the power of the atmosphere, being the coin moving through the air under the influence of the fields we live in, is something people have always sensed and perhaps projected or identified with the gods. The power of this space belongs to the big picture. People call it by various spiritual and religious names. Call it whatever you like, contact with it surely is good for you. I call it the Tao, the universe, and space–time dreaming. It is responsible for the processmind's dance of the ancient one.

In any case, the big picture includes all the little ones. If you follow the big picture some of the time, you notice things moving together, easily. However, as soon as you get excited about doing things all by yourself—"I MUST DO THEM"—then you will soon sense something moving against you. OK, that is the beginning of a going down, then sink, let a minor *deluge* happen to get reconnected with the ancient dance again.

Let me sketch this overall process. Remember Figure 4.2 from chapter 4? I will repeat it here and call it Figure 24.2. Recall that most of us begin moving like the normal little *u*, like a sailboat, heading toward Z, our goal. I do that all the time. But as I sail towards my goal, I experience some disturbing energy, X, pushing down against me, like the wind that is against where I am headed. I am sailing to Z, but I am troubled by the wind going in the direction of X. That is the way most of us live, by pushing against the wind.

CR PARTS (VECTOR) View	PM "CURVED" Space View

Here, *u* compensates for X so *u* fights crosswind X	Here there are *No* forces on *u* in curved space and *u* goes forwards with PM *DANCE*

24.2 Two ways of Sailing through Life.

In the second diagram (to the right in Figure 24.2), you see another way of dealing with this issue. As soon as I start out toward Z, the resistance, X, comes in and I can let go and feel: "Aha! I notice I am a *u* with a mind of its own and there is an X, which is not in total agreement with what I am doing and so I can let go and follow space–time dreaming and its wiggly, meandering path." In other words, keep your mind on what you want to do and let nature get you there.

Audience 1: I am just wondering how this approach applies in communication. For instance, I am thinking about how, when it feels very important to get something across but very risky to express a voice, there may be resistance.

Arny: Flow with it. Feel, know, and express the resistance, the X in the open, before your communication partner has to. Take their side, then take yours, follow your processmind. Then invite the other to add or subtract. Flow with the process as if the goal is not the point you wanted to make but the way you are making it, the way you are traveling so to speak.

Audience 1: You are saying that you, yourself, should pick up the whole process of X + *u* and the processmind?

Arny: Why not? *u* + X are your family and they are both in the air! If you think you are being criticized for something, bring out the critic before the critic can even speak. The critic is somehow needed to be part of the larger process.

Audience 2: I think that my son is like the big wind X, pushing against the sailboat in your metaphor. I get to the end of the day, I'm tried and I still need to clean the bathroom. My kid is 4 years old. He won't clean up after himself.

Arny: Then pick that process up for him, "I don't want to pick up all this stuff. This is not for me! I just want to play with my stuff over there!" Scream and yell for him! See what happens.

Audience 2: Oh, yes, he likes that!! That's play!

u (Mother) cleans. X (Child) says "NO!"

Mother FLOWS with FIELD

24.3 Mother Flows with the Field.

It's normal not to flow; but if you don't flow, the feeling of unwellness lurks. In every field where you are moving toward something and you feel a slight resistance that you are not going to flow with, flickering thoughts are likely to occur: "I'm not feeling so good today... I'm tired... am I getting sick? Do I have a cold? What is going on here?! I have got to get there!" This *u*-destruction is built into the field. Nature prefers you to flow and let *not-doing* happen.

Now let's think about all of us children, all people. There are 7 billion people on this planet and there will be 9 billion by the end of the century. Very often I think that 9 billion means more water pollution, more air pollution, bursting cities, climate change, and more conflict around all these areas. I am hoping that by your getting a little bit closer to your space–time dreaming, you will be able to help depolarize these various conflict areas and make them more creative. I think that is one of the big background goals of nature.

Enough theory. Now let's get down to practice. Let's focus on relationships in organizations and then on small group work, which is an extension of relationships. All this will be a preparation for working later on world issues. So let's begin with organizations. If you don't have a relationship situation with somebody in an organization, you can choose any relationship, but if you have both please focus on the organizational relationship problem.

As before, we shall feel the field of the problem between you and that person in the organization. That is the really important part. Does that field feel really tense, buzzing, frozen, or explosive? Whatever the field feels like, we are going to ask you to identify the worst X and also *u*'s response to the X in that field, and we are going to, once again, shift into our universe dance and see how it moves us smoothly and unpredictably, with moments of unstable equilibrium. Notice when you are moving and where you go off balance. Then we are going to look back again from a distance. The idea is to gain a great distance and look back and see what it advises you about that relationship. Make sure, when you are in your universe dance, to catch whatever intuition or advice flits past very, very quickly. Catch it!

[Arny then demonstrates this work with an audience member who has a relationship with someone in another organization who is very nasty! The audience member is very loving. Her processmind then showed her how to use the other person's nasty energy and power beneficially.]

Arny: Thank you for bringing your family, you and that organizational relationship, *home*. The discovery was that aspects of that situation are actually perfect for you. It is the most elementary thought. So, therefore, I would say to that troublesome person, "How wonderful that you stand so strongly for something, even if I don't believe in that! Your standing so strongly for something is a great model for me. Now I can and must say, I can't stand you! Woof!" and let things flow. Go on between this *strong* behavior and your normal loving way of doing things. Let your organizational relationship become an exciting (not just miserable) process where everyone is in the *family* and at home in the universe.

QUESTIONS ABOUT BUDDHISM

Audience 1:   My question is, how can we know that we have really connected with the processmind? In my country, Thailand, in the Buddhist practice of *vipassana*, we spend a lot of time, the whole life, 20 or 30 years, trying to connect with the processmind through unfolding the mental constructs, imagination. Maybe we spend many lives. From my experience I know I am connected when I realize that my breathing, my feeling, my thought, and every phenomenon that occurs in my dreambody is not mine but is a part of the universe and nature. But I could not yet do that in movement. Not in the moment.

Arny: Learning to connect with space-time dreaming in movement is a meditation. It takes time, as you said. It has taken me some years to get there, and sometimes I have it and sometimes I don't. But when I am there and when others are there… I know I am there when I begin to sense that something is dreaming me. It is not that I have a dream or that *I* am moving, but, actually, I am in touch with the thing that is dreaming me, the thing that is moving me, breathing me. It is similar to what you said. I feel dreamed.

So that is one aspect of it. Following the flow, being open to what is happening, I sometimes experience it when I am working with people, sometimes even in large groups. I'll suddenly have a sense of, "Why not this? Why not that?" I never tell people that they should feel that way, holding both sides, but it is something that they can feel.

Audience 1: That is different from my Buddhist practice, because in our practicing we don't follow flow, we are witnessing.

Arny: I love the witnessing part of Buddhism. As a witness there is also a moment when I realize something very paradoxical. It makes me laugh when I even think it. When I am being moved, I know that's my goal, but being moved makes me realize that actually my life is none of my business! My life, this movement, is none of my business! [Laughs] In this moment, I am witnessing and flowing at the same time. Then that processmind connection relaxes and I might return to consensus reality again. It's a process.

24.4 Life is Predictable and Unpredictable.

Audience 2: Can you expand on that idea a little bit?

DANCE OF THE ANCIENT ONE

Arny: Life in that dance of the ancient one is my business for my normal identity, my most common identity—I need to do this and I want to do this—but this perspective tires me. Then I allow myself to be moved and to have a process and, at the same time, to witness that process. Then the thought arises that my life is none of my business. That thought makes me feel happy. It is like aspects of *vipassana*: it is not your breath, it is not your heartbeat, your process is none of your business. Movement happens, but there is no mover.

But I don't insist that people make a program out of this... You smile when I say that. Life is predictable, because there is a general direction, but how you move depends upon the moment!

Audience 1: Then do you have an observer inside you?

Arny: Yes, but in my deepest processmind state, it is more like something is looking at itself. What Buddhism sometimes refers to as the witness, I call the universe looking at herself. She says, "Oh, so that is happening now, ok!" She is discovering herself with me. What great questions! I would not say these things publicly except for your questions!

Audience 1: Have you heard about *nirvana*?

Arny: *Nirvana* is something I have heard about, yes. I love *nirvana*! It is the state of stillness, of feeling free of suffering. It's freedom from your little *u*'s dictatorship, from its ambitions, greed, hatred, et cetera.

Audience 1: I just want to hear from you, from the Processwork point of view, what do you think about *nirvana*?

Arny: Ha! I want more of it! I love it! Yes. Mmmm, let me ask myself. "What, Arny, do you think about *nirvana*?" Aha! I suddenly looked at Amy! It's the sense of wellness and peace and timelessness! I have it for short periods of time. Everyone has it for short periods of time. But, as I have been saying, it is perhaps the fourth great instinct. People seek it through drugs, and so forth, so it is a really big drive. Processmind gives us peace even while we are doing things. But *nirvana* is not a permanent goal in Processwork. Our normal human processes seek *nirvana*, and then they seek the diversity of the *deluded* mind. Appreciate both without a goal of one or the other, that's what I mean by enlightenment. No hierarchies!

Audience 1: In Buddhism, in my country, it is a little different, approached with different meaning. I like your answer!

Arny: I grew up in an intense city situation, and so I had to learn how to fight, and that was good. But I always knew I needed more. One of my hopes is to bring fluidity to all moments in life, to experience *nirvana* in the midst of conflict with another, to remember everyone is in my family.

I suffered from turning against people who wanted to hurt me. I learned how to fight, and that was good, but it was not enough. If I only could have said at that time, "Sure, you are trying to be powerful, you are also struggling for life, you are trying to stand for who you are!" But I could not say it. I embraced them later on, but it was not early enough for me. I should have known this when I was five! And it can be learned when you are five. That's my goal for kindergarten!

Audience 1: Would you tell us about your first experience in which you connected with your processmind?

Arny: Yes, I do remember, we all remember our first time [laughter]! My first experience of being connected with the processmind occurred, I think, when I was three. That was when I said to myself, "Adults are kidding. They all look so stiff and weird!" Now, I experience the processmind in the middle of the night every night, dreaming me. Everyone does that, too. Something moves you to dream. I love your questions!

I said before that the old leadership idea is that the leader, or the spiritual leader, usually is supposed to have the most awareness or the most power. But my feeling is that awareness is shared. I can't do it all the time, and when I can't do it, then Amy does it. When Amy can't do it, then you do it. It is a community experience, a world experience, as the case may be. The power and the awareness are shared.

STREETWORK AND WORLDCHANGE THEATRE

We are, and you are, learning to be close to your deepest self while in the midst of tensions. Can you facilitate, make a home for people to work in, and make a home for the various sides in the midst of world problems? That is what we will focus on next.

Some people can make that home for all sides without any training whatsoever. I am not at all sure if you can train this skill because it goes far beyond the skill level. Everyone has the potential and develops it automatically now and then in life. I want to bring that potential out more. Make a home for yourself and for your critics and use their energies, not the content but the energies. In this way you may be able to gain the confidence of all kinds of people from different cultures, races, ages, sexual orientations, health situations, mental states. Try to communicate with people you normally cannot speak with!

Break into groups of four or five and work on a worst community, national, or world issue. What issues would you be interested in working on?

- The wisdom of indigenous people is often rejected or corrupted by Western cultures.

- The tension with Iran regarding nuclear weapons and the possibility that the United States is going to encourage an attack. The bomb itself is a ghost role.

- Afghanistan and the US military's burning of the Koran.

- Human trafficking is a big issue in Portland. I work with girls who have been trafficked. It is now the second leading illegal business in the world. Slavery and prostitution, second only to drugs. I have been working with the youth who are victims of it and thinking of it in relationship to world issues, male and female. What is it that is driving men to do this on a global scale?

- Bringing more of the feminine into positions of power so that there is a more balance and less sexism.

- The shame of the colonizer that perpetuates the problem and makes moving forward impossible.

Audience: Just noticing the feelings the topics bring up, it is so much to hold and hear!

Amy: Thank you, that is very helpful. Then let's hear only one or two more, very briefly, then we can go into it.

- The whole destruction of the ethnosphere, including language and culture.
- The Middle East, the Palestinian scene, the tension around the Muslim world. The widespread religious tension and lack of openess to diversity.

OK, now make sure you stay as close as you can to your space–time dreaming. People were saying yesterday that space-time dreaming brings in something different or new rather than just playing out roles and getting involved only in that way.

Exercise: Bringing Your Earth Family Home

Small Group and Street Theatre with Four or Five People

1. (15 minutes) All Together: Spin the pen to choose someone to be the exercise guide-timer-participant. All discuss troublesome world issues for you for 10 minutes. Then spin the pen to discover which issue the group will focus on. Whomever the pen points to will choose the issue most important to them and say what the worst energy, X, is for her or him in that issue. Don't process this further yet. First break up so each can do some inner work.

2. (10 minutes) Inner work.

    a. Each of you, recall and imagine that chosen, worst national or world issue. What does its atmosphere feel like to you? Feel that atmosphere and ask, what is the worst energy, X, within it for you? Feel and express that X energy with a motion and put some words to it to find out what it's really expressing and wants. Next, make a sketch of this X energy on your paper and name it. Then ask yourself, what part of you, u, is most disturbed by the X energy? Feel and then express that u energy with a motion, say words that go with it, and find out what it's expressing and wants. Make a sketch and name it on your paper.

    b. Stand, if you can, and choose a favorite earth spot. Look around and notice where you find the X + u energies there. Feel the earth again and imagine that it begins to breathe and move you back and forth as you express its X + u energies.

c. Now, feel and imagine that you move up into the space above the earth and that you continue to rise up even further into the universe. Feel the universe's space all around you and sense it beginning to move and dance you unpredictably with moments of unstable equilibrium. Wait until you feel loose and your dance becomes surprising and somewhat unpredictable. Care for yourself and those around you.

d. Now bring this dance back to earth by looking back at the X + u energies. Continue dancing until your universe mind gives you a hint about the X + u relationship and how it might help you facilitate this issue. Make notes. Then all come together again.

3. (45 minutes total) All Together: Group Process

a. (25 minutes) Chosen Timer-Guide-Participant:

Read all of this section before starting!

Now bring your earth family home to the universe. Each of you, re-feel your universe dance with its unpredictable wiggles. Now, the person whose issue was chosen should begin to express her or his X + u. Then others join in with their X's + u's. Everyone can switch roles and bring in ghost roles as you continue to facilitate with your universe dances. If you get lost or become too *pulled in*, take a moment to re-feel your universe dance and its detachment and let it guide you further. Continue until a solution or insight occurs or until the time is up.

b. (20 minutes) Finally, discuss what you or we learned and then create a 2 to 4 minute street theatre out of some important moment or resolution in your group process. Choose a narrator who will first say one sentence about the problem and possible learning and solution. Finally, decide how you would show this as a street theatre for the world.

AFTERWARDS

Groups showed their street theatre work; people acted out roles and created dynamic brief skits of 3 minutes each speaking about a world problem and then showing solutions.

Street Theatre in Greece

When we worked in Greece, we were saddened by the pain of the people experiencing severe economic depression. The suicide rate in that country has escalated to 40% above normal. But when the Greeks did their street theatre work, we were amazed.

We were also amazed at their resiliency. One of the small groups came forward from the very large group in Athens and pronounced, in front of everyone, that they had worked on unemployment. They had lost their jobs and also their sexual libido. That small group showed us what the dance of the ancient one brought to them. One person began by playing the boss that was firing people. Then everyone took that role and they fired one another. The result was that everyone lay flat on the floor. Some minutes passed as we all watched and wondered, "What next?" Then from the stillness, individuals began to arise from the floor, slowly at first, one after the other. Then suddenly and shockingly, they began a slow sensuous dance. They danced for minutes in front of everyone showing that yes, they had been downed. They had found their sensuality again and this led everyone in that large hall to dance, showing that the difficult outer financial crisis and atmosphere did not tyrannize them. It was hopeful and an amazing concluding moment to our work in Greece.

Days later Greece voted on their future. One of the results was that more liberals than ever were chosen to be part of the government. Greece suffered, she went down, and showed signs of rebirth in 2012. And one person from that large group street theatre was elected into the Greek parliament.

The themes of depression, death, and dying are something we frequently saw in many groups around the world during the global recession in 2012. Perhaps there is something for everyone to learn from such times. Perhaps dying, or at least *going down* once in a while is good for everybody! A lot of world issues are about death and stopping it and doing your best. *Death* is a ghost role in the simplest sense of letting go of your attachment to who you are in a given moment. *Die* out of the position you have and switch roles once in a while for creative solutions and more community.

I know the media is not everything, but I would love to get some of these skits that you have done in front of your groups out to the media.

I am amazed how you people could come together and show creative solutions for a renewed world! Thank you.

....

Σ   *FOR REFLECTION ON CHAPTER 24*

- Be yourself, the other person, and the field between you.
- Change organizations by acting out parts of groups for them.
- In a big picture, all the little pictures are at home.
- *Nirvana* is a moment in the process when you are the home for your family, for all members of a conflict situation.
- *Die* at least once a day for good health.
- Your life may be none of your business.

CONCLUSION

What? Life Is None of my Business?

Please don't only turn against conflict, it is not our central problem. We shall never be able to stop it. Conflict with conflict doesn't work for long. It's only a first step. This first step by now, however, is a very old story. In that old story, *bad* people create conflict, and the *good* ones must stop them. Okay, the old story is a first step. But the next step is to appreciate each side of the diversity issue behind conflict. Use the energies better. But then create a facilitator's new story.

In the new story, facilitators become more like the universe itself, we become the home for all that is. Become the home for all parts of yourself. Be an open space for all the various energies in your relationships and family scenes. Be the facilitator who models sustainability for organizations. Be the person who carries the sense of home with her and is, herself, all the parts and energies.

In the new story, the world is still made out of concrete rigid things, but not only. It is also interconnected by the dance of the ancient one. See the city as a real place, but don't forget that it is also a living entity. Economic problems, ecological difficulties, and practical problems of all kinds seek and need a larger picture, one in which the ancient dance of the universe—as modeled by you—values the parts and reminds us of the dance. It reminds us that we often get stuck with apparently unsolvable problems in part because those problems are not only between us but are also between various energies, the squares and curves of the universe.

DANCE OF THE ANCIENT ONE

C.1 The New Facilitator.[100]

**The New Facilitator creates a home by
showing that parts are aspects of one dance.**

I know this view is far out. But it is my view that we are not far out
enough. It is not easy to speak or write about a Tao that can't be said.
No linear, purely rational mind of anyone, including mine, can totally
comprehend this Tao. However, our bodies and dreams understand.
They remind us to rest, fantasize, flow, and to get up and dance. All of
us adults have a problem remembering this while trying to carry out
our work on this complex little planet of which we are fixed parts. But
the child in us remembers. Walk straight ahead and then occasionally
let the universe make a *hop!*

If you are an adult and are shy about being a spontaneous child,
you are not alone. Even Einstein was shy about bringing forward his
general relativity theory that not only unified space and time but also
curved what was believed to be linear space. Curve? Yes, in a world
valuing and praising rational straight forward thinking, curving is an
altered state. I called that almost ecstatic state the fourth great drive.
Remember, be careful, get there consciously, and don't only use chemical substances. Be a complete human being, with all levels of awareness, with your quantum self and everyday mind.

Meditate while mediating for yourself and the world. If you forget that, it might help to sometimes consider that you yourself are a
wave without a beginning or end. Not quite like Schrödinger's quantum wave but not much different either. For you, too, can be both alive
and dead at the same moment. Like that wave, something about you,

too, never began and may never end. Today this sounds a little strange. No? But don't forget Aboriginal Dreamtime thinking and the Tibetan Bardos that imply the importance of the time in between things and the magic of the space between us all.

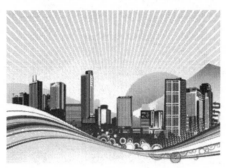

C.2 The New Facilitator's City.

Take care of yourself and also remember that perhaps your life is none of your business. Don't wait for a near-death experience or to become an astronaut to recall the power of the force fields around us, the space in the universe. It is a common metric, and when you feel it, you will communicate best with everyone. From this viewpoint, what we normally consider people are actors on a stage which itself is, paradoxically enough, an actor as well.[101] We are still ourselves on this stage, and, at the same time, we are the ancient one dancing. This dance brings the universe closer to everyday reality on earth.

Around the world today, people everywhere are fighting for democracy and expressing their hopes for universal equal rights and freedom. This democracy is a crucial first step. But democracy is weak in relationship skills. So remember to fight for the right to dream and remember deep democracy's essence: the dance of the ancient one.

Today, after a great deal of experience with individuals from nearly all cultures, small and massive organizations and nations, I am convinced that our whole family—you, me, and all those we love and are in conflict with—will appreciate being brought *home* to the universe's space–time dreaming.

C.3 Universe on Earth.

APPENDIX 1

The Processwork Paradigm

DREAMBODY HISTORY FOR READERS WHO ARE UNFAMILIAR WITH PROCESSWORK

In the late 1970s I realized that process had its own solutions. Have a symptom? Fight it, then follow it. Following nature became the center of my work. In the 1980s I showed how body experiences and symptoms appear in our dreams[102] and how dreams can be seen in our body signals.[103] Then I realized that we needed a new paradigm to bridge mind and body. Processwork, also known as process oriented psychology, is a paradigm that bridges both psyche and matter, inner and outer. The basic idea is that observable empirical reality is partly organized by dreams and the dreaming process. All dreams are not just *fantasies* that are *out there* somewhere but are observable as momentary body signals in everyday reality.

Extensions of the process paradigm made it possible to understand shamanism and work with psychiatric situations and near-death and coma-like events, as well as with small- and large-group conflict work and organizational development.[104] Process thinking has been helpful in understanding the psychology of quantum physics,[105] earth-based psychology, and approaches to unified field theories.[106]

I suggested in my 1980 book, *Dreambody*, that body symptoms and signals are organized by a *field*, which I called the dreambody. Later, I developed methods for working with visible body signals to follow this moving, dancing process as we go through the day and when dreaming at night. Dreambody work stresses body feeling or proprioception. Now, in the present book, the idea of space–time dreaming becomes an essence-level experience of the dreambody. In my previous book, *ProcessMind*, I spoke of the earth's field moving us. The present book's space–time dreaming gives us a more universal perspective on this earth experience.

My idea of the processmind was implicit in my early work and has developed over the years. In my first work, while still identifying as a Jungian analyst, I called this the unconscious, that later became known as the dreambody. As Processwork developed, I called aspects of this organizing principle the global dreambody, the quantum mind, the intentional field, and the big U (a vector, referring to experiences of the organizing principle as seen in psychology, quantum physics, and gravity field). The processmind's space–time dreaming includes all these previous terms and goes beyond them to include the spaces of the entire universe. It is an interdisciplinary concept which tries to pull together many fields, as the following diagram suggests (see Figure A.1).

A.1 Space-Time Dreaming
Fields in Science, Organizations, and Spiritual Experience.

Space–Time Explained

National Aeronautics and Space Administration

Newton's Gravity or Curved Spacetime?

According to Newton's theory of gravity (1687), all masses "pull" on each other with an invisible force called "gravity". This force is an inherent property of matter, and it is directly proportional to an object's mass. In our solar system, the Sun reaches out across enormous distances and "pulls" smaller masses, like planets, comets, and asteroids, into orbit around it, using its force of gravity.

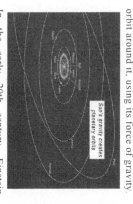

Sun's gravity creates planetary orbits

In the early 20th century, Einstein discovered a contradiction between Newton's theory of gravity and Einstein's theory of special relativity (1905). In special relativity, the speed of light is the speed limit of all energy in the universe. No matter what kind of energy it is, it cannot transmit across the universe any faster than 299,792 km/sec. Yet Newton's theory assumed that the Sun's force of gravity is *instantaneously* transmitted to the planets, at a speed much faster than the speed of light. Was gravity unique in its ability to fly across the universe, or did masses react to each other for a different reason?

{ In 1916, Einstein published his theory of general relativity, which transformed space from the Newtonian idea of vast emptiness with nothing but the invisible force of gravity to rule the motion of matter, to an ephemeral fabric of spacetime, which "grips" matter and directs its course through the universe. The spacetime fabric spans the entire universe and is intimately connected to all the matter and energy within it }

How does this change in thinking explain the motion of the planets, or the orbits of the moon and satellites around Earth? Theoretically, when a mass sits in this spacetime fabric, it will deform the space and altering the shape of space and altering the passage of time around it. In the case of the Sun, the spacetime fabric would curve around it, creating a "dip" in spacetime. As the planets (and comets and asteroids) travel across the spacetime fabric, they would respond to this dip and follow the curve in spacetime and travel around and around the Sun. As long as they never slow down, the planets would maintain regular orbits around the Sun, neither spiraling in toward it nor flying off into outer space.

To create a simple model of this idea, place a heavy weight in the center of a suspended bedsheet. Roll some small balls across the sheet at different points and observe how they curve in toward the central weight.

The balls are not "pulled" in by the mass's gravity; they are simply following the curve in spacetime caused by the mass's presence.

For more information, comments or questions, contact GP-B at www@relegyro.stanford.edu or visit http://einstein.stanford.edu/

Gravity ProBe

Thanks to NASA. (with my {} marks)[107]

DANCE OF THE ANCIENT ONE

ENDNOTES

1. Edgar Mitchell speaking to the City of Petaluma after receiving its Key to the City award http://vimeo.com/53941638

2. A 1930 statement by Einstein, found in L. Kostro, 1988, "Einstein and the Ether." Electronics & Wireless World, 94, 238–239.

3. Einstein, "Sidelights of Relativity," translated by J. G. Jeffrey and W. Perret, Methuen, London, 1922, republished unabridged, and unaltered, Dover, NY, 1983, pp. 16, 23.

4. John Wheeler, p. 14, *Journey into Gravity and Spacetime*. Scientific American Library, NY, 1999. He quotes the 10th-century Chinese poet, Su Tung-p'o in his description of sailing on Yangze rivers.

5. Max Tegmark, 2003, discusses "mathematical democracy," which sounds similar to my deep democracy concept: "that mathematical existence and physical existence are equivalent, so that all mathematical structures exist physically as well."

6. From an interview with John Wheeler, 2003, on The Science Show, Radio National Australia. Thanks to Susan Kocen for finding this quote.

7. *ProcessMind: A User's Guide to Connecting to the Mind of God.*

8. The Gaia hypothesis, also known as Gaia theory or Gaia principle, proposes that all organisms and their inorganic surroundings on Earth are closely integrated to form a single and self-regulating complex system, maintaining the conditions for life on the planet. From http://en.wikipedia.org/wiki/Gaia_hypothesis

9. See C.G. Jung. 1952/1993, 'Synchronicity: An Acausal Connecting Principle' in Volume VIII of his *Collected Works*. Bollingen, Switzerland: Bollingen Foundation. ISBN9780691017945.

10. W. Heisenberg, *Physics and Beyond*. Cambridge University Press, Cambridge, UK, 1971, p. 101.

11. Lao-tzu, *Tao Te Ching*, Chapter 25, translated by S. Mitchell, also see online, for example, http://academic.brooklyn.cuny.edu/core9/phalsall/texts/taote-v3.html

12. See, for example, my *Sitting in the Fire* or my *Deep Democracy of Open Forums*.

13. The development of Processwork is an exciting story onto itself, told in part by previous books on various subjects ranging from inner work, to relationship and coma work, to psychotic states, large-group conflicts, quantum physics... many applications. See also, Amy Mindell's books, and those of Arlene and Jean Claude Audergon, Julie Diamond and Lee Sparks Jones, Gary Reiss and Pierre Morin, to mention but a few. Also see the various training centers around the world: http://www.iapop.com/centers/

14. John Wheeler, p. 14, *Journey into Gravity and Spacetime*. Scientific American Library, NY, 1999. He quotes the 10th-century Chinese poet, Su Tung-p'o in his description of sailing on Yangze rivers.

15. Stephen Hawking, *A Brief History of Time*, p. 125.

16. See John Wheeler's and Richard Feynman's thoughts about fields http://en.wikipedia.org/wiki/Field_%28physics%29#cite_ref-Feynman_2-1

17. John Wheeler's whale can be found in my *ProcessMind*, page 66.

18. I will explain more about the details of relativity in chapter 7. See also Appendix 2.

19. op cit. Einstein, on the "power" of space, said that the universe mysteriously affects the material domain. "The ether of the general theory of relativity is a medium which is itself devoid of all mechanical and kinematical qualities, but helps to determine mechanical (and electromagnetic) events."

20. See Max Tegmark's 2011 Scientific American article, for example, at http://teachphysics.org/wp/max-tegmark-and-parallel-universes-scientific-american-pdf-download/

21. http://en.wikipedia.org/wiki/File:Hasegawa_Tohaku,_Pine_Trees.jpg

22. Jung's autobiography, *Memories, Dreams, Reflections*, edited by Aniela Jaffe. From p. 209. The bold type in the quote is mine.

23. "Tao Te Ching", Wiley translation *Way and Its Power the Tao Te Ching* (Mandala Books) by Arthur Waley (Dec 31, 1977)

24. See the interview around that Conference title: *Edges of experience: Jung, process work and collective change: Luisetta Mudie interviews Arnold Mindell,* from http://www.cgjungpage.org/index.php?option=com_content&task= view&id=587&Itemid=401

25. See June Singer Interview Amy and Arny Mindell for example http:// www.aamindell.net/download/2009/03/JuneSingerinterview.pdf

26. C.G. Jung edited by Aniela Jaffe in *Memories, Dreams, Reflections,* Princeton University Press, 1965, pp. 208–9.

27. C.G. Jung, Stages of Life, CW 8, § 771.

28. As quoted in *Stephen Hawking's Universe* (1985) by John Boslough, Ch.... he Final Question, p. 77

29. Bradford Keeney, *Ropes to God: Experiencing the Bushman Spiritual Universe,* quote from the foreword.

30. http://www.nationalpost.com/opinion/columnists/Physics+metaphysics+k nowledge+wisdom/3134524/story.html#ixzz0qskeYuE5

31. E. Salaman, "A Talk with Einstein," *The Listener,* 54 (1955): 370-371.

32. This is something Jung suggested in his 1936-1941 seminar on childhood dreams called, "Kinderträume," Seminare, 2001 Walter Verlag Stuttgart.

33. *ProcessMind,* pp. 42-43.

34. See *ProcessMind,* p. 80

35. This phrase comes originally from the Polish-American scientist and philosopher Alfred Korzybski http://en.wikipedia.org/wiki/The_map_is_ not_the_territory meaning models of reality are not reality.

36. Op.cit. Einstein 1920 address to the university of Leyden (in the "Works of Albert Einstein," last paragraph of "Ether and the General Theory of Relativity").

37. Quoting from the work of Lao-tzu's disciple Chuang-tzu and Confucius' grandson Tzu-ssu, Mitchell tells of the Taoist master "Shadow" speaking to the student "Penumbra" who asked, "When the Tao moves, you move; when it stops, you stop. Don't you find it depressing to have no power of your own? Shadow said, "On the contrary. With no decisions to make, my mind is always at ease. All I have to do is follow. You can't imagine how much freedom there is in just going along for the ride...." Page 27, Mitchell, Stephen, *Second Book of the Tao,* Penguin, NYC, 2009.

38. From Wikipedia Jan 2012, we read; Dé/Te 德 basically means "virtue" in the sense of "personal character," "inner strength" (virtuosity), or "integrity." The semantics of this Chinese word resemble English virtue, which developed from a (now archaic) sense of "inner potency" or "divine power" http://en.wikipedia.org/wiki/Tao_Te_Ching#Title

39. *Quantum Mind*, Section III, Taoism and Relativity.

40. Albert Einstein, "Mein Weltbild" (1931) ["My World-view", or "My View of the World" translated as the title essay of his book, *The World As I See It*, (Philosophical Library, New York, 1949).

41. Thanks to http://atropos.as.arizona.edu/aiz/teaching/a250/bh.html

42. Chapter 5 by Edmund Bertschinger, Edwin F. Taylor and John Wheeler, to be published by Person Addison Wesley, San Francisco, CA, USA.

   The whole quote from Einstein is: "The basic demand of the special theory of relativity (invariance of the laws under Lorentz-transformations) is too narrow, i.e., that an invariance of the laws must be postulated relative to nonlinear transformations for the co-ordinates in the four-dimensional continuum...This happened in 1908. Why were another seven years required for the construction of the general theory of relativity? The main reason lies in the fact that it is not so easy to free oneself from the idea that coordinates must have an immediate metrical meaning."

43. Isaac Jacobson, *His Life and Universe*, p. 320.

44. Einstein, Op. cit 1920 address to the university of Leyden (in the "Works of Albert Einstein," last paragraph of "Ether and the General Theory of Relativity."

45. In: Einstein, Lorentz, Weyl, Minkowski, 1953 [first published in 1923].

46. This is a paraphrase of Wheeler, John A. (1990), *A Journey Into Gravity and Spacetime*, Scientific American Library, San Francisco: W. H. Freeman.

47. Op.cit

48. Incas of Andes regarded S-T as a single concept, named pacha (Quechua: pacha, Aymara: pacha).[2][3][4] Stephen Hart, Peruvian Cultural Studies: Work in Progress Paul Richard Steele, Catherine J. Allen, Handbook of Inca mythology, p. 86, (ISBN 1-57607-354-8), Shirley Ardener, University of Oxford, *Women and Space: Ground Rules and Social Maps*, p. 36 (ISBN 0-85496-728-1) kept this understanding until now. R.C. Archibald (1914) Time as a fourth dimension: Bulletin of the American Mathematical Society 20:409.

49. Shirley Ardener, University of Oxford, *Women and Space: Ground Rules and Social Maps*, Berg Publishers; 1st edition (April 22, 1993 p. 36) (ISBN 0-85496-728-1).

50. p. 2, "An Introduction to General Relativity, Hughston, L.P., and Tod, K.P. London Math Society, Student Texts 5, Cambridge University Press, 1990, New York.

51. "The Bardo" in Selected Writings, page 554 in *The Collected Works of Chögyam Trungpa, Volume Six*.

52. *ProcessMind*, Chapter 1, page 9 and following.

53. Ibid. thanks to the work of Gabreila Samadhi; see her at http://gabrielasa-madhi.files.wordpress.com/2012/04/lightbody.jpg

54. http://lightworkers.org/blog/103997/tweleve-light-bodies

55. My book, *The Dreambody*, came out in 1982 about 10 years earlier than his name, "Dreambody" in Tibetan Buddhism for this light or subtle body. The Dalai Lama tells us in *Cultivating a Daily Meditation*, (Publisher: Ltwa; 2nd rev. ed. March 1, 1991).

56. Mindell, Arnold, *Coma: Key to Awakening*, Shambhala, Boston, 1989, Lao Tse Press, Portland 2010.

57. http://www.soundstrue.com/podcast/transcripts/lamasurya-das.php?camefromhome=camefromhome

58. See my Rainbow Medicine summary in *ProcessMind*, chapter 11, see figure 11.1.

59. Grimm, Jacob and Wilhelm, *Fairy Tales*. London: Routledge & Kegan Paul, 1959.

60. *Dreambody*, Sigo Press, p. 98 and ff, 2nd ed. Lao Tse Press, 2000; 3rd ed. Deep Democracy Exchange, 2011.

61. His original lecture where he said, "Turn on, tune in, drop out" was given to 30,000 hippies in Golden Gate Park in San Francisco. http://en.wikipedia.org/wiki/Turn_on,_tune_in,_drop_out

62. *Coma: Key to Awakening*, p. 84.

63. "The least-action principle is an assertion about the nature of motion that provides an alternative approach to mechanics completely independent of Newton's laws. Not only does the least-action principle offer a means of formulating classical mechanics that is more flexible and powerful than Newtonian mechanics, [but also] variations on the least-action principle have proved useful in general relativity theory, quantum field theory, and particle physics. As a result, this principle lies at the core of much of contemporary theoretical physics." Thomas A. Moore "Least-Action Principle" in *Macmillan Encyclopedia of Physics*, John Rigden, editor, Simon & Schuster Macmillan, 1996, Volume 2, p. 840.

64. I am thankful to Prof. Edwin Taylor of MIT, for his elucidation of this most basic physical principle, is least action.

65. Edwin Taylor, op. cit.

66. Edwin Taylor and Jon Ogron Institute of Physics. "Quantum physics Explains Newton's Laws of Motion" where he says, "The deepest principles of nonrelativistic quantum mechanics—Explore all paths!—to the deepest principle of classical mechanics....Follow the path of least action...The old truths of the classical world come straight out of the new truths of the quantum world."

67. See Edwin Taylor's 2003 article in Journal of Physics; "A call to action" American Journal of Physics, Vol. 71, No. 5, pp. 423–425, May 2003 This "flying" is my interpretation of the path of maximal aging. Also note that it was Richard Feynman that came up with the idea that you must try all paths. Also note: "When action is not least," C.G. Gray and Edwin F. Taylor, American Journal of Physics, Vol. 75, No. 5, May 2007, pages 434-458. Action is a minimum along a sufficiently short world line in all potentials and along world lines of any length in some potentials. For long enough world lines in a majority of potentials, however, the action is a saddle point, that is, a minimum with respect to some nearby alternative curves and a maximum with respect to others. The action is never a true maximum.

68. See my more complete discussion of Feynman's ideas in *ProcessMind*, pp. 138-139.

69. Columbia University (1958), as quoted in Symposium on Basic Research (1959) by Dael Lee Wolfe, p. 66.

70. Thanks to internet Host on Madness Radio, Mr. Will Hall for interviewing me on extreme states. Some of this chapter was taken was taken from that interview. http://www.madnessradio.net/madness-radio-physics-dreaming-and-extreme-states-arnold-mindell

71. Thanks to Stephen Hawking and Leonard Mlodinow for their book, *The Grand Design*, Bantam Books, New York City, 2010 where they mention this story about the wolves. "In Viking mythology Skoll and Hati chase the sun and the moon. When the wolves catch either one there is an eclipse. When this happens people on earth rush to save the sun or moon by making as much noise as they can in hopes of scaring off the wolves."

72. Op.cit. see 70.

73. In *ProcessMind*, I imply the same, based upon quantum, not relativity, theory (p. 218): "Nonlocality in physics and psychology points to the reason why inner work is outer work as well. All our inner work is world-work, and worldwork is our inner work. Your psychology is not contained by your physical boundary; you can't have personal psychology that belongs only to you. This means that in an altered state of consciousness characteristic of the dreaming process, parts of the universe become your family and your community, just as the people around you. What you experience is a piece of the universe that is, at the dreaming level, a piece of the universe experiencing you."

74. See, for example, www.en.wikipedia.org/wiki/Naropa

75. In *Metaskills*, Amy Mindell defines metaskills as the feeling attitudes behind skills.

76. Davies, Paul, 2010, *The Eerie Silence: Renewing Our Search for Alien Intelligence*, Houghton, Mifflin, Harcourt, New York.

77. Thanks to http://www.theoservice.org/node/290 for this alchemical picture.

78. See Jung's Psychology and Alchemy, *Collected Works*, Vol 12. See for example; http://www.jungiananalyticpraxis.com/individuation.htm

79. Thanks to Dr. Joe Goodbread for reminding me of this situation.

80. In *Yoga, Immortality and Freedom*, p. 273. Eliade speaks of a dead man in life.

81. Eliade, Mircea, *A History of Religious Ideas*, Vol. 1 translated by Willard R. Trask, University of Chicago Press, London, p. 220.

82. Rozack, Theodore, *Voice of the Earth*, Phanes Press, Grand Rapids, MI, 1992.

83. Tyler Volk, CO2 Rising, #2, http://www.youtube.com/watch?v=2T7LSbyQ3bs

84. Here is Amy Mindell's "Coastal Town" at http://youtu.be/ofDqq6gbd9c

85. See Mark Freier for more. 2006. "Time Measured by Kairos and Kronos" © Whatif Enterprises, LLC.

86. Thanks to Ellen and Max Schupbach of the Deep Democracy Institute for creating this forum.

87. Mindell, *Quantum Mind*, op.cit.

88. James and Margaret Adams Leeming, Oxford Press, 1994, New York.

89. Earlier (page 80) I spoke about Stephen Hawking's question, "Why is there something rather than nothing," and concluded (pages 88 & 93) that there is a continuous process beyond the consensus reality concept.

90. James and Margaret Leeming, op. cit.

91. David M Raup and J. John Sepkoski. 1982. "Mass Extinctions in the Marine Fossil Record." Science, Ner Series, 215(4539), 1501–1503.

92. November 2011, Wikipedia on Extinction Event http://en.wikipedia.org/wiki/Extinction_event#Causes

93. http://epa.gov/oia/toxics/asgm.html

94. Mercury is a chemical with the symbol Hg. It has also been known as quicksilver or hydrargyrum because "hydr-" signifies water and "argyros" is silver. Mercury is the only metal that is liquid at ordinary temperatures. You can dig it out of the mountains.

95. See Wikipedia on Alchemy for more general information.

96. Mindell, *Shaman's Body*, 1992.

97. Ibid.

98. Op.cit.

99. The Dalai Lama speaks about the "Middle Way" in his book by that name.

100. Thanks to iCLIPART.com for the pictures on this page I adapted for this book.

101. Thanks to John Wheeler again, op.cit. for the idea of space-time being an actor, and thanks to IPAD free wallpaper; see: http://ipadwallpaper.eu/wallpapers/2/new-moon-city-nights.jpg

102. See my *Dreambody* (Sigo Press, 1980; LaoTse Press, 2000); and *Working with the Dreaming Body* (Routledge & Kegan Paul, 1985).

103. See my *Dreambody in Relationships* (Routledge & Kegan Paul).

104. See *City Shadows, Coma Key to Awakening, Leader as Martial Artist, Sitting in the Fire, Quantum Mind.*

105. My *Quantum Mind.*

106. See my *Earth-Based Psychology* and *ProcessMind.*

107. Thanks to NASA and Stanford, downloaded April, 2012 at: http://science.nasa.gov/media/medialibrary/2004/04/10/16Nov_gpb_resources/Vip_Lithos-2.pdf

INDEX

Bushmen's "rope" 79

C

callings, symptoms as 126
carbon dioxide, volcanic
    eruptions and 228
cashmere goats, air pollution
    and 287
Castaneda, Carlos 223, 270, 277
Challenger disaster 192
channel theory 18
charged scenes 203
Chief Joseph of the Nez
    Perce 242, 269
childhood dreams
  processmind and 82–83
  symptom experiences and 126
children, flow between
    realities for 87
Christianity 168
chronos 51
Chuang Tzu 247
city shadows 159–163
City Shadows (Mindell) 155
climate change
  panic and 280
  social/economic issues and 3
cocreation 259–260
coffee 129, 136
coherence
  congruence and 243–248
  defined 241–242
coherence-decoherence-
    coherence cycles 256–262
coherent point 264
Columbia 215–218
Coma, Dreambody Near Death
    (Mindell) 114, 117
Coma (Mindell) 144
comatose states 65
comawork 114–115
common ground 281–282
  relationships and 182
  space-time as 25
communication 280–281

entropy and 37
  space-time dreaming and 323–324
community(-ies)
  conflict and 198–202
  finances and 303–304
  in organizations 192
  processwork for 167
community processes, participants in
  189
compassion 32
complex coupled processes
  gold mining as 265–267
  understanding/defining 267–268
complex(es)
  having a 99
  hungry ghosts as 118
computers 240
conflict
  community and 198–202
  with conflict 334
  divorced energy and 194
  facilitation and 178, 334
  marginalized people and 203–219
  mediating and basics of 196
  and the oneness 17
  process-oriented ecology and 233
  process oriented economics and
    305
  role switches and 197
congruence, coherence and 243–248
connections
  ecology and 228
  with strangers 307
conscious divining 13
consciousness 66
consensus reality 12, 18
  background possibilities and 34
  boundaries and 61
  coherence-decoherence cycle and
    257
  economics and 300
  extreme states and 163–164
  field experiences vs. 83–84
  illness, medical attitude and 135
  polarities and 47

shamanism vs. 276
time/space, concepts of 96
useful generalizations within 99
consensus reality fields 298–299
contagion, finances and 303
Copenhagen interpretation
of the quantum world 34
coupled processes
in Earth System 228
of ecology 266–267
creation myths
cleansing 254–256
deluge/drought and 254–256
Islamic 16
Judeo-Christian 16
patterns of 251–253
quantum physics and 42
re-beginnings and 43
self vs. other in 13

D

dakini 169
Dalai Lama 112, 304
Dancing Shiva 101, 146
dark energy 78
dark matter 78
death 88. *See also* near-death
experiences
bardos and 109–110
childhood dreams and 145
comawork and 114
dying before you are killed 204
fear of 18, 116–117, 148
relaxation of everyday mind and
131–132
decoherence 241
benefits of 242
space–dreaming and 260
deep democracy 34, 318
deluge 254–256
as a cleansing 43
coherence–decoherence cycle and
258
processwork and 46
re-beginning after 264

democracy
deep 34, 318
fight for 336
multiple realities as 33–34
deniers 223, 234–237
depression 84, 253, 320
detachment, seeking 202
determinism, randomness vs. 26
deterministic processes 282
diamond body 146
dictators
internal or external 187
reappearance of 320
as role 194, 288
A Dictionary of Creation Myths 251
diversity, decoherence and 256
divining 13
consciously 13
processmind field 83
Taoism and 23, 25
divorced energy 194
Don Juan 94, 150, 270
double signals
experiencing others' 169
incongruence and 244
parallel worlds and 18
tokenism as 205
dreambody 112, 127, 144
Dreambody (Mindell) 126, 338–339
dreamers, marginalization of 159
dreaming
as common ground 27
dreaming (Aboriginal Australian) 83
dreamland
body signals and 145
consensus reality and 18, 177
as part of reality 144
unconscious as 66
dreams
joining in others' 159–163
dream talk, as common ground 27
dreamwork, entropy and 37
"dropping out" 138
drought 254–256
drugs 136, 138

duct tape 249
dying before you are killed 204

E

Earth Based Psychology (Mindell) 22
eco-deniers 223
ecological processes,
        coupling and 266–267
ecology 222–237
  deniers 234–237
  home, concept of and 249–251
  psychological change needed for
        229
  system mind in 224–227
  as taoism 227–230
  as a theory of everything 239–241
economic differences, rank and 205
eco shamans 223
Eidgenössische Technische
        Hochschule 6
Einstein, Albert 4, 9, 25, 26,
        95, 96–99, 101–102, 108, 335
elders 318
elementary particles 12, 35
emptyness, fear of and death 110
energy 77
enlightenment 119–122
entanglement 68–75, 198
entropy 36
  in creation myths 43
  dreamwork and 37
  order and 44
  reversing, to slow time 38–41, 46
environment
  body experience as reflection of
        286–293
  body symptoms and 278–286
environmental problems 233
ether, relativity and 102–107
Eve 16, 255
Everett, Hugh 10, 34
extra-terrestrial consciousness 179
extreme states
  insanity and 158
  necessity of, to the whole 163–164

F

facilitation 329–333
  conflict and 178, 334
  global field/mood and 300
  leadership role in 300
  love and 32–33
  meditating and 199
  organizational problems and
        189–190
  shamanizing and 182
  sustainable 189
"family members," conflict/
        tensions as 275
Feynman, Richard 10, 35,
        79, 150, 163
field picture 97
fields 15–16, 338
  awareness edges and 298–299
  in background 69
  global fields 299
  moods as 299
  in physics 81
  states of conciousness as 49
  virtual particles and 79
first attention 184
flirts
  defined 34–35
  as synchronicity 69
  Te and 89
flow, of fields 69
four "halves" of life 115–118
free fall 172–173
Fukushima Roshi, Keido 83

G

Gaia concept 5
Gandhi, Mohandas 204, 304
Garden of Eden 255
Gautier-Downes, Catherine 235
Genesis 253, 255
ghost roles 298, 311, 314
global fields 299
global village concept 319
global warming 3, 260

Lao Tse 59, 65
leadership
  awareness and 298–300
  empathy and 195
  possibilities, being open to all 192
  rank and 189
  roles 188
Leary, Timothy 138
least action 146, 147
Lee, Bruce 314
life
  four "halves" of 115–118
  healing and spirit of 132
light body, space-time
    dreaming as 111–112
love 32–35
Lovelock, James 5
luck 301, 305
lunar eclipse 156–157

M

magnetic field 81
Ma (Japanese concept of) 50, 232
mandalas 258
Manhattan (New York City) 230, 231
marginalization 203–219
  of minorities 211
  9/11 and 207
  zen mind and 207–208
Massachusetts Institute of
    Technology (MIT) 6
Matus, don Juan 277
Maxwell, James Clerk 44, 45
Maxwell's demon 45, 46
mediation 194–202, 335–336
medicine
  allopathic 230
meditation 194–202, 335–336
  comawork and 114
  process-oriented 196
Memories, Dreams, Reflections
    (Jung) 111
Menken, Dawn 64
mental illness 155–164
  nonconsensus reality oriented 158

social norms and 155
mercury 265–267
metacommunicator 149
Metaskills (Mindell) 288
Minkowski, Hermann 108, 109
minority status, power within 211
Mitchell, Stephen 94
MIT (Massachusetts Institute
    of Technology) 6
money 301
  deep democracy of 300–315
  universe mind and 312–315
Mongolia 287–288
mono-causality 276
moods, fields as 299
Mount St. Helens 228
muddles 86
multiverse 15. *See*
    also parallel universes/worlds
mu-shin 242, 252
myoclonic spasms 25, 282
Mysterium Coniunctionis (Jung) 111
mythbody 144, 145
mythic patterns 145

N

Nagual 94, 223, 277
Naropa 169–172
Nataraja 83, 146, 187, 188, 198
Nataraja dance 190
nature, as process 65
Navajos 258
near-death experiences
  bardos and 110
  comawork and 114–115
  connection to universe from 40–41
  enlightenment during 120
  fighting 135
  seeking space-time during 296
  superpositions in 113
Newton, Isaac 98
New York City 157
Nez Perce 242
9/11 terrorist attack 207
Nirvana 168, 327

healing and 131–132
Maxwell's demon and 46
mythbody and 145
nirvana and 327
relationships and 168–169, 177–185
as unified theory of psychology 82
ProcessMind (Mindell) 5,
109, 137, 338
process-oriented ecology
222–237, 239
decoherence cycles and 256–262
as deep democracy of ecology 232
deniers 234–237
process-oriented economics 297–317
leadership and awareness 298–300
money, deep democracy of 300–315
personal finances and 309–311
universe mind and 312–317
process-oriented meditation 196
process-oriented psychology 61
process paradigm 3–10, 59–77
as bridge between parallel worlds 22
for complex global issues 3–4
politics of 75–77
processwork and 61–63, 64–66,
338–339
seeing into the other and 63–64
space-time dreaming 5–8
synchronicity and 68–75
processwork 7
channel theory 18
coherence and 243–244
comawork and 114–115
congruence and 243–244
deluge and 46
edges and 61
four "halves" of life 115–118
group dynamics and 189
history of 338–339
hungry ghosts and 119
Jungian psychology and 61–63
leadership and awareness 298–300
love and 32–35

mental illness and 159–160
organizations, facilitating with
186–193
origins of 60–61
parallel worlds and 18
synchroniscity 68–75
psi function 244
psychology
physics and 6
process-oriented 61
pushing 266–267, 279

Q

Quantum holism 232
Quantum Mind (Mindell) 33, 245
quantum physics 12
congruence/coherence and 245–248
creation myths and 42
entanglement 67–68
psychology and 12
synchronicity and 69
quantum vibes 247
quantum wave function
244–246, 250
quibits 87–88

R

racism 205
rainbow body 118–119
rainbow medicine 125–133
finding spirit in the bottle 132–133
Spirit in the Bottle fairy tale and
128–132
randomness, determinism vs. 26
random processes 282
rank 311–312
consciousness of 188–189
financial 301
tokenism and 204–207
victim 206
realities, entangling 162
re-beginnings 43
recurring problems 21, 171–176
"recycling the bad guys" 288
reincarnation 150

relationships 31, 177–185
  coherence–decoherence cycle and
    256
  coupled processes and 266–267
  entanglement 67–68
  fighting 180–182
  kairos in 50
  leadership and 192–193
  organizing story 168
  problems in 86
  process-oriented ecology and 233
  rank consciousness and 188–189
  unus mundus and 183–184
relationship spirit 42–56
relationship work 31
relativity, general theory of
    96–99, 102–103, 335
Ricklin, Franz 60, 62–63
rigidity, fluidity vs. 149
Rinzai sect (Zen Buddhism) 242
roles 311–312
  financial 302–303
  opponents as 320
  people vs. 194–195
role-switching 52, 197
Rubber Sheet Universe Analogy 104
Rumi 75

S

sadhana 310
same-sex marriage 212
Schrödinger, Erwin 19, 335
Schrödinger's cat 19, 178
science, spiritual traditions
    and 101–102
secondary processes 18, 19, 282
second attention 184
second law of
    thermodynamics 37, 45
self-abuse 136
self-knowledge, entropy and 38
self-reflection 17
September 11 terrorist attacks 207
sexism 205
shamanism 70

essence of money in 306
marginalization of 276
processwork and 137
relationships and 182
Shaman's Body (Mindell) 277
Shannon, Claude 36
sharing 304
Shiva 188, 198, 251
signal congruence 243
Singer, June 64, 65
Sitting in the Fire (Mindell) 205
smog 157
snake, in Judeo-Christian
    mythology 16, 255
social norms 155
space
  hyperbolic nature of 97–99
  time separated from 96
space-time 4
  consensus reality and 108–109
  as universal common ground 27
space-time dreaming 5, 7, 25
  altered states and 159–163
  approaching global problems with
    44
  body symptoms and 134, 284–286
  coherence–decoherence cycle and
    260
  communication and 323–324
  dakini as personification of 169–
    170
  edges of 319–325
  energies of the universe and 79
  entanglements as 68
  ether and 103
  facilitation of 201
  free fall and 100–101
  hungry ghosts and 119
  as interdisciplinary concept 339
  leadership and 195
  as least action 146
  mental illness and 155–164
  myoclonic spasms and 282
  Nagual as 223
  necessity of extreme states 163–164

six bardos of 112
Tibetans 256, 258
Tilopa 170, 186, 187, 198
time
creation of, in Christian mythology 255
entropy, reversing to slow time 38–41, 46
space, as separated from 96
stepping out of 152, 270–272
Tohaku, Hasegawa 50
tokenism 204–207
trashers, learning from 261
tree, as symbol of processmind 130
Trungpa, Chogyam 109
trying all paths 147
Tucker, Wilma Jean 175
twice born concept 203

U

u 47–48
death and 148
as primary process 18
u-destruction 324
unconscious 60, 64
unified field theory 251
universe talk 155–164
unpredictable movements 143
unus mundus 23, 78, 179–180, 198, 268
US Army 238–239

V

victim rank 303
vipassana 325, 327
vitamins 129
volcanoes 228
Volk, Tyler 230
von Franz, Marie-Louise 60, 62

W

war 287–293
wave(s)
entanglement and 69

as symbol of process 22
wonder as 13
weak force fields 81
Western religions, hungry ghosts and 118
whale, as metaphor for the universe 18
Wheeler, John 3, 8, 18, 103, 106
Wheel of Life (Tibetan) 256
witnessing, in Buddhism 326–327
wonder 13–15
defined 32
and desire for self-reflection 43
Einstein and 96
wood, as energy source 129
worldchange theatre 329–333
world conflict 196
worldwork 52
wu-wei 89, 270

X

X 47
conflict in organizations and 189
as secondary process 19

Y

Yachats, Oregon 19, 231
Yahweh 101
Yggdrasil 24
yin-yang symbol 23, 245
Yoga Sutras 131

Z

Zen Buddhism 252
Zen mind 73, 83, 207–208

BIBLIOGRAPHY

Ardener, Shirley. 1993. *Women and Space: Ground Rules and Social Maps*. University of Oxford, UK: Berg.

Dalai Lama & Geshe Thupten Jinpa. 2009. *Middle Way, Faith Grounded in Reason*. Sommerville, MA: Wisdom.

———. 1997. *Sleeping, Dreaming, and Dying*. Boston, MA: Wisdom.

———. 1991. *Cultivating a Daily Meditation* (2nd rev. ed.). Dharamsala, India: Ltwa.

Davies, Paul. 2010. *The Eerie Silence: Renewing Our Search for Alien Intelligence*. New York: Houghton, Mifflin, Harcourt.

Einstein, Albert. 1922/1983. "Sidelights of Relativity," trans. J. G. Jeffrey & W. Perret. London, UK: Methuen. Republished unabridged & unaltered, New York: Dover.

———.1950. "On the Generalized Theory of Gravitation." Scientific American, 182(4), 13.

———. 1949. *The World As I See It* . New York: Philosophical Library.

———. 1931/2007. *Cosmic Religion: With Other Opinions and Aphorisms*. New York: Covici-Friede.

———. 1926/1971. "Letter to Max Born," December 4, 1926, in *The Born–Einstein Letters*, edited by Max Born. New York: Walker.

———. 1923/1963. *The Principle of Relativity*. A. Lorentz, A. Einstein, H. Minkowski, H. Weyl, H. Sommerfeld (Eds.). New York: Dover.

———. 1920. "Ether and the General Theory of Relativity," from http://www.zionism-israel.com/Albert_Einstein/Albert_Einstein_Ether_Relativity.htm

Eliade, M. 1969. *Yoga, Immortality and Freedom*. Princeton, NJ: Princeton University Press.

Feynman, Richard. 1988. *QED: The Strange Theory of Light and Matter*. Princeton, NJ: Princeton University Press.

Goswami, Amit, Richard E. Reed, & Maggie Goswami. 1993. *The Self-Aware Universe: How Consciousness Creates the Material World*. New York: Tarcher/Putnam.

Gribbon, John. 1998. *Q Is for Quantum: An Encyclopedia of Particle Physics*. New York: Touchstone Books.

Grimm, Jacob & Wilhelm. 1959. *Fairy Tales*. London, UK: Routledge & Kegan Paul.

Harris, I. C. 2004. *The Laughing Buddha of Tofukuji: The Life of Zen Master Keido Fukushima*. Bloomington, IN: World Wisdom.

Hawking, Stephen & Leonard Mlodinow. 2010. *The Grand Design*. New York: Bantam Books.

———. 1996. *Brief History of Time*. New York: Bantam Books.

Heisenberg, Werner. 1971. *Physics and Beyond*. Cambridge, UK: Cambridge University Press.

Hughston, L. P., & K. P. Tod. 1990. *An Introduction to General Relativity*. [London Math Society, Student Text 5]. New York: Cambridge University Press.

I Ching or *Book of Changes*. 1990. Translated into German by Richard Wilhelm, English translation by Cary F. Baynes. Princeton, NJ: Princeton University Press.

Isaacson, Walter. 2007. *Einstein; His Life and Universe*. New York: Simon & Schuster.

Jung, C.G. 1965. *Memories, Dreams, Reflections*. Aniela Jaffe (Ed.). New York: Vintage Books.

———. 1930/2001. "Kinderträume," Seminare. Stuttgart, Germany: Walter Verlag.

———. 1966. "Structure and Dynamics of the Psyche." Vol. 8 *Collected Works*. Trans. R. F. C. Hull. Gerhard Adler, Michael Fordham, & Herbert Read (Eds.). Bollingen Foundation. Princeton, NJ: Princeton University Press.

Keeney, Bradford. 2003. *Ropes to God: Experiencing the Bushman Spiritual Universe*. New Haven, Australia: Leete's Island Books.

Kostro, L. 1988. "Einstein and the Ether." Electronics & Wireless World, 94, 238–239.

————. 1952/1993. "Synchronicity: An Acausal Connecting Principle." In Volume 8 of the *Collected Works of C.G. Jung*. Bollingen Foundation. Princeton, NJ: Princeton University Press.

Lao Tse. *The Tao Te Ching*. See online: http://www.duhtao.com/translations. html

Lao-tzu. *Tao Te Ching*. Chapter 25, translated by S. Mitchell (see, for example, http://academic.brooklyn.cuny.edu/core9/phalsall/texts/taote-v3.html)

————. Tao Te Ching. 1977. *Way and Its Power the Tao Te Ching*. Arthur Wiley translation. Mandala Books. http://www.mandalabooks.com/

Leeming, David Adams & Margaret Adams Leeming. 1994. *Encyclopedia of Creation Myths* (2nd ed.). Santa Barbara, CA: ABC-CLIO.

Mindell, Amy. 2008."Bringing Deep Democracy to Life: An Awareness Paradigm for Deepening Political Dialogue, Personal Relationships, and Community Interactions." Psychotherapy and Politics International, 6(3), 212–225.

————. 2007. "World Work and the Politics of Dreaming, or Why Dreaming Is Crucial for World Process," November, http://www.aamindell.net/ blog/ww-themes

————. 1994. *Metaskills: The Spiritual Art of Therapy*. Tempe, AZ: New Falcon. Reprinted by Lao Tse Press (Portland, OR), 2001.

Mindell, Arnold. 2010. *ProcessMind: A User's Guide to Connecting with the Mind of God*. Wheaton, IL: Quest Books.

————. 2007. *Earth-Based Psychology: Path Awareness from the Teachings of Don Juan, Richard Feynman, and Lao Tse*. Portland, OR: Lao Tse Press.

————. 2004. "The Edges of Experience: Jung, Processwork and Collective Change." Interview with Luisetta Mudie, on the "Jung Page." Available from http://www.cgjungpage.org/index.php?option=com_content&task =view&id=587&Itemid=40

————. 2004. *The Quantum Mind and Healing: How to Listen and Respond to Your Body's Symptoms*. Charlottesville, VA: Hampton Roads.

————. 2002. *The Deep Democracy of Open Forums: How to Transform Organizations into Communities*. Charlottesville, VA: Hampton Roads.

————. 2000. *Dreaming While Awake: Techniques for 24-Hour Lucid Dreaming*. Charlottesville, VA: Hampton Roads.

————. 2000. *The Quantum Mind: The Edge Between Physics and Psychology*. Portland, OR: Lao Tse Press, the Deep Democracy Exchange (Portland OR) 2012.

———. 1995. *Sitting in the Fire: Large Group Transformation Through Diversity and Conflict*. Portland, OR: Lao Tse Press, the Deep Democracy Exchange (Portland OR) 2012.

———. 1993. *The Shaman's Body: A New Shamanism for Health, Relationships and Community*. San Francisco, CA: HarperCollins.

———. 1992. *The Leader as Martial Artist: An Introduction to Deep Democracy*. San Francisco, CA: HarperCollins.

———. 1989. *Coma, Key to Awakening: Working with the Dreambody Near Death*. Boulder, CO: Shambhala. Reprinted as *Coma: The Dreambody Near Death*, by Lao Tse Press (Portland, OR), 2009.

———. 1989. *The Year One: Global Processwork*. London & New York: Viking-Penguin-Arkana.

———. 1987. *The Dreambody in Relationships*. London & New York: Viking-Penguin-Arkana. Reprinted by Lao Tse Press (Portland, OR), 2000, and the Deep Democracy Exchange (Portland OR) 2012.

———. 1982. *Dreambody: The Body's Role in Revealing the Self*. Boston, MASAD Sigo Press. Reprinted by Viking-Penguin-Arkana (London & New York), 1986; by Lao Tse Press (Portland, OR), 2000; by Deep Democracy Exchange (Portland, OR), 2011.

Mitchell, Stephen. 2009. *Second Book of the Tao*. New York: Penguin.

Moore, A. 1996. "Least-Action Principle," in Macmillan *Encyclopedia of Physics* (Vol. 2), John Rigden (Ed.). New York: Simon & Schuster Macmillan.

Onsager, Lars. 1931. "Reciprocal Relations in Irreversible Processes." Physics Review, 37, 405–426.

Pauli, Wolfgang. 1955. "The Influence of Archetypical Ideas on the Scientific Theories of Kepler." In *C.G. Jung & W. Pauli, The Interpretation of Nature and Psyche*. Bollingen Series L1. New York: Pantheon Books.

Plato. *Timaeus*. n.d. Stanford Encyclopedia of Philosophy. Available from http://plato.stanford.edu/entries/plato-timaeus

Radin, Dean. 2006. *Entangled Minds: Extrasensory Experience in Quantum Reality*. New York: Paraview Pocket Books.

Rozack, Theodore. 1992. *Voice of the Earth*. Grand Rapids, MI: Phanes Press.

Siegel, R. K. 1989. *Intoxication: Life in the Pursuit of Artificial Paradise*. Rochester, VT: Park Street Press. Reprinted as The Universal Drive for Mind Altering Substances by Inner Traditions International (Rochester, VT), 2005.

Steele, Paul Richard & Catherine J. Allen. 2004. *Handbook of Inca Mythology*. Santa Barbara, CA: ABC-CLIO.

Stuart, Cheshire. n.d. "Collected Quotes from Albert Einstein." Retrieved 6 Dec 2004, from http://rescomp.stanford.edu/~cheshire/EinsteinQuotes.html

Suzuki, Shunryu. 1995. *Zen Mind, Beginner's Mind* (34th ed.). New York: Weatherhill.

Taylor, Edwin F., Edmund Bertschinger, & John Wheeler. 2000. *Exploring Black Holes, An Introduction to General Relativity*. San Francisco, CA: Person Addison Wesley, to be republished soon.

———. 2003. "A Call to Action." American Journal of Physics, 71(5), 423–425.

Tegmark, Max. 2003. "Parallel Universes." In *Science and Ultimate Reality: From Quantum to Cosmos*, honoring John Wheeler's 90th birthday. J. D. Barrow, P. C. W. Davies, & C. L. Harper (Eds.). Cambridge, UK: Cambridge University Press.

———. 2011. Scientific American. Retrieved from http://teachphysics.org/wp/max-tegmark-and-parallel-universes-scientific-american-pdf-download/

Trungpa, Chogyam. 2004. *The Collected Works of Chögyam Trungpa*. Boston, MA: Shambhala.

Wheeler, John. 2000. Edwin F. Taylor and John Archibald Wheeler, *Exploring Black Holes: Introduction to General Relativity*. New York: Addison Wesley Longman.

———. 1999. *Journey into Gravity and Spacetime*. New York: Scientific American Library.

———. 1989. *Information, Physics, Quantum: The Search for Links*. Proceedings of the 3rd International Symposium on the Foundation of Quantum Mechanics, Tokyo, Japan.

Wolf, Fred Alan. 1995. *The Dreaming Universe: A Mind-Expanding Journey into the Realm Where Psyche and Physics Meet*. New York: Touchstone.

———. 1984. *Star Wave: Mind, Consciousness, and Quantum Physics*. New York: Macmillan.

ABOUT THE AUTHOR

Arnold Mindell, Ph.D., a graduate of MIT and the C.G. Jung Institute, Switzerland, is the author of over twenty books including *Riding the Horse Backwards* (with Dr. Amy Mindell, Lao-Tse Press, 2001), *Dreambody* (Deep Democracy Exchange, 2011), *The Shaman's Body* (Harper-SanFrancisco, 1993), *Quantum Mind* (Deep Democracy Exchange, 2012), and *ProcessMind* (Quest Books, 2010).

He is known throughout the world for his innovative synthesis of dreams and bodywork; integrating Jungian therapy, group process, consciousness, shamanism, quantum physics, and conflict resolution.

In the 1970s, Mindell began to develop Processwork, which is also known as process oriented psychology. His work has given rise to a new paradigm with applications in a diversity of areas including individual psychotherapy, personal meditation practice, medicine (including coma and near-death experiences), large group and change management processes, and environmental issues.

Dr. Mindell travels widely in the US and abroad with his partner and co-researcher, Dr. Amy Mindell, holding workshops and making frequent appearances at professional conferences and on television and radio shows. They live in Oregon, and work as consultants and facilitators for groups, cities, and governments worldwide.

Deep Democracy Exchange publishes books, films, music, visual art, and other forms of media that contribute to the research and development of transdisciplinary approaches to both overcome and learn from the challenges that we face as a species and as a planet.

Other Books by Arnold Mindell

Dreambody: The Body's Role in Revealing the Self

River's Way: The Process Science of the Dreambody

Working with the Dreaming Body

Working on Yourself Alone: Inner Dreambody Work

The Dreambody in Relationships

City Shadows: Psychological Interventions in Psychiatry

The Year 1: Global Processwork

Coma: Key to Awakening

The Leader as Martial Artist: An Introduction to Deep Democracy

Riding the Horse Backwards: Processwork in Theory and Practice, with Amy Mindell

The Shaman's Body: A New Shamanism for Transforming Health, Relationships, and Community

Coma: The Dreambody Near Death

Sitting in the Fire: Large Group Transformation Using Conflict and Diversity

Quantum Mind: The Edge Between Physics and Psychology

Dreaming While Awake: Techniques for 24-hour Lucid Dreaming

The Dreammaker's Apprentice: Using Heightened States of Consciousness to Interpret Dreams

The Deep Democracy of Open Forums: Practical Steps to Conflict Prevention and Resolution for the Family, Workplace, and World

The Quantum Mind and Healing: How to Listen and Respond to Your Body's Symptoms

Earth-Based Psychology: Path Awareness from the Teachings of Don Juan, Richard Feynman, and Lao Tse

ProcessMind: A User's Guide to Connecting with the Mind of God

Deep Democracy Exchange

Welcome

Welcome inside a publication of Deep Democracy Exchange, the publishing house of the Deep Democracy Institute.

We produce books, films, music, visual art, and other media that contribute to the research and development of transdisciplinary approaches to both learn from the challenges that we face as a species and as a planet, and overcome them. Although these challenges may seem overwhelming at times, they also serve as catalysts to create new knowledge and further unlikely connections, both in terms of communities as well as in terms of scientific thinking. Along with the growing complexity of our world, we also see a growing interest in finding holistic, all inclusive perspectives that can address our yearning to understand ourselves as individuals and as part of the whole.

Deep Democracy Exchange sees itself as a crossroad where the scientist, the mystic, the leader, and the everyday traveler can meet together in that quest.

In this spirit, we are very proud to publish Arnold Mindell's *Dance of the Ancient One* as the first in our ToE (Theory of Everthing) Series.

Deep Democracy Institute
A Global Thinktank

We research, develop, and implement Deep Democracy solutions for organizations, governments, communities, teams and individuals worldwide.

We consult, facilitate, coach and train using the Deep Democracy and Processwork approaches in the USA, Europe, Russia, Africa, the Middle East, South America and Central Asia.

Contact us at
info@deepdemocracyinstitute.org

Or look up our schedule of events
at www.deepdemocracyinstitute.org

Contact us at
ddx@deepdemocracyexchange.com

or look for our publications at
www.deepdemocracyexchange.com

Made in the USA
San Bernardino, CA
15 March 2016